Daring Raids of
World War Two

Daring Raids of World War Two

Heroic Land, Sea and Air Attacks

Peter Jacobs

Pen & Sword
AVIATION

First published in Great Britain in 2015 by
Pen & Sword Aviation
an imprint of
Pen & Sword Books Ltd
47 Church Street
Barnsley
South Yorkshire
S70 2AS

ISBN 978 1 78346 333 6

A CIP catalogue record for this book is available from the British
Library

Typeset in Ehrhardt by
Mac Style Ltd, Bridlington, East Yorkshire
Printed and bound in the UK by CPI Group (UK) Ltd,
Croydon, CRO 4YY

Pen & Sword Books Ltd incorporates the imprints of Pen & Sword
Archaeology, Atlas, Aviation, Battleground, Discovery, Family
History, History, Maritime, Military, Naval, Politics, Railways, Select,
Transport, True Crime, and Fiction, Frontline Books, Leo Cooper,
Praetorian Press, Seaforth Publishing and Wharncliffe.

For a complete list of Pen & Sword titles please contact
PEN & SWORD BOOKS LIMITED
47 Church Street, Barnsley, South Yorkshire, S70 2AS, England
E-mail: enquiries@pen-and-sword.co.uk
Website: www.pen-and-sword.co.uk

Contents

Acknowledgements

A book such as this could never be produced without the help of many people. First and foremost, I would like to thank the staff at the National Archives in Kew, who continue to maintain an excellent facility and provide an outstanding service for all members of the public. The same can be said for the staff at the Imperial War Museum (London, Manchester and Duxford), the RAF Museum (Hendon and Cosford) and those at the Air Historical Branch (RAF) based at Northolt. All have provided me with great support over the years.

In addition to these excellent museums and institutions, I was fortunate to spend a full career as an officer in the Royal Air Force. This gave me privileged access to service establishments, unit records and squadron diaries. I was also fortunate to spend my last few years in the Service at the RAF College Cranwell, which boasts one of the finest libraries in the country, and this gave me access to a great deal of material. Furthermore, during my career, which spanned five decades, I was privileged to meet many wartime veterans. Although very few are still with us today, they always seemed happy to share their personal memories with me, something I shall never forget. From all of these museums, institutions, establishments and individuals I have been able to build a wonderful archive of information, personal accounts and images; the images used in this book have been credited accordingly.

To include the stories of thirty daring raids under one cover means I can only provide a short account of each. Many of these stories have been given far more coverage in other books and so I must pay my own tribute, and give thanks, to all the authors that have taken the time to tell each tale in much greater depth. My research naturally took me to a number of published sources, and for the enthusiast wishing to learn far more about a particular raid I recommend each and every one of them. The Bibliography provides a fuller list, but amongst the many excellent books I have read are (to name just a few): *Night Raid* (the audacious raid at Bruneval) by Taylor Downing;

Operation Suicide (Cockleshell Heroes) by Robert Lyman; *The Dambusters Raid* (John Sweetman); *The Small Scale Raiding Force* (Brian Lett); *Pegasus Bridge* (Stephen Ambrose); *Arnhem: A Tragedy of Errors* (Peter Harclerode); and *Target Tirpitz* (Patrick Bishop). Over the years some of these stories have become immortalized on the big screen. Great films, such as *The Dam Busters*, *Heroes of Telemark*, *The Cockleshell Heroes*, *Sink the Bismarck* and *A Bridge Too Far*, all inspired me in my younger years to the point that I just wanted to join the armed forces – and so I did. Most importantly though, films such as these have meant that the daring exploits they portrayed will live on for generations to come and so, on behalf of a most grateful nation, I must thank the film-makers of days gone by. Not only did they inspire me, but I suspect they have inspired many others over the years.

For a long time I have felt there was a place for a book such as this, as it gives the reader a good understanding of the courage and bravery demonstrated by members of the British Armed Forces during the Second World War, whichever service or theatre they were operating in. And so I would like to thank the team at Pen & Sword for agreeing to let me tell these stories in one volume, and to Laura Hirst, in particular, for helping to make it happen. I have always thought that writing the book is the easy part but turning it into what you see today is something else.

Last, but by no means least, I would like to pay tribute to all those who took part in the raids included in this book, many of whom did not live to tell the tale. Without their courage there would be no stories to tell.

Introduction

Amongst the titanic strategic battles of the Second World War, countless daring raids were carried out by British units across all operational theatres – by land, sea and air. These raids varied in size enormously. Some involved thousands of men, such as at Dieppe, Arnhem and in the jungle of Burma, while others were carried out by a handful of men and, in some cases, by just a couple of individuals. Included in this latter category is a raid carried out by two men in a canoe on an enemy vessel in the enemy-occupied harbour at Boulogne, and a mission carried out by two men who, night after night, swam ashore from a midget submarine to carry out vital reconnaissance of the beaches that were soon to become centre stage for the Allied invasion of Normandy.

While some raids have since been immortalized in dramatic form on the big screen and have become household names, such as the legendary Dam Busters, others, no less daring or dramatic, have disappeared into forgotten archives, only to be remembered by those who took part. The latter could happen for any number of reasons. Some took place thousands of miles from Britain or involved specialist units of which little was known back home at the time, such as the raid on Barce in North Africa by the Long Range Desert Group (LRDG) and a raid carried out by two midget submarines against Japanese cruisers in the Johore Straits of Singapore at the very end of the seemingly forgotten war in the Far East. Some ended in dramatic failure, such as the disastrous reconnaissance of Saint Honorine-des-Pertes, while others were deliberately not publicized back home, such as at the Litani River, where a British commando raid on Vichy forces resulted in French casualties. However, while some raids went largely unheard of at the time, others were seen as great opportunities to provide the British public with some much needed good news. The sinking of the mighty German battleship *Bismarck*, for example, or the successful commando raid at Vaagso on the west coast of Norway, both during 1941, was news considered too good not to tell, and those who took part returned home as heroes.

A pattern of raids emerged as the war progressed. In 1940, when Britain's survival was the priority, there were often not the resources, nor the expertise for that matter, to strike back at the enemy. But the formation of new organizations, such as the Army Commandos and the Special Operations Executive (SOE), formed by British Prime Minister Winston Churchill to 'set Europe ablaze', introduced new players into the raiding game, who quickly became specialists in their trade. At that stage of the war it was vital to hit back at the enemy in any way possible, but some of the early commando raids were hastily planned and, therefore, resulted in disaster. One commando raid towards the end of 1941, for example, on what was believed to be General Erwin Rommel's headquarters in North Africa, ended in failure and brought an end to what some considered to be raiding of a rather gung-ho nature. The intelligence on which the raid had been planned turned out to be hopelessly wrong and it cost the Commandos one of their finest men.

From the end of 1941 until the Allied invasion of north-west Europe in 1944, there were many British units capable of taking the war to the enemy in a variety of ways. In addition to the conventional forces of the Royal Navy, British Army and the Royal Air Force (RAF), there were many other smaller units operating within the Services: the Small Scale Raiding Force, the Combined Operations Pilotage Parties, 101 Troop, the Royal Marines Boom Patrol Detachment and the Long Range Desert Group to name just a few. The importance of co-ordinating with other organizations soon became apparent but, even as the war progressed, this did not always happen as it should. For example, when a small group of Royal Marines carried out one of the most physically demanding of all raids, by paddling 60 miles up a river to attack enemy shipping in the Nazi-occupied French port of Bordeaux, in a story better known as the Cockleshell Heroes, they did so without the knowledge that the SOE was planning its own raid against the same port.

Of the many British raids carried out during the Second World War, some were quite audacious to say the least. Had their stories not be true then some would struggle to believe them. These include the raid on St Nazaire, often described as the most daring raid of them all, when a Royal Navy warship was packed with explosives and rammed at full speed into the dry dock to put it out of action, and the legendary Bruneval raid; what better way was there to find out how an enemy radar worked than to capture one, dismantle it and then take the key components back to Britain for analysis? And then there was the raid carried out by the SOE to steal three enemy vessels from a neutral Spanish port off the west coast of Africa, later described as one of the SOE's classic raids, and so it goes on.

The significance of all of these missions varied enormously. Some helped gain a tactical advantage in a bigger overall battle, for example at Lake Comacchio in Italy, while others gathered important intelligence, such as those carried out across the Channel by the Small Scale Raiding Force. Some proved a point, such as the first low-level daylight raid by Lancaster bombers at Augsburg deep into southern Bavaria, which demonstrated the capability of the RAF's new four-engine heavy bomber, while others had repercussions far beyond the locality of the raid itself, such as the commando raid on the Channel Island of Sark that resulted in Hitler's notorious Kommandobefehl, his Commando Order, stating that all Allied commandos captured by German forces should be killed immediately, even if in uniform or if attempting to surrender. Even now, some raids continue to be the subject of great debate as post-war historians argue whether they were a success or not: one such example is the low-level raid by RAF Mosquitos on the prison at Amiens. The fact that so much resource was applied to sinking or neutralizing the mighty German warships – *Bismarck*, *Tirpitz*, *Scharnhorst*, *Gneisenau* and *Prinz Eugen* – shows just how feared these ships were at the time, particularly by Churchill; had these great warships have been allowed to roam the Atlantic then the war may have had a very different outcome. And while contemplating how the Second World War might have turned out, who knows what the outcome might have been had the raid on the Vemork hydro-electric plant at Telemark in Norway, and the subsequent sinking of the *Hydro* ferry on Lake Tinnsjø, not been successful? Often described as the SOE's greatest raid of the war, it prevented the Nazis from acquiring deuterium oxide, otherwise known as heavy water, which could well have been used in the production of nuclear weapons – another subject of much post-war debate!

I have picked a selection of thirty raids and reconnaissance missions carried out on land, by sea and from the air, which I consider to be amongst the most daring of the Second World War. Rather than cover too many raids of a similar type, I have included a variety to cover all the Services and the main operational theatres, ranging from those involving thousands of men to those involving just a few individuals, to represent all those who fought with such courage in those parts of the world: from northern Norway to the Channel Islands and to the west coast of Africa, and from north-west Europe to North Africa, the Middle East and the Far East. In the case of those carried out from the air, I have been mindful to include raids carried out by a variety of aircraft from the RAF and the Fleet Air Arm – the Battle, Blenheim, Beaufort, Swordfish, Mosquito and Lancaster – again, to represent all the brave crews who flew these types. Whatever the scale of the operation or its location, the raids I have picked all required strong leadership and extreme courage from those who took part. It goes without saying that not all were a success. In fact, some went disastrously wrong, but the men who carried out these raids did so in the knowledge that they might not return. Many were decorated for their deed, some more than once, and where this is the case I have abbreviated all awards as follows: Victoria Cross (VC); Distinguished Service Order (DSO); Distinguished Service Cross (DSC); Military Cross (MC); Distinguished Flying Cross (DFC); Distinguished Conduct Medal (DCM); Conspicuous Gallantry Medal (CGM); Distinguished Service Medal (DSM); Military Medal (MM); and Distinguished Flying Medal (DFM).

These are thirty stories of the extreme courage and bravery of men who often did not live to tell the tale. I have told them in chronological order to show where they fitted in to the overall context of the war rather than attempt to try and rank them in any other way. When putting them together I was very much aware that selecting these raids is like asking someone to name their thirty favourite films, novels or music tracks – everyone has their own idea. In the end, it is a matter of personal choice, but this is my selection. All have inspired me throughout my life and I only hope they inspire you too.

Enjoy the book!

Chapter One

Bridges at Maastricht

12 May 1940

Since its inception by Queen Victoria in 1856, the Victoria Cross has rightly taken precedence over all other awards within the British Commonwealth. Its award exemplifies unadulterated valour, in which rank or class plays no part. The fact that the award was made to airmen on just thirty-two occasions during the Second World War is an indication of its rarity, and for two members of the same crew to each receive a VC is unique. And so the story of daring raids rightly starts with these two men, Donald Garland and Thomas Gray: the pilot and observer of a Fairey Battle, who so gallantly faced a seemingly impossible task.

The Fairey Battle was a single-engine light bomber. It was powered by the same Merlin engine that gave the RAF fighters, the Spitfire and Hurricane, such great speed and performance, but, unlike the fighters, the Battle was weighed down by a three-man crew and an internal bomb load of four 250lb bombs. Although it had a rather sleek appearance, the Battle was 100mph slower than the new generation of fighters entering service, was limited in range, lacked manoeuvrability and was extremely vulnerable to anti-aircraft fire from the ground. In the air, its defence consisted of a single machine gun in the starboard wing and another mounted in the rear cockpit. In truth, the Battle was an obsolete aircraft, but had been retained by the RAF at the outbreak of war as there was no adequate replacement at the time.

For the aircrew of 12 Squadron, the first eight months of the Second World War had proved relatively uneventful. Since being rushed to northern France at the outbreak of war as one of ten short-range bomber squadrons of the RAF's Advanced Air Striking Force, operations had been relatively few and far between and had been limited to a series of reconnaissance missions.

The squadron had become settled at its grass airfield near the village of Amifontaine, some 25 miles north-west of Rheims.

Then, during the early hours of 10 May 1940, everything changed. The period that has since become known as the Phoney War came to a sudden and dramatic end as German forces attacked northern France and the Low Countries. The main German thrust had seen its armoured units cut-off and surround Allied units in Belgium and, in doing so, they had captured several vital bridges spanning the Albert Canal.

Two of these bridges were on the Dutch/Belgian border at Vroenhoven and Veldwezelt, on the western side of Maastricht. On the morning of 12 May, volunteers from 12 Squadron were called on to carry out a short-notice and high-priority raid. The volunteers that came forward had no idea of what the raid would involve and had been given no time to prepare; as the six crews made their way to briefing they were still coming to terms with the squadron's losses on the opening afternoon of the German offensive, just two days before, when three of the four Battles sent out to bomb enemy positions advancing through Luxembourg had failed to return.

As the volunteers listened to the briefing they soon realized they were facing a most daunting task. Their targets were two bridges at Maastricht, the ones at Vroenhoven and Veldwezelt, which had not been destroyed by retreating ground forces and were now allowing German forces to pour into Belgium. Tasked with leading a first section of three aircraft to attack the concrete bridge at Vroenhoven was Flying Officer Norman Thomas, while the second section, with the task of attacking the metal bridge at Veldwezelt, was to be led by a 21-year-old Irishman, Flying Officer Donald Garland.

Having captured the bridges intact, the Germans were not prepared to let them be destroyed and so considerable resources, including anti-aircraft guns and fighter cover, had been allocated to their protection. The Battle crews were, therefore, briefed to expect Hurricanes over the target area, with the task of sweeping ahead of the Battles and engaging any Luftwaffe fighters lurking in the vicinity.

Thomas and Garland formed their plan. They decided to carry out different types of attack to give the enemy defences more of a problem, which would hopefully give the Battle crews more chance of success rather than having all six aircraft approach Maastricht at the same height and at the same time. Thomas elected to lead his section to the target at 6,000 feet and to then carry out a diving attack on the bridge at Vroenhoven, while Garland chose to approach and attack the bridge at Veldwezelt from a low level.

It was just after 8.00 am when the crews climbed into their Battles at Amifontaine. One aircraft was unserviceable and so Thomas would have to carry out the attack on the bridge at Vroenhoven as a pair, with the other Battle flown by 20-year-old Pilot Officer Tom Davy. Minutes later the Battles were climbing away towards Maastricht. Meanwhile, eight Hurricanes were getting airborne from nearby Berry-au-Bac, but instead of being the hunters and sweeping the area in readiness for the Battles, the Hurricanes soon became the hunted as a large formation of Messerschmitt Bf 109s swooped down upon them.

The two Battles arrived in the target area to find the Hurricanes were already fighting for their own survival and could not offer any fighter protection at all. The task facing the Battle crews was now greater than ever. As Thomas and Davy approached Vroenhoven they were soon spotted by the German defences on the ground and an intense barrage of flak opened up. Through the smoke and patches of cloud they could see their target but they were then spotted by the 109s defending the bridges.

Undaunted and completely focused on their task, Thomas and Davy commenced their attack from the south-west. As the two Battles headed towards their target they soon found they were also running the gauntlet of enemy fighters as they dived down through the anti-aircraft fire towards the bridge. Both Battles were hit repeatedly during their attacks but Thomas and Davy managed to press on towards the bridge, finally releasing their bombs before turning away in a desperate bid for safety.

Although their bombs hit the target, causing some damage to the structure, the bridge remained intact. Now badly hit and struggling to maintain any control of his aircraft, 'PH-F', Thomas could not make it back to friendly lines and ordered his two crew members, Sergeant B. T. P. Carey, the observer, and the wireless operator/air gunner, Corporal T. S. Campion, to bail out before the aircraft crashed near the bridge; all three survived to be taken as prisoners of war.

Davy's aircraft, 'PH-G', had also been hit, but his air gunner, a 21-year-old Canadian, Aircraftman 1st Class Gordon Patterson, had twice managed to hold off attacking enemy fighters to enable his pilot to complete the attack. Then, having released its bomb load, the plane made a steep climbing turn towards the covering cloud just as it came under further attack from another 109 above. Patterson again held off the attacking fighter and the 109 was last seen entering cloud and trailing smoke.

By now there was a long trail of smoke behind Davy's aircraft and both Patterson and the observer, Sergeant G. D. Mansell, reported the port fuel tank to be on fire. They were just 3 miles north-east of Maastricht as Davy gave the order to his two crew members to bail out. With his crew gone, Davy then headed back towards Allied lines. The fire had seemingly gone out and so he decided to remain at the controls. He could see that he was desperately losing fuel but he managed to make it back across the lines and force-landed just a few miles from his home base.

Although badly damaged, the aircraft was later taken to Amifontaine and, as things turned out, would be the only Battle of the five to have taken part in the raid to return. Davy would later be awarded the DFC for his courage during the attack on the bridge at Vroenhoven and for getting his aircraft back across friendly lines. His observer, Mansell, managed to evade capture and made it back to Allied lines, but Patterson had suffered a broken bone in his left foot and a broken arm, so he could not escape. He was subsequently captured and treated in hospital in Liège. Gordon Patterson was later awarded the DFM for holding off the marauding 109s long enough to enable their attack on the bridge to take place; his award was the first Canadian DFM of the Second World War.

The second section, led by Garland, had taken off from Amifontaine just a few minutes after Thomas and Davy. The three Battles headed off towards their target at low level beneath a layer of cloud. Garland's observer in 'PH-K', Sergeant Tom Gray, was one of seven brothers from Wiltshire and just a few days away from his twenty-sixth birthday. He had joined the RAF as an apprentice at the age of 15, and after leaving Halton had served as an engine fitter before volunteering for flying duties; this was to be his first bombing sortie of the war. Making up the crew was the wireless operator/air gunner, Leading Aircraftman Lawrence Reynolds, from Guildford in Surrey, who was just 20 years old.

Flying in Garland's section were Pilot Officer I. A. McIntosh in 'PH-N' and 28-year-old Sergeant Fred Marland in 'PH-J'. By the time they could all see the bridge at Veldwezelt, the three Battles had already been spotted from the ground and a barrage of flak awaited them. Even before they could start their bombing run, McIntosh's aircraft had been hit in the main fuel tank and had burst into flames. Quickly jettisoning his bombs, McIntosh turned away and managed to make a forced landing near Neerharen to the south-east of Genk in Belgium. He and his two crew members, Sergeant N. T. W. Harper and Leading Aircraftman R. P. MacNaughton, were all captured.

Not wishing to hang around a moment longer than necessary, the two remaining Battles quickly commenced their attack. Without flinching, Garland and Marland flew head-on into the barrage of fire, seemingly ignoring the flak that greeted them. Despite the intensity of the anti-aircraft fire, Garland coolly led the two remaining Battles in a shallow dive-bombing attack on the bridge. After releasing his bombs, Garland's aircraft came under further attack, this time from the enemy fighters. Looking across to where the other Battle was making its attack, he witnessed Marland's aircraft suddenly pitch up, roll out of control and then dive into the ground near Veldwezelt; Marland, his observer, 24-year-old Sergeant Ken Footner, and his wireless operator/air gunner, 22-year-old Leading Aircraftman John Perrin, were all killed.

Garland's bombs had hit the western end of the bridge, causing it some notable damage, but he now found he was in the most hopeless of situations. The Battle was no match for the 109s now swooping in numbers on their helpless prey, and was promptly shot down. The aircraft came down in the village of Lanaken, just 3 miles to the north of Veldwezelt; there were no survivors.

Of the fifteen crew members of the five Battles that had taken part in the raid, six were killed and seven were taken as prisoners of war. Although it was such a tragic loss, it is fortunate that one of the Hurricane pilots sent to sweep the area had witnessed the bravery of the Battle crews over the bridges at Maastricht, and he would later report the outstanding courage and determination displayed during the attacks despite such overwhelming opposition.

In the *London Gazette* of 11 June 1940 it was announced that Donald Garland and Thomas Gray were both to be posthumously awarded the Victoria Cross; the first RAF VCs of the Second World War. Their citation concluded:

Much of the success of this vital operation must be attributed to the formation leader, Flying Officer Garland, and to the coolness and resource of Sergeant Gray, who navigated Flying Officer Garland's aircraft under most difficult conditions in such a manner that the whole formation was able successfully to attack the target in spite of subsequent heavy losses.

Nearly a year later, Garland's mother attended the investiture ceremony at Buckingham Palace to receive the award to her son. She had four sons, but tragically they would all die while serving with the RAF during the Second World War.

Chapter Two

Italian Fleet at Taranto

11/12 November 1940

The latter half of 1940 had seen Britain fighting for its survival, and the heroics of the RAF's few during the Battle of Britain had ensured the nation was safe from invasion, for the time being at least. As the year drew towards a close there was no realistic way of taking the war to the enemy other than from the air. Newly formed and specialist organizations, such as the Commandos and the SOE, would soon enable Britain to strike back at the enemy in a number of ways, but, at the time, these organizations were still finding their feet. And so it is no coincidence that the second of the most daring raids carried out during 1940 was from the air, although it was not carried out by the RAF, but by outdated biplanes of the Fleet Air Arm.

The Fairey Swordfish, known affectionately to its crews as the 'Old Stringbag', was made of a metal airframe covered in fabric. It had a fixed undercarriage and an open cockpit with a three-man crew. Yet the old Swordfish achieved some spectacular successes during the early years of the Second World War, and one of the most notable was against the Italian fleet at Taranto, a raid that would be remembered as one of the most daring in the Fleet Air Arm's history.

Italy's entry into the war in June 1940 had seen the first exchanges between British and Italian forces in North Africa and a change in control of the Mediterranean sea lanes that were vital to the reinforcement of both sides. Conscious of the threat posed by the Italian fleet to the Royal Navy in the Mediterranean, the British Prime Minister, Winston Churchill, was quick to order an attack against the fleet at its base of Taranto.

A large coastal city in southern Italy, Taranto faces the Ionian Sea, and its shallow harbour and port lie on the shores of the Gulf of Taranto on the Salentine Peninsula in the north-east corner of the 'instep' of the boot of

Italy. In November 1940 the port was an important home base for the Italian
fleet, with six battleships, seven heavy cruisers, two light cruisers, and more
than twenty destroyers using the two anchorages of Mar Grande and Mar
Piccolo in what was effectively an outer and inner harbour.

The ships were well protected by quite formidable defences. At just 40 feet
deep, the harbour was considered too shallow for an underwater attack but,
just in case, torpedo nets across the opening to the outer harbour protected
the ships. There was also a line of barrage balloons stretching across the
outer harbour and along its eastern side to provide protection from a low-
level air attack, and a vast array of anti-aircraft defences; both on board the
ships and at the numerous batteries around the harbour.

Initially planned for 21 October, the Royal Navy's celebrated Trafalgar
Day, the raid, called Operation Judgement, was to be carried out by
Swordfish from the carriers HMS *Illustrious* and HMS *Eagle*. However,
repairs to the *Eagle* led to the decision to postpone the attack until the
night of 11/12 November, with the newly commissioned *Illustrious*
providing the aircraft for the attack. It would be the first time in history
that a major air strike would be carried out against an enemy fleet from an
aircraft carrier.

Because of the distance from *Illustrious* to Taranto, the third crew member
of the Swordfish, the Telegraphist Air Gunner (known as the TAG), was
replaced by an auxiliary fuel tank fitted in the central part of the aircraft,
in the position normally occupied by the observer. This gave the aircraft
60 gallons (270 litres) of additional fuel to ensure it had sufficient range to
carry out the attack, meaning the observer was now required to occupy the
rear part of the cockpit.

The plan was for twenty-one Swordfish – sixteen from *Illustrious* (nine
from 815 Squadron and seven from 819 Squadron), augmented by five
aircraft from *Eagle* (two from 813 Squadron and three from 824 Squadron)
– to attack in two waves. The first wave would consist of twelve aircraft and
was to be led by Lieutenant Commander Ken Williamson of 815 Squadron,
while the second wave of nine, led by Lieutenant Commander John Hale
of 819 Squadron, would attack an hour later. Eleven Swordfish armed with
a single modified 18-inch Mk XII torpedo were to be the primary strike
aircraft, while six aircraft would carry six 250lb semi-armour piercing

bombs. The remaining four aircraft would carry a mix of 250lb bombs and parachute flares to carry out diversionary attacks.

The shallow harbour meant the torpedoes would have to be dropped from a very low altitude and so the simple modification to the torpedo-carrying aircraft consisted of a drum fitted beneath the fuselage with a wire connected to the nose of the torpedo; when the torpedo was launched the wire would pull the nose of the torpedo up so that it would 'belly-flop' into the water rather than enter the water in a more conventional nose dive. Breakaway wooden fins were also fitted to provide aerial stability for the torpedo prior to it entering the water.

A final aerial reconnaissance sortie during the early evening of 11 November, timed to coincide when *Illustrious* was positioned off the Greek island of Cephalonia, some 170 miles south-east of Taranto, provided final confirmation that the ships were at anchor in the harbour. Then, at 8.35 pm the first aircraft took off into the evening sky.

Climbing cumbersomely into the air, the twelve Swordfish formed up 10 miles from the carrier before setting course for Taranto. It was a cold evening in the open cockpit but conditions were ideal for the raid, with the moon nearly full, a little more than half of the sky covered by a thin layer of cloud above and a light westerly wind. Just over two hours later the twelve aircraft began their approach towards Taranto from the south-west. The first wave was tasked with attacking targets in both the outer and inner harbours. Passing over the small island of San Pietro to the west of the Mar Grande at 4,000 feet, the Swordfish descended to commence their attack.

Two aircraft, flown by Lieutenants Lancelot Kiggell and Charles Lamb, ran north-easterly towards the outer harbour. Their task was to drop flares along the eastern side of the Mar Grande and to then bomb any targets of convenience. As they approached the harbour they were spotted by the enemy gunners around the shore and on board the ships. The sky soon became illuminated by flares followed by intense anti-aircraft and machine-gun fire. Approaching the south-eastern corner of the line of barrage balloons, Kiggell released his magnesium flares and then broke to the north to look for any targets. Spotting an oil storage depot he carried out a dive-bombing attack before turning for safety. Lamb, seeing the area illuminated by Kiggell, followed and bombed the same oil depot before also turning away.

Making a gentle descent, Williamson led the first three torpedo-carrying Swordfish straight across the bay and towards the eastern side of the Mar Grande. Turning left, he then flew north-eastwards along the eastern edge of the outer harbour towards the line of flares and where he knew a number of ships were at anchor.

The technique for attacking a warship at night was to approach the target from as low as possible, below the horizon, and to silhouette the ship using whatever ambient light was available and by making best use of any light generated from flares or enemy fire. With a maximum speed barely exceeding 100mph when carrying a war load, the Swordfish presents itself as a big, painfully slow and vulnerable aircraft. Yet its slow speed meant that it was an extremely manoeuvrable aircraft in the hands of the right pilot and, flying no more than 30 feet above the waves, Williamson commenced his long run-in towards the ships. Having passed safely between two destroyers, the first major Italian warship that appeared in front of him was the battleship *Conte di Cavour*. At 23,000 tons, she presented an irresistible target. By now there was a concentrated cone of fire coming towards the Swordfish, but Williamson kept heading straight for the centre of the bright inferno in front of him. Each second took him closer and closer to his target, although the intense firing was making it almost impossible to maintain an accurate target run. Staying as low as he dared, Williamson closed to within 1,000 yards of the ship before easing the Swordfish up just enough to release his torpedo.

Behind Williamson, the two other Swordfish wove their way through the outer ring of barrage balloons as both Sub-Lieutenants Philip Sparke and Gus Macauley crossed the breakwater. Unable to identify their primary target, the battleship *Littorio*, Sparke and Macauley chose instead to follow Williamson and to head for the *Conte di Cavour*, pressing home their attacks under intense fire.

On board the *Conte di Cavour* there was nothing anyone could do to prevent the torpedoes from hitting their target, but seconds later the anti-aircraft fire rattled into Williamson's Swordfish, taking it and its crew into the sea. It was just at that point that their torpedo struck the *Conte di Cavour*, tearing a hole nearly 30 feet wide in its side below the waterline, causing it to list and then grounding her with most of the hull underwater. The torpedoes dropped by Sparke and Macauley missed their target and exploded close to the battleship *Andrea Doria*.

The second flight, led by Lieutenant Neil Kemp, accompanied by Lieutenants Henry Swayne and Michael Maund, had been well to the north of Williamson and attacked from the west. Kemp passed to the north of San Pietro and descended north-eastwards towards the centre of the outer harbour. He could now make out the silhouettes of a number of Italian warships against the night sky and headed straight for the *Littorio*, one of the two most modern battleships in the Italian fleet.

Kemp's Swordfish came under increasingly heavy fire from the gun batteries on San Pietro and on the headland protecting the northern part of the Mar Grande. The guns on board the cruisers in the harbour now joined in, but despite the wall of anti-aircraft fire Kemp pressed on towards his target. He was now skimming the wave tops and making it harder for the Italian defenders to pick him out against the dark sea. At nearly 40,000 tons, the *Littorio* was a big target, and the silhouette of its vast length of 780 feet filled the horizon in front of Kemp. Then, at a range of 1,000 yards, Kemp released his torpedo.

Swayne had become separated from his leader and so chose to head eastwards across the Mar Grande and then make a sharp turn to port so that he could attack the *Littorio* from the east. His final run-in to the target coincided with that of Kemp, and the distraction of the other Swordfish attack allowed Swayne to close to around 400 yards from the ship before releasing his torpedo.

In what had been a classic pincer attack, the two Swordfish struck devastating blows: Kemp's torpedo blowing a large hole in the starboard bow of the *Littorio* while Swayne's struck the port quarter. The third aircraft in the formation, that of Maund, headed for the *Littorio*'s sister ship, the *Vittorio Veneto*, although she was fortunate and survived unscathed; Maund's torpedo appearing to explode on impact with the seabed.

A few minutes later it was the turn of the four bomb-carrying Swordfish, led by Captain Oliver Patch, a Royal Marines officer serving with 824 Squadron, to carry out their attacks. Their task was to bomb the line of cruisers and destroyers moored against the quayside of the Mar Piccolo. Starting from a height of 8,000 feet, Patch ran in from San Pietro and crossed the Mar Grande to the western side of the Mar Piccolo. Finding it initially hard to locate the warships from such a height, particularly as he was looking down into a mix of fire and shadows, he pressed on before identifying two cruisers as his target. Patch then commenced a dive-bombing attack and released his bombs from 1,500 feet, hitting the *Libeccio* before making his escape towards the east.

Unable to locate any ships in the gloom, the pilot of the second Swordfish, Sub-Lieutenant Bill Sarra, carried on along the southern shore of the Mar Piccolo and bombed a seaplane base before heading away. The two other Swordfish, flown by Sub-Lieutenant Tony Forde and Lieutenant John Murray, had become separated from the lead pair and so they ran in from further east. Forde flew across the Mar Piccolo from the north-east and delivered his attack on two cruisers from a height of 1,500 feet, while Murray attacked from the eastern end of the Mar Piccolo by flying along the southern shore at 3,000 feet and dropping his bombs along a line of four destroyers.

By the time the Swordfish of the first wave had completed their attacks, seven of the second wave, including the five torpedo-carrying aircraft, were just 50 miles from Taranto. Transiting just below the cloud at a height of 8,000 feet, the Swordfish crews could already see the fires and anti-aircraft fire ahead of them. Twenty minutes behind them was one of the two bomb-carrying Swordfish. It had been delayed on take-off but was now on its way, although the ninth aircraft had been forced to return to *Illustrious* after the straps carrying the auxiliary fuel tank had broken, causing the tank to fall into the sea.

The plan for the second wave was much the same as the first, the only difference being the direction of attack, which was to be from the north-west. The two flare-dropping aircraft were dispatched from the main formation just before midnight and flares were dropped along the eastern side of the outer harbour by Lieutenants Richard Hamilton and Ron Skelton before they both bombed an oil storage depot and headed unscathed back towards *Illustrious*.

Fires were still raging and dense smoke filled the air from the earlier attack as Hale and the four other torpedo-carrying Swordfish commenced their run-in towards the warships. The Italian defences were fully alerted to what was going on as Hale started his target run from the north at 5,000 feet before descending gradually and heading straight for the *Littorio*. Keeping as low as he dared, Hale pressed on, taking his Swordfish to 700 yards from his target before launching his torpedo from a height of just 30 feet. With his torpedo on its way, Hale turned hard to starboard just as he reached the line of barrage balloons.

Close behind him was the Swordfish of Lieutenant Gerald Bayly. He had followed Hale into the harbour but had soon come under intense anti-aircraft fire. His Swordfish was hit repeatedly, but Bayly bravely pressed on towards the heavy cruiser *Gorizia*. Whether he managed to release his torpedo or not is unknown, but the Swordfish succumbed to the relentless fire and plunged into the sea just to the west of the cruiser.

The third Swordfish, flown by Lieutenant Charles Lea, had also followed Hale in to the attack. Flying well astern of Hale, Lea had managed to identify the *Caio Duilio*, one of the older battleships of 25,000 tons. Despite intense fire he carried on closer and closer to his target, finally releasing his torpedo from just 500 yards. Then, weaving between even more intense anti-aircraft fire coming from two cruisers nearby, Lea made his escape as his torpedo hit the battleship amidships on the starboard side, causing a mighty explosion and flooding the ship's magazines.

Next to attack was Lieutenant Michael Torrens-Spence. Following the line of Hale ahead of him, he also chose the *Littorio* for his target, but his Swordfish had been spotted and was already under intense fire. Torrens-Spence pressed on just above the waves, his target clearly visible against the night sky. He kept closing until the battleship was just 700 yards away, then he finally released his torpedo and turned for safety, his undercarriage clipping the waves as he weaved his way through the line of barrage balloons to make his escape.

Running in across the Mar Piccolo and then crossing the town, the final torpedo-carrying Swordfish, of Lieutenant John Wellham, turned hard right towards the centre of the Mar Grande. The sky was illuminated from the previous attacks and the Swordfish was spotted by the Italian defenders just as Wellham started his dive towards the ships. His aircraft was struck several times, causing him to temporarily lose control, before he levelled out amongst a group of battleships. Pressing on regardless, he could see the *Vittorio Veneto* in the distance and descended down to wave-top height to commence his torpedo run. Despite being hit twice on the port wing by flak, which shattered the aircraft's ribs and ripped the fabric apart, causing aileron damage, Wellham continued on towards the huge silhouette of the *Vittorio Veneto*, now getting ever closer. Finally, at a range of just 500 yards, he released his torpedo. As he broke off towards safety his aircraft was hit yet again, but Wellham managed to retain control and take the stricken Swordfish safely back to the *Illustrious*.

The last Swordfish to attack was that of Lieutenant Ed Clifford. He was more than twenty minutes behind the rest of the second wave, and by the time he arrived in the vicinity of Taranto the anti-aircraft fire was relentless. Rather than position himself to the north-west of the harbour, as was originally planned, Clifford elected to run-in from overland to the east of the inner harbour and head across the dockyard for the far side of the Mar Piccolo. As he turned left and descended to 2,500 feet to carry out his bombing run, the Swordfish came under intense anti-aircraft fire. Having spotted two cruisers in the Mar Piccolo, the *Trento* and *Miraglia*, Clifford then ran across the two ships and dropped his bombs, hitting the *Trento*, before turning hard to the north for safety.

By 3.00 am eighteen of the Swordfish were back on *Illustrious*. Behind them they had left a scene of total devastation. The *Conte di Cavour* had been severely damaged and, despite the attempts of those on board during the hours after the attack, the ship was grounded and would play no further part in the war. The destroyer *Caio Duilio* had suffered one significant hit and was lucky not to suffer a worst fate, but she would nonetheless require extensive repairs and it would be five months before she was able to put back to sea. It was to be the same outcome for the *Littorio*. Having been hit by three torpedoes, once on the port side and twice on the starboard, the battleship had also suffered extensive damage from severe flooding and would be out of action for the next five months. The *Trento* had been fortunate to escape any serious damage, as the bomb that had passed through its deck had failed to explode, but it would still be out of action for several weeks. Two destroyers, the *Libeccio* and *Pessagno*, had also been hit and damaged by unexploded bombs, and the Swordfish had also caused extensive damage to the surrounding port.

On board *Illustrious*, the heroic tales of bravery and courage started to be told. Although the raid had expected to suffer losses of up to 50 per cent, the reality was that just two Swordfish had failed to return. One was that of the leader of the first wave, Ken Williamson, and his observer, Norman Scarlett, but both crew members had miraculously survived the impact on hitting the sea and were subsequently captured and taken as prisoners of war. The only other loss was the second Swordfish of the second wave; sadly, its crew, Lieutenants Gerald Bayly and Henry Slaughter, were both killed.

Consideration was briefly given to conducting a follow-up attack the next evening, using fifteen of the Swordfish, but this idea was cancelled due to the weather; besides, the imminent departure of the undamaged Italian warships for Naples would have meant there was little point.

Unsurprisingly, the success of the raid resulted in an initial announcement of six gallantry awards for those who had taken part. There were DSOs to the leaders of each wave, Ken Williamson and John Hale, and four DSCs: to the observers of the two lead aircraft, Lieutenants Norman Scarlett and George Carline, and to Captain Oliver Patch and his observer, Lieutenant David Goodwin. However, the captain of *Illustrious* felt this was insufficient recognition for the outstanding bravery shown by the Swordfish crews and so an additional two DSOs and fourteen DSCs were later announced, with the remaining members of the raid receiving a Mentioned in Despatches. Those DSOs announced later were presented to the two crew members of the final Swordfish to attack, Lieutenants Ed Clifford and George Going, who had flown to Taranto and then pressed home their attack completely alone.

Also included in the later awards was a bar to his DSC for Sub-Lieutenant Philip Sparke, who had received his first DSC during the Dunkirk evacuation earlier in the year and who would subsequently be awarded a second bar, albeit posthumously, for his outstanding courage during strikes against Vichy French shipping off the Syrian coast just six months later. At the time of his death Philip Sparke was just 21 years old, but he would not be the only survivor of Taranto to be killed later in the war: fourteen more would die in action, six of whom were casualties of the devastating bombing of *Illustrious* just a few weeks later.

Although Taranto was not the first large-scale attack by Swordfish of the war – that had been achieved in the Norwegian campaign earlier in the year – it was the most effective and was the first all-aircraft ship-to-ship engagement in the history of warfare. In just one raid the brave crews of the Old Stringbag had succeeded in halving the capability of the Italian fleet in the Mediterranean; the balance of sea power in the Med had swung towards the Allies in just one night.

Not surprisingly, the heroism shown by those who took part in the raid has never been forgotten; Taranto remains one of the most celebrated events in the Royal Navy's calendar to this day. But the raid not only had an immediate effect in the Mediterranean. Elsewhere in the world, others could see the dramatic impact on naval power by an air-launched torpedo attack. Prior to the raid, most naval strategists had believed that deep water was required for a torpedo attack to be successful, but Taranto had proved this not to be the case. Most historically though, and unbeknown to anyone at the time, watching closer than anyone else were the heads of the Japanese Navy. The attack on Pearl Harbor was just a year away.

Chapter Three

Attack on the *Gneisenau*

6 April 1941

W hat chance would one aircraft, armed with only one torpedo, have of crippling a mighty German warship located in a virtually impenetrable harbour and protected by a thousand guns? Certainly no one would ever have planned such a raid, and any aircraft daring to try and pierce such a defence would have only the remotest chance of survival. But that was exactly the position Flying Officer Kenneth Campbell found himself in at dawn on 6 April 1941. His target, the *Gneisenau*, was in his sights and he would get no second chance.

The fact that Britain was an island meant it was vital to keep its sea routes across the Atlantic open. Germany's two large and very capable battle cruisers, the *Scharnhorst* and the *Gneisenau*, each displacing 32,000 tons, and quicker and more heavily armed than the Royal Navy's capital ships in the Atlantic, posed a real threat to the merchant convoys supplying Britain. By early 1941 it was estimated the two battle cruisers had, between them, sunk more than a million tons of Allied shipping, and they were soon to be joined by the *Bismarck*, the largest warship in the world at the time. If this was allowed to happen, it was clear that the three mighty warships would create havoc in the Atlantic and potentially starve Britain into defeat.

At the end of March the two battle cruisers went into harbour at Brest, on the west coast of France, having just completed their successful Atlantic patrol. This provided a rare opportunity to attack the ships in harbour and so a bombing campaign was ordered by the RAF, to commence immediately, in an attempt to sink the two ships. However, despite a number of bombs dropped against the two ships during a week-long campaign, there was no success. More than a hundred aircraft had attacked on the night of 30/31 March without achieving any hits, and another similar sized force had attacked four nights later, but found it difficult to locate the ships. A further raid the following night had only produced one hit on the dry dock in which the *Gneisenau* was lying, despite more than fifty bombers being involved in the attack.

Bomber Command's attempts to sink the ships had proved costly in terms of resources. More than 250 sorties had been flown during the week and four aircraft had been lost, but only one bomb had landed anywhere near the ships. The RAF now turned to Coastal Command. An aerial reconnaissance sortie revealed the *Scharnhorst* was moored up alongside the harbour quay and was well protected by torpedo nets, but the *Gneisenau* had been moved out of the dry dock and into the inner harbour, and was now considered vulnerable to attack from a torpedo-carrying aircraft such as the twin-engine Bristol Beaufort.

An attack was immediately ordered for the following day, 6 April, soon after dawn, with the task falling to 22 Squadron. The squadron was operating a detachment of aircraft from St Eval in Cornwall, having moved to the south-west from its home base at North Coates in Lincolnshire. From St Eval its Beauforts were within striking distance of the Atlantic ports along the Bay of Biscay on the west coast of France, but only six aircraft were available for the raid, with only three of the crews torpedo-trained. The plan, therefore, was to attack in two formations of three, with one formation bombing the torpedo nets while the second wave of three torpedo-carrying aircraft would carry out the main attack against the *Gneisenau*.

The three pilots chosen to carry out the torpedo attack against the *Gneisenau* were Flying Officer John Hyde, Sergeant H. Camp and Flying Officer Kenneth Campbell. Born and raised in Scotland, Campbell was still only 23 years old. He was serving with his first operational squadron, having arrived just six months before, and this was to be his twentieth operational sortie. His three crew members were a Canadian observer, Sergeant Jimmy Scott, a wireless operator, Sergeant William Mulliss, and Flight Sergeant Ralph Hillman as air gunner.

The Beaufort crews knew that the harbour at Brest was heavily defended by an estimated one thousand guns of various calibre. Furthermore, the harbour benefitted from the natural protection of hills around it. The reconnaissance photographs had shown the *Gneisenau* to be moored just 500 yards from a harbour mole, which meant the crews would have to deliver their torpedoes with extreme accuracy. Then, having released their torpedo, the pilot would have to make a steep turn away from the high ground beyond the harbour.

The crews knew from the outset that their chances of achieving any success were incredibly slim, but even so, the raid did not get off to a good start. The aircraft were due to take off soon after 4.30 am but heavy rain at St Eval overnight had turned the airfield into a swamp and had prevented two of the bomb-carrying Beauforts from getting airborne. Even then, the one that did manage to get airborne got lost due to the bad weather, which was not helped by the fact that it was still dark. The three torpedo-carrying aircraft had fared little better. One also got lost in the heavy rain and the other two became separated because of misty conditions over the sea.

The one Beaufort to have pressed on was that flown by Campbell. Unaware of what was happening elsewhere, he arrived at the planned rendezvous point a short distance from the harbour at Brest. It was now starting to get light and, with no sign of the other Beauforts, he decided to circle over the sea some distance from the harbour and watch for visible signs of the bomb explosions from the first wave. But, as it approached 6.00 am, there were still no signs of any such activity in or around the harbour.

Campbell knew that he would soon lose the cover of the murky dawn, as it was getting lighter by the minute. He had to make a decision, and, not knowing what had happened to the others, he decided to press on alone. Undaunted, he started his run-in towards the harbour. With no signs of any other Beauforts around, he knew that his attack would have to be made with absolute precision. There would be no second chance.

The *Gneisenau* was secured alongside the wall on the north shore of the harbour, protected by the stone mole bending round it from the west. On the rising ground behind the battle cruiser stood a protective battery of anti-aircraft guns with other batteries clustered thickly around the two arms of land, encircling the outer harbour. In the outer harbour, and near to the mole, were moored three heavily armed anti-aircraft ships that were guarding the cruisers. Campbell knew that even if he could succeed in penetrating these formidable defences, it would be almost impossible to avoid the high ground beyond the harbour. Yet he still decided to take his chances and to run the gauntlet of defences in order to press home his attack.

As Campbell took the Beaufort down to just above the waves, he was immediately greeted by a wall of flak as the anti-aircraft gunners spotted him running in at low level. As he crossed the mole he passed the three anti-aircraft ships below the height of their masts as he hugged the waves as close as he dared. As the only attacking aircraft everything was thrown his way as he ran the gauntlet of concentrated anti-aircraft fire. The final seconds of the run-in would have seemed like an eternity, but he then popped up to 50 feet, just high enough to release his torpedo at minimum range. Finally, with the torpedo gone, he started a steep banking turn away to port and towards the safety of the cloud above.

As it turned out, Campbell's run-in and torpedo release had been textbook, bordering on perfection, but as he turned away to avoid the high ground and to seek the cover of cloud, his aircraft presented an easy target to the gunners. All the guns in the area caught the Beaufort in a devastating burst of fire and it plummeted into the harbour. The crew stood no chance.

The result of Campbell's attack was that the *Gneisenau* was severely damaged below the waterline and the mighty battle cruiser was soon back in dry dock undergoing major repairs to its starboard propeller shaft; she would be out of action for nine months. It was an incredible achievement, given that Campbell had attacked alone and with only one torpedo, to inflict as much damage as he did. He had known that his attack would have to be carried out with precision, and it was.

Such was the bravery of Campbell and his crew, the Germans gave the four airmen a funeral with full military honours. When news of the lone and gallant attack by Campbell and his crew filtered through to London, through the network of the French Resistance, it was announced that Kenneth Campbell was to be posthumously awarded the Victoria Cross. The fact that he managed to launch his torpedo with such accuracy, in the face of intense anti-aircraft fire from all around, is testament to the skill and bravery of the young Scot. By pressing home his attack at close quarters in the face of overwhelming enemy fire, and on a course fraught with extreme peril, Kenneth Campbell displayed valour of the highest order.

Chapter Four

Sink the *Bismarck*

24–27 May 1941

The success at Taranto had brought an air of confidence to the Swordfish crews of the Fleet Air Arm. Although the raid against the Italian fleet had been extremely hazardous, the dramatic impact an ageing biplane could have against a large warship was there for all to see. But it was not the Italian fleet that would ultimately present the biggest threat to the Royal Navy, or to Britain – that would come from the large warships of the German Navy.

One of the biggest threats to naval shipping in the Atlantic came from the German battleship *Bismarck*. Launched in 1939 and completed the following year, the *Bismarck* was more than 820 feet (250 metres) in length, displaced 50,000 tons, boasted a vast array of heavy guns and had a speed of 30 knots. By May 1941 she was ready to break out into the Atlantic Ocean where she could add to the havoc already being caused by German U-boats and other surface ships.

Under Operation Rheinübung (Rhine Crossing), the latest in a series of raids by the Germany Navy against Allied shipping, the *Bismarck* and the heavy cruiser *Prinz Eugen* sailed separately from Gotenhafen during the night of 18/19 May 1941. Proceeding under escort, they rendezvoused in the western Baltic and then set course for the northern Atlantic. Five nights later they entered the Denmark Strait near the coast of Greenland, having transited through the Norwegian Sea to keep well clear of Britain and the Royal Navy. But the German naval group had been spotted and tracked along the way, and were now being shadowed by two Royal Navy cruisers. A number of ships of the Home Fleet were already en route to intercept the German raiders and, during the early morning of 24 May, the *Bismarck* and *Prinz Eugen* were engaged by the Royal Navy's mighty battle cruiser HMS *Hood* and the battleship *Prince of Wales*. The two opposing surface groups were still more than 12 miles apart but the sea battle raged, and resulted in the sinking of the *Hood* within just a matter of minutes, her magazines exploding following fatal hits from the *Bismarck*. Although the *Prince of Wales* continued the action, she had suffered badly as a result of multiple hits and was forced to make her escape under the cover of a smokescreen.

Although striking a vital blow, the *Bismarck* had not escaped unscathed. She had been hit near the bow, causing fuel tanks to rupture and a serious oil leak, and forcing her to head for Brest to undergo repairs. With the *Prinz Eugen* detached to continue the mission, *Bismarck* drew off the pursuit and every effort was now made by the Germans to provide the great battleship with as much protection as possible from all available U–boats in the area.

With the *Bismarck* heading for safety, she was shadowed by the damaged *Prince of Wales* and the out-gunned cruisers *Norfolk* and *Suffolk*. Determined to avenge the loss of the *Hood*, the British Admiralty also realized this was too good an opportunity to miss and set about getting more British forces to the scene as fast as possible. More ships of the Home Fleet, including the newly commissioned aircraft carrier HMS *Victorious* with nine Swordfish on board, had earlier sailed from Scapa Flow. Escorted by four destroyers, the *Victorious* was soon dispatched from the main surface group towards the *Bismarck* and was now just over 100 miles away as the Swordfish were being prepared to make an attack.

It was just after 10.00 pm when the nine Swordfish of 825 Squadron took off from *Victorious*. It was already starting to get dark as the squadron commander, Lieutenant Commander Eugene Esmonde, led the Swordfish towards the *Bismarck*. At 31 years old, Esmonde, an Irishman, was an extremely experienced pilot and had commanded 825 since before the war. It was an extremely professional and effective unit with some of the Swordfish recently fitted with ASV (air-to-surface vessel) radar, which enabled the *Bismarck* to be located in the cloudy and squally weather conditions.

By the time Esmonde led his squadron through cloud in preparation for an attack, it was nearly midnight. As they broke cloud, the Swordfish were still more than 5 miles away from the *Bismarck*, but they had been spotted against the cloudy background and were already under attack. The intense anti-aircraft barrage put up by the battleship succeeded in hitting Esmonde's aircraft and caused his formation to break up. With severe damage to his starboard lower aileron, Esmonde had little option but to press home his attack alone from his current position on the port bow of the *Bismarck*, skimming the wave tops and closing to within 1,000 yards before launching his torpedo from a height of 100 feet. Close behind him were the two other Swordfish of his flight, flown by Sub-Lieutenant John Thompson and Lieutenant Neal Maclean. Both pilots succeeded in getting their torpedoes away despite the volley of anti-aircraft fire coming at them.

The second flight of three aircraft, led by Lieutenant Percy Gick, had arrived out of position for their attack and so circled before commencing their run-in towards the battleship. The two Swordfish of Lieutenant Bill Garthwaite and Sub-Lieutenant Pat Jackson followed Gick into the attack and, keeping as low as they dared, managed to escape much of the barrage as they pressed on towards the *Bismarck*, before releasing their torpedoes from a height of no more than 50 feet.

The leader of the third flight, Lieutenant Henry Pollard, decided to lead his formation away from the barrage and take a longer route to the target, but one of the Swordfish, that flown by Sub-Lieutenant Alex Houston, lost sight of his leader and the *Bismarck*, which left just Pollard and Sub-Lieutenant Bobby Lawson to carry out an attack.

The Swordfish all returned safely to the *Victorious* during the early hours of 25 May, but, given the attack had taken place at night, and in difficult weather and sea conditions, it is hardly surprising that this first airborne attack against the *Bismarck* did not cause any direct damage, although it had caused the battleship to take constant evading action and crucially delayed its escape towards safety. For his leadership, skill and courage during the raid Eugene Esmonde was awarded the DSO. There were also awards for his observer, Lieutenant Colin Ennever, and for Percy Gick and his observer, Sub-Lieutenant Valentine Norfolk, as well as awards for Henry Pollard and Bill Garthwaite; all five were awarded a DSC. Esmonde's telegraphist air gunner, Petty Officer Airman Stan Parker, and two other TAGs, Leading Airmen Les Sayer and Ginger Johnson, were all awarded the DSM, and there was a Mention in Despatches for Sub-Lieutenants David Berrill, Leslie Bailey and Bobby Lawson.

The idea of a follow-up attack at dawn was cancelled due to increasingly poor weather, but later that day the Swordfish flew off the carrier again in an attempt to relocate the *Bismarck*. The weather proved too bad for a sighting, leaving the German battleship to continue its escape to safety, but her loss of fuel had meant a reduction in speed. For now the *Bismarck* had temporarily lost her pursuers, but she was sighted again the following morning by a long-range Catalina aircraft of RAF Coastal Command. The chase was back on and soon to arrive on the scene was the Royal Navy aircraft carrier HMS *Ark Royal*, having been dispatched from Gibraltar alongside the battle cruiser HMS *Renown*, the cruiser HMS *Sheffield* and a number of escorting destroyers.

Using a pair of Swordfish to maintain a shadow of the *Bismarck*, the *Ark Royal* prepared the rest of her aircraft for an attack. During the afternoon, fourteen Swordfish, led by Lieutenant Commander James Stewart-Moore, took off from the *Ark Royal* to attack the *Bismarck*, but poor weather meant the battleship could not be located and nearly resulted in the sinking of the *Sheffield* instead.

Time was now running out to sink, or at least slow down, the *Bismarck* before she reached the safety of the French coastline at some time during the following day. Desperate to try again before nightfall, a second attempt was mounted in the evening with fifteen Swordfish from 820, 810 and 818 Squadrons taking part in the attack; this time with their torpedoes fitted with an impact detonator and set to run at a more shallow depth.

The weather conditions were still terrible as the fifteen aircraft, led by Lieutenant Commander Trevenen Coode, took off from the *Ark Royal* just after 7.00 pm. Once formed up, they headed for the *Bismarck*, keeping below the medium-level cloud to avoid icing conditions that would present a serious threat to the old aircraft. An hour and a half later they arrived in the area to find the cloud layered, which made it difficult to maintain six separate flights, but there were enough breaks to allow them to descend below the cloud base at 2,000 feet to carry out their attacks.

Just before 9.00 pm, the first section, led by Coode, and now including a fourth aircraft that had been unable to maintain formation with its own section, made their descent. Beneath the cloud Coode realized they were still nearly 5 miles from the *Bismarck* and in no great position to attack. Deciding that a long and very slow run-in to their target from a less than ideal position would be suicidal, he took the four aircraft back into cloud to reposition and to get closer to the *Bismarck* before commencing their attack. Meanwhile, the second section of three aircraft, led by Lieutenant

David 'Feather' Godfrey-Faussett, had initially climbed above the lower layer of cloud to position for their attack but had then run into more cloud. With ice forming on their wings, they had lost sight of the lead section as it descended below cloud to carry out its attack. With no option but to dive down on the last known ASV bearing, Godfrey-Faussett led the two other Swordfish, flown by Sub-Lieutenants Ken Pattisson and Tony Beale, into attack, but as they descended back through the cloud Beale was unable to maintain position and had to break off.

The two Swordfish of Godfrey-Faussett and Pattisson broke cloud to find the *Bismarck* out on their starboard side and so were the first to attack. Hugging the waves and flying in line astern to make it as hard as possible for the ship's gunners to pick him out against the dark sea, Godfrey-Faussett pressed on through the screen of anti-aircraft fire to complete his attack. Pattisson, meanwhile, no longer able to see his leader, also headed straight for the battleship. As he edged closer towards his target, the Swordfish proved a slow and lumbering target for the *Bismarck*'s gunners. Pattisson's aircraft was hit by shrapnel from the shells exploding nearby, ripping the canvas from his airframe, but he pressed on regardless. Holding his aircraft straight and level, he carried on under intense fire during the final seconds of his run-in towards the *Bismarck*. Then, at a range of just 900 yards, and at less than 100 feet above the waves, he dropped his torpedo before jinking his way to safety.

The remaining aircraft of the third section had now joined up with the fourth section, led by Lieutenant Hugh de Graaff Hunter. The four aircraft descended to just above the lower layer of cloud at 2,000 feet and then separated briefly before joining up once again below the cloud to attack from the port side, just at the time that Godfrey-Faussett and Pattisson were completing their attack on the starboard.

It was then the turn of Coode and his formation. As they popped out of cloud on the *Bismarck*'s port beam they immediately came under intense and accurate anti-aircraft fire. As they pressed home their attacks and then broke away for safety, a torpedo released from one of the first pair of Swordfish was seen to strike the stern of the *Bismarck*.

The fifth and sixth sections, each consisting of a pair of Swordfish, had been unable to complete their attacks. The first pair had become separated in cloud, with one ending up out of position astern the *Bismarck* and under intense fire, while the other was driven off by a concentration of anti-aircraft fire after making two attempts. The second pair had also come under heavy fire and one aircraft was forced to release its torpedo too early, while the other had to break off and withdraw.

While all this was going on, Beale had reappeared ahead of the *Bismarck* and off her port bow. Determined not to return to the *Ark Royal* without having attacked, he pressed on alone amidst the heaviest barrage of anti-aircraft fire, as the *Bismarck* threw everything it could at the single Swordfish. Having released his torpedo, Beale and his crew watched in awe as the torpedo struck the battleship amidships on the port side, causing an enormous column of smoke and water rising well above her decks.

It was just after 10.00 pm when the first of the Swordfish made it back to the *Ark Royal*. Remarkably, all fifteen aircraft returned safely to the carrier, even though many had been damaged; one had been hit more than 150 times and two of its crew were wounded. Although they did not know what damage they had caused when they first gathered back on the *Ark*, the Swordfish crews had hit the *Bismarck* aft and caused significant damage to its propellers and rudders; this was probably a result of Ken Pattisson's attack, although at least one other torpedo, that of Tony Beale, was seen to have hit its target.

The *Bismarck* was now severely crippled. She could only maintain slow speed and was unable to manoeuvre. Later that night, shadowing aircraft reported that she was slowly turning in a circle, her port rudder jammed. It was the beginning of the end for the *Bismarck*. Throughout the night and into the following morning, the great battleship was repeatedly hit by Royal Navy ships closing in on their prey. A third air strike took off in bad weather the following morning and the Swordfish arrived in the area ready to attack but they were not needed. The *Bismarck* had reportedly been hit more than 400 times and her final moments came during the morning of 27 May. It may have been that she was scuttled by her own crew, or it may have been the torpedoes of HMS *Dorsetshire* that caused the *Bismarck* to capsize to port and roll over. Either way, she was swallowed by the chilling depths of the Atlantic as the Swordfish crews watched silently from above.

Understandably, there were many awards announced for the sinking of the *Bismarck*, including the DSO to Trevenen Coode for his outstanding leadership of the final Swordfish attack, and a DSC to his observer,

Lieutenant Edmund Carver. There was also a DSC for 'Feather' Godfrey-Faussett, Hugh de Graaff Hunter, Ken Pattisson and Tony Beale, as well as a DSC for Sub-Lieutenant Peter Elias and a DSM for Leading Airman Harry Huxley, the observer and TAG of one of the two Swordfish that had initially shadowed the *Bismarck* when the *Ark Royal* had first arrived on the scene.

What the outcome of the pursuit might have been without the heroic intervention of the Swordfish crews will never be known, but what is clear is that the damage caused by one or more of the torpedoes launched in their final attack on the ship crippled the *Bismarck* to the point that there was to be no escape. The capability of the *Bismarck* was never in doubt, as its swift destruction of the Royal Navy's mighty *Hood* had proved, and who knows what she might have gone on to achieve had it not been for the extreme bravery of the crews of the Old Stringbags.

Chapter Five

Litani River

9–10 June 1941

Having covered four daring raids from the air, it is time to turn attention to the Commandos, which had been formed during 1940 after the Fall of France. Because Britain had no special forces at the time, the Prime Minister, Winston Churchill, had proposed the formation of a new organization, made up of volunteers, to carry out offensive action against the enemy. Churchill gave the organization the name Commandos, taken from his days as a war reporter in the Boer War when he had witnessed for himself the significant losses inflicted on the British Army by the Boer's irregular forces, known as 'commandos'. Although the vision had initially been for the British Commandos to carry out offensive action against the enemy's extended and quite vulnerable coastline in north-west Europe, it is to the Middle East, and a campaign that is rarely given any historical recognition, that we go first to look at an early and very daring commando raid, and it would be the first time that commandos would attack a heavily defended position.

The Allied invasion of Vichy French-controlled Syria and Lebanon, called Operation Exporter, commenced in June 1941. The fact that little was known of the campaign during the war can be put down to there being little, if any, coverage given to the campaign back home. Politicians believed that any public knowledge of Allies fighting against French forces would probably have a negative effect in those countries involved. Even after the war, the campaign has remained largely unknown, but the action involving the men of 11 (Scottish) Commando at the Litani River was as fierce as anything the commandos had encountered at that stage of the war.

For several months the leader of the Free French, General Charles de Gaulle, had been pressing for an invasion of Vichy French Syria, but British forces were stretched across the Mediterranean and North Africa. Then, in

May 1941, an agreement was signed between Vichy France and Germany, allowing the Nazis access to military facilities in Syria.

The outcome was the launching of an Allied offensive to prevent the Germans from using Syria and the Lebanon as havens to launch an attack on Egypt. Hostilities commenced on 8 June and, in support of Exporter, 11 Commando was tasked with capturing the Qasmiye Bridge that crossed the Litani River, about 50 miles south of Beirut, in what was then Syria, but is now southern Lebanon. The river flows east–west at that point and crossed the planned Allied line of advance northwards towards Beirut. Capturing the bridge would ease the Australian 7th Division's advance along the coastal road from Haifa to Beirut, and it would be the first of a series of major actions lasting more than a month.

Commanded by Lieutenant Colonel Dick Pedder, 11 Commando had been drawn largely from Scottish regiments and sent to the Mediterranean in early 1941 as C Battalion of Layforce, a rather ad hoc formation made up of a number of commando units under the overall command of Colonel Robert Laycock. The intention was that Layforce would carry out a campaign of harassment against the enemy in the Mediterranean, but things had not turned out quite as planned, and by the time they arrived in theatre the strategic situation had much changed. A planned raid on the Greek island of Rhodes had to be cancelled, a supposedly daring raid on the Italian-held town of Bardia turned out to be unopposed, and the decision to send commandos to Crete to fight a rearguard action during the evacuation of the island, a role that commandos had not been specifically formed to do, had resulted in heavy losses. None of these early operations had involved Pedder's men. They had instead been given the task of carrying out garrison duties on Cyprus, a role that had left the men of 11 Commando still looking for an opportunity to make their mark – an opportunity that finally came during Exporter.

The plan was for the commandos to carry out an amphibious assault at dawn, landing from the sea at the mouth of the Litani to coincide with the Australian 21st Infantry Brigade's attack on the river. The enemy was known to be holding the ground along the line of the Litani River, with a second bridge, situated at Kafr Badda, crossing another river flowing parallel to the Litani about 2 miles to the north. The whole area was known to be heavily defended. In-between the two rivers, and to the east of the coastal road connecting Sidon and Tyre that crossed the two bridges, there were a number of enemy installations, including two main gun batteries and a barracks. Once ashore the commandos were to outflank the enemy and to attack them from the rear. They would then secure both the Qasmiye and Kafr Badda bridges before the enemy had time to destroy them, which would allow the Australian infantry to cross both rivers and advance towards Beirut. As the amphibious assault was planned for 8 June, the commandos left Cyprus four days prior to that, and two days later boarded their landing ship, HMS *Glengyle*. They then set sail from Port Said with a naval escort.

Pedder had a raiding force of more than 20 officers and 450 men, but he had been given little information regarding where the landing was to take place. A motor gunboat was launched so that the naval beach master and a local guide could carry out a quick reconnaissance of the coastline along the intended landing beaches. They came back reporting a large swell and heavy surf along the coast, particularly in the final few hundred yards of the beaches, which made the likelihood of the flat-bottomed landing craft being able to go ashore without capsizing quite slim. With the commandos laden with their heavy equipment, this would most likely result in several casualties. Furthermore, the forecast was not good, as it was looking unlikely there would be any change to the sea conditions for the next forty-eight hours.

Nonetheless, the decision was made to attempt a landing at dawn the following morning as planned, and during the early hours of 8 June the *Glengyle* arrived at the dropping-off point about 4 miles off the mouth of the Litani River. The eleven landing craft were lowered and the commandos packed inside with all their equipment and ammunition. The swell was quite severe and there was still a major concern about the conditions. Opinions differed, particularly between Pedder, who argued that the risk was worth taking in order to retain the element of surprise, and the beach master who had carried out the reconnaissance of the coastline. The final decision belonged to the skipper of the *Glengyle*, Captain Christopher Petrie, who, at that early part of the operation, still retained overall responsibility for whether the assault was launched or not. Reluctantly, Petrie made the decision to abort the mission.

With the commandos back on board and the landing craft raised, the *Glengyle* headed back to Port Said, arriving back during the afternoon. The commandos now waited anxiously while Pedder was summoned to a quick meeting on board another ship to find out what was to happen next. He soon arrived back on the *Glengyle* to tell his men the operation was back on and they were to set sail at once. It had been just over an hour since the *Glengyle* had arrived back in port and, to the disbelief of those on board, she was once again heading out to sea.

The *Glengyle* reached the dropping-off point during the early hours of 9 June. Fortunately, the swell had subsided enough to make the lowering of the landing craft easier than before. By now the Australian attack was well underway. Unfortunately, however, the earlier decision to abort the mission had been made in full view of the enemy. The motor gunboat carrying out the reconnaissance along the coastline had been spotted and it had become obvious to the enemy what was going on, so by the time the Australian infantry had advanced the defenders had simply blown the Qasmiye Bridge.

The second bridge at Kafr Badda, however, was still intact and so Pedder had to modify his plan. He split his force into three parties: X, Y and Z. The original plan had been to land the parties on both sides of the mouth of the Litani and to seize the Qasmiye Bridge, but because the bridge was no longer the main objective, all three parties would now land to the north of the estuary on separate beaches between the two rivers.

X Party comprised of 2, 3 and 9 Troops, and was to land closest to the Litani to carry out the main assault on the north bank of the river. The men were to be led by Major Geoffrey Keyes, Pedder's second-in-command and the oldest son of Admiral Sir Roger Keyes, the Director of Combined Operations. Keyes had just celebrated his twenty-fourth birthday and had already been in action in Norway prior to serving in the Middle East. His task now was to destroy an enemy position at Aiteniye and to then seize the enemy fortification on the north bank of the river from its rear. His party were then to hold the area to allow the Australians time to build a pontoon bridge across the river.

Pedder, meanwhile, was to lead Y Party, consisting of 1, 7 and 8 Troops. His party would land just to the north of Keyes's group and provide support during the main assault by taking a gun battery and capturing the enemy barracks just over a mile inland, after which Pedder's group would support the main attack in whatever way it could. The third group, Z Party, made up of 4 and 10 Troops, and under the command of Captain

George More, would land furthest north, some 2 miles from the Litani River and at the mouth of the second river. More's task was to capture and hold the bridge at Kafr Badda, and so prevent the enemy from reinforcing the area along the coast road from the north, and to capture an enemy gun battery to the east.

Soon after 3.00 am the lead commandos of X Party boarded four landing craft and headed off towards the shore. It would be another hour before daylight. As before, there had been a lack of information during the briefing and so the landing party had been given little idea of how to find the right landing spot. Although there was a reasonable amount of moonlight, it proved a difficult task.

In the end, X Party landed just before 5.00 am about a mile south of where they should have been and on the wrong side of the river. Fortunately, the landing was unopposed. It was now getting light and Keyes quickly realized they had landed on the south side of the river. With no alternative but to mount a frontal attack against heavily armed troops in a fortified position, Keyes ordered his men to move rapidly across the beach towards the river. At that point the whole beach area came under heavy fire, including mortar and artillery fire, as well as that from heavy machine guns. The fire was coming from the same enemy fortification to the north-east of their position that they should have been attacking from the rear.

During their advance to the river the men of X Party soon became pinned down, particularly from sniper fire from the enemy bank, and suffered a number of casualties. One section led by Captain George Highland, with 21-year-old Lieutenant Eric Garland alongside him, managed to work its way forward on the far right, and out of sight of the main enemy position. But faced with only open and flat ground ahead there was little in the way of protection, and they soon became pinned down by an enemy sniper.

As Keyes surveyed the scene, the casualties started to mount; two of his corporals and a sapper were killed. They could get no further. For the best part of half an hour the commandos remained where they were, but they had now been joined by some Australian infantry supporting the commandos' attack on the river. Using a combination of crawling and sprinting across the open ground, and using whatever cover he could find, Keyes managed to reach Highland's advanced position. He arrived to find that Highland and Garland had just teased out the enemy sniper who had kept his small group pinned down for so long; with his position now exposed, the hapless Frenchman was soon cut down by a burst of commando machine-gun fire.

With the sniper taken care of, and with supporting artillery fire now raining down on the enemy, the commandos had an opportunity to cross the river. A small canvas boat was brought up to the river and positioned amongst some rushes as cover. With the help of the Australians, and with Garland and a handful of commandos on board, the men paddled their way across the river, which, at that point, was just 30 yards wide. Although the river was relatively narrow at that point, it was fast flowing and reaching the other side was hard work, but the Australians soon set up a ferry service to take more commandos to the northern side.

Keyes and his men had now been ashore for more than four hours. Meanwhile, the central group, Pedder's Y Party, consisting of 8 officers and nearly 150 men, had gone ashore in 4 landing craft. They had landed at around 4.30 am just over a mile from the river and had come under fire before they even reached the beach. With the landing craft crews keen to drop off the commandos and withdraw as quickly as possible, many of the latter were left to struggle ashore in water that was chest high. The commandos then ran quickly across the open beach, covering the short distance of just 20 yards or so in record time, before heading inland over the dunes and crossing the coastal road. It was then that they encountered more heavy enemy fire from the higher ground ahead.

Although Y Party had somehow managed to arrive at their positon in reasonably good shape, progress was slow and their radio had been damaged. Pedder had no way of communicating with the other two parties and so he was forced to get his men to break out of their cover and into the open. But, as they pressed on towards the barracks, it was impossible to co-ordinate an attack, and it was not long before the commandos became pinned down once more.

Fortunately, one of Pedder's officers, Lieutenant Blair 'Paddy' Mayne, who was leading 7 Troop and would later become a founding member of the Special Air Service, had managed to join up with elements of 8 Troop. They were soon able to press on and then head south towards the river.

But it was 1 Troop and Pedder's headquarters who encountered the fiercest opposition. Undaunted, Lieutenant Gerald Bryan led his men on beyond the barracks to one of the guns. He arrived to find the gun unmanned and the crew taking cover nearby. The other guns nearby were manned and were firing on the commandos, but Bryan's men succeeded in getting the captured gun in action and firing on those emplacements still in the hands of the enemy.

Elsewhere amongst Pedder's group, the commandos mounted an assault against the barracks but they were met by heavy machine-gun and sniper fire. Casualties soon started to mount as Pedder ordered his men to withdraw towards a gulley for shelter. It was at that point that Dick Pedder was killed. It was a savage blow. Other officers had also become casualties. Captain Bill Farmiloe and Lieutenant Donald Coode had both been killed and the last remaining officer, Gerald Bryan, who had now taken over command of the men, was then wounded; Bryan would, nonetheless, manage to keep the enemy at arm's length for two hours before he was taken prisoner.

With all his officers gone it was left to Regimental Sergeant Major Lewis Tevendale to regroup and rally the men and head for the river. They managed to reach some cover, but after several hours of continuous fire they were finally overrun; with no other option, the commandos surrendered.

Meanwhile, further to the north, George More's Z Party also had no way of communicating with the other groups; a landing craft had hit a submerged rock during its approach to the beach and the radio set had been soaked, rendering it nothing short of useless. The other landing craft seem to have been caught on a sandbank and so the commandos had to make their way in chest-high water. They then had to make their way across the beach and open ground under sporadic enemy fire, a distance of several hundred yards, before they were able to find any cover. Although they encountered more enemy fire once they arrived at the coastal road, Z Party managed to mount a frontal attack on the enemy. The Vichy troops were outfought and seemingly had little stomach for a heavy fight. By 6.30 am the commandos had seized the bridge intact.

Having overrun many vacant enemy positions, where the occupants had clearly departed in a hurry, the commandos of Z Party started rounding up prisoners. For most of the day they managed to hold off the enemy, although the flatness of the surrounding terrain made it difficult. They also succeeded in capturing four gun emplacements and a transport pool, as well as take a number of prisoners. It was only when a number of enemy armoured vehicles arrived that More was forced to withdraw his men. Some headed off east in a group led by Lieutenant Tommy Macpherson before going south to reach the Australian lines, while More led others off south, still under heavy enemy fire, to join up with Y Party. However, the latter were soon caught in open ground and, unable to communicate with the commandos further south, suddenly found themselves coming under fire from all directions. Amongst the five men killed was one of the young officers, 21-year-old Lieutenant Geoffrey Parnacott. Three other men were wounded, and with no hope of getting to safety, they surrendered.

Back at the river, the commandos of X Party were busy crossing the Litani. More boats had been made available, but it was now already early afternoon and had taken more than three hours to ferry the men across. As more men reached the far side, the commandos gradually gained a stronger foothold on the northern bank. Led by Highland and Garland they slowly cleared the enemy positions and captured the enemy redoubt, although it came at a cost, with several commandos killed and wounded during the assault on both sides of the river.

Having crossed the river, and now fearing a counter-attack, Keyes consolidated his position. Several prisoners had been captured and sent back across the river using the boats. Throughout the afternoon more and more Australians crossed the river. A pontoon bridge had been built, and by the early evening Keyes was able to hand over command of the fortification to the new arrivals.

The surviving commandos remained at the river overnight before the enemy forces in the area surrendered the following morning. Keyes was then ordered to withdraw at midday and to leave the redoubt to the Australians. One stroke of fortune was that George More and the commandos captured during the fighting the previous day were now released. Their captors from the day before had now become prisoners of the Australians. Keyes then led his men off southwards and by that night they were safely back at Haifa.

The men of 11 Commando returned to Cyprus on 15 June. They had acquitted themselves well and had achieved the objectives of the revised plan; they had crossed the Litani River and held the north bank long enough to allow the Australian Brigade to cross the river and move on towards Beirut. The commandos had landed with only enough ammunition to last for eight hours, but they had ended up having to fight for more than twenty-four. But it had been at a cost. Of the more than 450 men that had left Cyprus just 11 days before, 45 had been killed and a further 85 wounded.

But despite the courage and determination of the commandos, they had been let down even before they set foot on the beaches, particularly by weak intelligence and poor navigation. There is no doubt that casualties would have been far fewer had the commandos been landed in the right place. This was down to the fact that Pedder had been given insufficient information about the coastline and landing beaches before leaving the *Glengyle*, and X Party's landing beach had been misidentified during the run-in before daylight. This had left Keyes and his men fighting all morning to get to the place where they should have been from the start.

After the raid, Geoffrey Keyes was given command of 11 Commando and awarded the Military Cross. Also awarded the MC were George More and Gerald Bryan, while Eric Garland received a bar to his MC, which he had won earlier in the war during the retreat to Dunkirk. Amongst the other awards, RSM Tevendale was awarded the DCM.

Chapter Six

Raid on Bremen

4 July 1941

By the end of June 1941 Hitler had turned on Russia and Bomber Command was increasingly taking the offensive into the heart of Germany. Until that point, Bomber Command's major raids had been at night, but a number of smaller daylight raids had also been carried out across the Channel, against targets in northern France and the Low Countries. It was now that Winston Churchill decided he wanted to strike at the heart of the Reich by day, while many of Hitler's forces were engaged in the east.

A number of targets were drawn up for the units of 2 Group Bomber Command, and the list included Germany's second largest port of Bremen. This was to be Operation Wreckage and the precision raid would be carried out at very low level by two squadrons based in Norfolk: 105 Squadron at Swanton Morley and 107 Squadron at Great Massingham, a satellite airfield of West Raynham.

The squadrons were equipped with Blenheim IV light bombers. With a crew of three, the aircraft had a maximum speed of just over 250mph and carried 1,000lb of bombs internally (either 4 x 250lb or 2 x 500lb). Chosen to lead the raid was the commanding officer of 105 Squadron, Wing Commander Hughie Edwards. Edwards was an Australian and had only recently been given command of the squadron after the previous commanding officer had been killed. For the past few weeks the 105 crews had been carrying out low-level attacks against enemy shipping, during which Edwards had been awarded the DFC, while the crews of 107 Squadron had recently returned to East Anglia after two months with Coastal Command carrying out anti-submarine patrols and attacks on enemy shipping from their base in Scotland. Its squadron commander, Lawrence Petley, had, like Edwards, recently taken over command after the loss of the previous squadron commander.

The first two attempts to carry out Wreckage both ended in the mission having to be aborted en route to Bremen. First, on 28 June, when the raid was led by Petley; the decision to abort came under scrutiny and resulted in criticism. The Air Officer Commanding (AOC) 2 Group, Air Vice-Marshal Donald Stevenson, decided that Edwards should lead the next attempt and that 107 Squadron be replaced by 21 Squadron, based at Watton and led by Wing Commander Tim Partridge. The second attempt took place two days later, this time led by Edwards, but halfway to the target they ran into a thick blanket of fog. Not wishing to suffer the AOC's displeasure for a second time, Edwards decided to press on towards the coast of Germany for another 100 miles in appalling visibility but it eventually proved impossible to carry on and so he reluctantly made the decision to return to base.

Operation Wreckage remained a high priority and so a third attempt was ordered on 2 July, but was twice postponed by 2 Group. Then, finally, on 4 July, the raid was ordered once more. This time, just like the first, the crews of 107 were to get another chance to take part in the raid with 105, and Edwards was again instructed to lead the raid.

The briefing took place the evening before. Bremen was vital to the German war effort and so there were numerous targets to choose from, including an oil refinery, aircraft factories and naval construction yards, all located in the built-up area of the port between the main railway station and the docks. Unsurprisingly, the port and surrounding area were heavily defended. An outer ring of at least twenty heavy 105mm gun batteries were backed up by an inner ring of twenty-plus 88mm batteries and numerous other anti-aircraft defences, including 37mm and 20mm gun emplacements situated around the port and town that had been mounted anywhere possible, including on large buildings overlooking the area. There were also several barrage balloons rising to a height of 500 feet and protecting the outer perimeter against air attacks. As a preventative measure, the Blenheims were fitted with cable cutters along the leading edge of the wing that were designed to cut through the steel cables connecting the balloons to the ground, although in reality these did not always work as well as had been hoped. With balloons and hundreds of guns protecting the area, Bremen was a fortress, and with the raid being carried out at very low level there would also be hazardous high-voltage pylons, large dockyard cranes and high buildings to encounter.

No approach to any of the specified targets was considered safe or even less risky than any other line of attack.

The crews were disappointed to learn there would be no fighter escort, but their attack on Bremen would hopefully benefit from a diversionary raid by Blenheims of 226 Squadron from nearby Wattisham against a seaplane base on the East Frisian island of Norderney. There was also a raid planned by Bomber Command for that night, and while the Blenheim crews were being briefed, a mixed force of Hampdens and Wellingtons were carrying out a bombing raid on Bremen. Not only was it hoped that some of the anti-aircraft defences around the port would be destroyed, but that the defenders would be kept awake well into the night, and so either be sleeping or less alert when the Blenheims carried out their attack the following morning.

That night the Blenheim crews got whatever sleep they could before getting up early on the morning of 4 July for the raid; the crews of 105 had now got used to the routine. Then, once again, soon after 5.00 am, fifteen Blenheims got airborne. The nine aircraft of 105 Squadron orbited their home airfield at Swanton Morley to wait for the six Blenheims of 107 Squadron and then, having all joined up as planned, they set out across the North Sea.

Having tested their guns, one of 107's aircraft encountered a problem and returned to base; two more soon followed for other reasons. Edwards was now left with twelve aircraft in his formation; the original nine from his own squadron and just three from 107. The formation continued in four vics of three; Edwards leading, with Sergeants Ron Scott to his left and Bill Jackson on his right. The weather was clear and not at all what the crews had hoped for. If the raid was to be successful then it very much depended on surprise and so it was important for the formation to reach Bremen without having been spotted; cloud would have provided some welcome cover when transiting over the sea.

Given the distance to the target and the limited range of the Blenheim when flying at low level, the route across the North Sea inevitably took them close to the line of Frisian Islands that run parallel to the northern coastline of Holland and Germany. Despite the crews flying as low as they dared, mostly below 50 feet, to avoid presenting a silhouette on the horizon for any lookouts on the islands, or for anyone on board enemy shipping in the area, the Blenheims were spotted at least three times. As they got closer to

Bremen their target became increasingly more obvious and so they could expect a hostile reception.

The Blenheims eventually coasted in over northern Germany near Cuxhaven before they turned south for Bremen. The sight of some cloud raised hopes of much needed cover, but hope soon turned to disappointment as the cloud was too thin and too high to offer the raiders any protection. Visibility was excellent, which, again, was greeted with a mixed reaction amongst the crews. They could easily see their targets, but then the defending gunners would just as easily see them. There would be nowhere to hide.

The port of Bremen is spread across the banks of the River Weser and the city lies some 40 miles inland from the mouth of the river. It was around 8.00 am when the twelve aircraft approached their targets from the north. As they edged closer and closer to the ground they were greeted by the inevitable flak, which seemed to come from everywhere. Edwards even flew under pylons to avoid presenting the defenders with an easier target, but two of 107s Blenheims were shot down, including that of the squadron commander, Lawrence Petley, who was killed.

The ten surviving Blenheims ploughed on through a mesh of crossfire. The pilots had now spread out to provide as wide a frontage as possible. This would give the defending gunners more of a problem and give the Blenheim crews a better chance of success, but it was almost impossible for all ten aircraft to escape unscathed. Two of 105's Blenheims soon fell to the flak. One was flown by 23-year-old Flying Officer Michael Lambert. As Lambert's observer, Sergeant Reg Copeland, directed him ever closer to the target, and his wireless operator/air gunner, Sergeant Fred Charles, hit back with everything he had, the Blenheim pressed on despite having repeatedly been hit. However, Lambert could no longer maintain any control and the Blenheim veered one way and then the other before coming down in a street where it exploded, its bombs still on board; there were no survivors. The second Blenheim to fall was flown by 20-year-old Sergeant William MacKillop. The young pilot had pressed on heroically towards the target and even managed to release his bombs, albeit short of the dock area, but he could maintain control no longer. The Blenheim then plunged into a factory and blew up, killing the crew.

Only eight Blenheims now remained, including just one from 107 Squadron. They all pressed on, weaving their way through the flak as each second took them closer to their target. The barrage of anti-aircraft fire was relentless as those defending Bremen threw everything they could at the attackers. Each Blenheim was hit time and time again, but still they continued through the colourful array of tracer and flak.

Finally, their target was in sight. Edwards, with all three of his formation still intact, now delivered his attack under intense fire. His aircraft had repeatedly been hit and his wireless operator/air gunner, Sergeant Gerry Quinn, had been wounded in the leg, but, completely undaunted, Edwards released two of his bombs over one of the main railway lines, putting one of Bremen's main lines of communication out of action, before he released his remaining bombs on a tunnel and then destroyed the overhead installations. He then attacked a train with his machine gun and pressed on to the suburban part of the town before circling above to maintain a watchful eye over the others as they made their attacks and to draw as much of the enemy fire as possible. Finally, having remained in the vicinity for nearly ten minutes, and having been hit several more times, Edwards turned for home.

Behind Edwards, his two wingmen, Ron Scott and Bill Jackson, had also pressed home their attacks. Scott hit a factory and storage depot as well as more railway lines while Jackson pressed on to the centre of the town, through a balloon barrage and in the face of extremely heavy fire from the ground. His aircraft suffered numerous hits while his wireless operator/air gunner, Sergeant Jim Purves, and his observer, Sergeant Bill Williams, were both wounded in the leg and foot. Having successfully bombed tramlines and buildings in the town, Jackson turned for home, his aircraft badly mauled.

While Edwards had been leading his formation into attack, the two other formation leaders, both down to just a pair, had led theirs. One of Edwards's flight commanders, Squadron Leader Tony Scott, known amongst the squadron as simply 'Scotty', led Pilot Officer Ben Broadley against their target, a propeller foundry. The two Blenheims buffeted their way through the wall of flak and delivered their bombs on target before pulling hard starboard over the Weser to take up a heading for home. The other pair, that of Pilot Officer Jack Buckley and Sergeant Bruce, dropped their bombs on an aircraft factory and caused considerable damage to several new aircraft as well as damaging the main aircraft production hangar. The last surviving aircraft of 107 Squadron, flown by Sergeant Leven, successfully attacked a goods yard and released his bombs before turning for home.

It was a long transit back to Norfolk but one by one the surviving Blenheims returned to Swanton Morley. Bruce was the first to return, then it was the turn of Ron Scott to land, then his namesake Scotty, followed by Broadley, Buckley and then Jackson. It had been a particularly difficult transit back for Jackson and his crew. In spite of his injuries, Williams had successfully navigated the aircraft back home, ably assisted by Purves, who himself was seriously wounded and suffering from considerable loss of blood. The aircraft had suffered considerable damage during the attack and had lost its hydraulics, which prevented the undercarriage from being lowered. Nonetheless, Jackson managed a perfect wheels-up landing and he managed to bring the badly damaged Blenheim to rest right next to the ambulance and fire tender that were standing by. Jackson, Williams and Purves would all later receive the DFM for their part in the raid.

It was now 11.00 am and six aircraft had returned. Then, finally, an hour later, Hughie Edwards returned; his aircraft almost a write-off, visibly scarred and still trailing parts of telegraph cables. After three attempts, Wreckage had finally taken place. News soon spread and back at HQ 2 Group in Huntingdon its results were considered a success; in fact, losses were less than had been expected. Tributes to the bravery of the crews started pouring in. The Chief of the Air Staff, Sir Charles Portal, wrote:

I have just read the first account of the Bremen raid today. Convey to the units concerned my warmest congratulations on a splendid operation. I am sure that all squadrons realise that besides encouraging the Russians, every daylight attack rubs into the Germans, the superiority of our units. You are doing great work.

The Commander-in-Chief Bomber Command, Air Marshal Sir Richard Peirse, was also keen to express his congratulations. His message to the squadrons was:

Your attack this morning has been a great contribution to the day offensive now being fought. It will remain an outstanding example of dash and initiative. I send you and your captains and crews my warmest congratulations and the admiration of the Command.

The AOC, Air Vice-Marshal Donald Stevenson, who had clearly been so disappointed with the fact that earlier attempts had to be aborted, wrote:

Please convey to the crews of 105, 107 and 226 Squadrons who took part in today's daylight attack on Bremen and Norderney, my deep appreciation of the high courage and determination displayed by them. This low-flying raid, so gallantly carried out, deep into Germany without the support of fighters, will always rank high in the history of the Royal Air Force.

News had also spread to the British media and soon the public were made aware of the heroic raid. A number of individuals who had taken part received personal recognition. In Edwards's crew there was a DFC for his observer, Pilot Officer Alistair Ramsay, and Gerry Quinn received a bar to his DFM. But the most notable award went to the gallant leader of the raid, Hughie Edwards, who was awarded the Victoria Cross; he was the first Australian airman of the war to receive the highest award for bravery. The announcement came in the *London Gazette* on 22 July, with the citation concluding:

Throughout the execution of this operation which he had planned personally with full knowledge of the risks entailed, Wing Commander Edwards displayed the highest possible standard of gallantry and determination.

Chapter Seven

Rommel's Headquarters

17/18 November 1941

Not all daring raids ended in success, or even partial success. Some ended in complete disaster. This in no way reflects the extraordinary bravery of those taking part: failure could be for any number of reasons, including poor intelligence. One such mission was the raid on the headquarters of General Erwin Rommel, the famous Desert Fox and commander of Axis forces in North Africa. The raid, called Operation Flipper, took place in November 1941, but instead of killing Rommel, it cost the life of its gallant young leader, Geoffrey Keyes.

The raid was planned for the night of 17/18 November 1941, the eve of Operation Crusader, a major British counter-attack in the desert to relieve the port of Tobruk and to drive Rommel's forces out of Cyrenaica. Killing Rommel, it was believed, would massively disrupt the enemy's most senior levels of command just at the point Crusader was getting underway. It would also have a major psychological impact on the troops of both sides fighting in the desert. It would boost the morale of the Allies while shattering those of the Axis powers, as the Desert Fox had become regarded as something of a super-general by those he led.

The plan for Flipper was for a raid to be carried out against a number of objectives behind enemy lines, the main one being Rommel's headquarters, which, it was believed, was in a villa near Beda Littoria. The villa was located 20 miles inland from coastal Apollonia in eastern Libya and some 250 miles behind enemy lines. The other objectives of Flipper were to attack a radio and intelligence facility at Apollonia, and to conduct attacks against two Italian headquarters: one at Cyrene (now Shahat), and the other further south near Slonta.

The overall operation was to be led by Lieutenant Colonel Robert Laycock, the former commander of Layforce, although the actual raid on

Rommel's headquarters, by far the most hazardous part of the operation, was to be led by Geoffrey Keyes. At 24 years old, Keyes was the youngest lieutenant colonel in the British Army. Since taking part in the action at the Litani River, 11 Commando had been disbanded, but more than a hundred men, including Keyes, had been retained as a troop in the Middle East Commando, an amalgamation of units, including the remnants of Layforce.

On 10 November two submarines left the port of Alexandria. On board HMS *Torbay* was Keyes, with two junior officers and twenty-five men, while HMS *Talisman* carried Laycock and his men. Then, on the night of 14/15 November, Keyes's raiding party landed safely on the North African coast. They went ashore in rubber dinghies and landed on the beach at Hamama where Keyes met up with Captain John Haselden, an Arabic-speaking intelligence officer operating behind enemy lines with a small reconnaissance team from the Long Range Desert Group. It had been Haselden's Arabic informants who provided the initial intelligence that Rommel was regularly seen entering a residence at Beda Littoria, from which it had been deduced that his headquarters was set up there.

Laycock had been less fortunate. Extremely poor weather, which had strengthened to a Force 7, and an excessively strong current, had meant that only he and seven of his men had made it ashore from the *Talisman*; the rest had been left on board the submarine.

With only thirty-six men ashore, and with such an ambitious raid ahead, the decision could easily have been made to abort the mission, but it was decided to press on, although the original plan had now to be changed. Instead of four detachments attacking four objectives, the plan was revised so that the men formed three groups. Laycock was to remain at the rendezvous point with three men to secure the beach while Keyes would lead the main raiding party to attack the headquarters, and Lieutenant Roy Cooke would take a small supporting group to destroy the communications lines from the headquarters near Cyrene.

Keyes, with Captain Robin Campbell as his deputy, led the men off up the escarpment shortly before first light. The weather was atrocious, and was forecast to remain so over the next few days, with torrential rain making progress difficult and, at times, slow. They spent the following day hiding at a wadi before Keyes led his men off under the cover of darkness. The rain continued to fall. Previously dry wadis had become flooded and it was mud the men had to encounter rather than sand, but the deteriorating weather did not deter the men. They covered the next 18 miles in total darkness and driving rain. It was hard going, particularly on the rising and rocky ground, which they had to cover under storm conditions, and without any local guides to help; the guides had been unable to get ashore and so were left behind on the submarine. Every time someone stumbled or fell behind, the group would have to stop and wait for him to catch up.

The following day they took cover in a cave, still 5 miles from their destination. That night, Cooke's small detachment left the main group to carry out their own mission, before Keyes and his group finally closed to within a few hundred yards of the villa.

Leaving part of his detachment to block the approaches to the residence, Keyes led a group of six men, including Robin Campbell and his sergeant, Jack Terry, towards the villa. It was just before midnight when they moved silently forward, passing sentry positions and then cutting the surrounding fence before crawling through. Fortunately, the sound of the heavy rain prevented them from being heard and the awful weather had meant that only one guard was seen; he was quickly and silently removed before the raiding party reached the villa.

Keyes had hoped to find a door or window open at the rear of the villa so that they could get inside, but the heavy rain meant that all the windows were closed and the doors locked. Versions of how the commandos finally entered the villa vary, and range from the German-speaking Campbell hammering on the door and demanding to be let in, to the commandos forcing their way in through the main entrance. Either way, the raiders were met by a German sentry who had come to the door, only to then get the shock of his life, which was now about to come to an end; he did not give up easily and had to be shot.

The sound of shots being fired now stirred everyone inside the villa. The element of surprise had well and truly gone, and in reality there was now little chance of escape. Keyes quickly led his men inside and into the large entrance hall. Leaving a man at the foot of the stairs to prevent any interference from the floor above, Keyes made his way down the hall and then stormed one of the rooms, firing as he went, while Campbell lobbed in a grenade. The room was found to be empty. Keyes then stormed a second room but its occupants were now fully aware of what was going on. The gallant young Keyes was gunned down as he entered the room. He fell back into the passage mortally wounded, and died soon after.

With stronger opposition inside the villa than had been anticipated, Campbell and Terry made a hasty retreat. Campbell was then mistakenly shot in the leg by one of his own men as he rushed out of the villa. Unable to get away, he was left behind. With both of his officers down, Terry quickly led the raiders away under the cover of darkness. Any thoughts of staying there to try and find Rommel were gone. It would have been suicidal.

The survivors of the raiding party eventually made it back to the beach to rendezvous with Laycock, but Cooke's group did not return; they had all been captured, although they had first managed to complete their mission. The weather was still too bad to make it back on board the submarines and so Laycock had to wait for the weather to improve. However, their position was now known by the enemy and there was no way the small group of raiders could hold off such a large force. Laycock ordered the men to scatter in small groups and to try and make it back to friendly lines by any method they could. But only Laycock and Terry made it back to Allied lines after more than a month in the desert. The rest were either killed, wounded or taken prisoner.

The strategic aim of the raid had been to kill Rommel and throw the Axis hierarchy into disarray just at the point the Allies were launching a major offensive. It did nothing of the sort. In fact, despite the many deeds of heroism performed that night, the raid was floored long before Laycock and Keyes had set off to carry it out. Although Rommel had been seen at the villa several weeks before, the fact was that it was not his headquarters at all. At the time the raid took place the villa was being used as a headquarters by a Panzer group. But that was all. Worst still, Rommel was not even in North Africa at the time. He had moved his headquarters nearer to Tobruk some weeks earlier, and at the time of the raid he had been in Italy celebrating his fiftieth birthday.

When Rommel later found out about the raid, the one thing that seemingly annoyed him the most was the fact that the Allies thought his headquarters was so far behind enemy lines. It is a fair point. Rommel always believed that his generals should be as close to the fighting as they could and so he always led by example. He was regularly at the front, often too close to the action, and surely this would have been known?

The failure of the raid proves the importance of having good and reliable intelligence: the information Keyes had been given was clearly inaccurate and out of date. Sadly, though, it had been an expensive lesson to learn and had cost many men, including Keyes, their lives.

Reportedly on the orders of Rommel, Keyes was buried in a local cemetery with full military honours; he now lies in the Benghazi War Cemetery. Geoffrey Keyes was later posthumously awarded the Victoria Cross. His citation concluded:

> *By his fearless disregard of the great dangers which he ran and of which he was fully aware, and by his magnificent leadership and outstanding gallantry, Lieutenant Colonel Keyes set an example of supreme self-sacrifice and devotion to duty.*

It has since been suggested that Keyes was killed by friendly fire but, whatever the truth, his bravery was beyond doubt and his award of the VC was the first of eight VCs won by commandos during the war. Robin Campbell, who had been wounded in the leg and left behind at the villa, was fortunate to be taken as a prisoner of war rather than executed by the Germans. He was awarded the DSO, while Sergeant Jack Terry received the DCM.

The raid on Rommel's so-called headquarters at the villa brought an end to such audacious and seemingly gung-ho raids. The raid also marked the end of the Commandos' first period of operations in the region. From now on raids would require better co-ordination with Combined Operations, and be provided with more accurate intelligence so that they could be better planned by those taking part and the chances of achieving success improved.

Chapter Eight

Vaagso

27 December 1941

Until 1941 the small island of Vaagso was largely unheard of beyond its locality on the western coast of Norway. Even today, Vaagso is probably not the first name that readily comes to mind when listing any of the Army Commandos' battle honours; except, perhaps, by those who served there or knew someone who did. Yet, the commando raid that took place there in December 1941 is significant because it was the first time British forces had carried out a truly combined amphibious operation that involved all three Services planning and operating together to achieve a common aim.

When Lord Louis Mountbatten replaced Sir Roger Keyes as Chief of Combined Operations at the end of October 1941, he did so under instruction from Winston Churchill to commence a series of raids that would keep the enemy defences alert from the North Cape of Norway to the Atlantic coastline of France. Mountbatten was much younger than his predecessor and was considered to be a man of action, and his appointment was to mark the beginning of a period of intense commando operations that had not been seen during their first eighteen months.

Occupied since June 1940, Norway was an obvious area to conduct commando operations as it was of strategic importance to both sides. The reasons ranged enormously, from the country's supply of iron ore, on which much of the German war effort depended, to the huge economic value of its fishing and, of course, its vast coastline, where the strategically important ports and fjords provided shelter for Germany's largest warships.

With Churchill's direction, a plan was put together to carry out a raid against German positions on the island of Vaagso. It would not be the first time that commandos had visited Norway. A raid had already taken place earlier in the year much further to the north, called Operation Claymore, when 3 and 4 Commandos landed on the Lofoten Islands. On that occasion the raid had targeted a number of fish–oil factories to disrupt the enemy's glycerine production and had proved to be a resounding success. A number of enemy vessels had been destroyed and more than 200 prisoners taken, while the returning commandos had been joined by more than 300 local volunteers wishing to escape to Britain.

The raid on the Lofoten Islands had provided the newly formed commandos with a much needed boost. It had also been given great publicity back in Britain to raise the morale of a public suffering the full extent of the Blitz, but it had fallen short in terms of a great amphibious operation, which the commandos had been formed and trained to undertake. While some might have considered a bloodless encounter against an undefended position to be a good operation, others felt what was needed was a commando raid of some magnitude, and one that was a truly combined and amphibious operation.

Ideally, Churchill wanted a raid on Trondheim to take some pressure off the Russians on the Eastern Front, and to provide a welcome break for the Royal Navy convoys heading for the Arctic port of Murmansk, but the British were not capable of making such a large-scale raid at that stage of the war. Nonetheless, Mountbatten wanted to make an impact for his first operation and was keen to go as far as he could towards meeting the prime minister's wish. And so a raid was planned against enemy positions on the small island of Vaagso – lying on the northern side of the mouth of the Nordfjorden between Bergen and Trondheim, and marking the entrance to a system of fjords in which the German Navy had established anchorages – and its tiny neighbouring island of Maaloy. The area was home to German coastal gun batteries and a garrison of over 200 troops and the raid, called Operation Archery, was to be the first truly Combined Operation of the war.

Overall responsibility for the naval contribution to Archery was given to Rear Admiral Harold Burrough, while Brigadier Charles Haydon, the commander of the Special Service Brigade, was given command of the non-naval aspects of the raid. Chosen to carry out the assault was 3 Commando, led by Lieutenant Colonel John Durnford-Slater.

Durnford-Slater was 32 years old. He had raised 3 Commando, credited as the first commando unit of the war, and had led the unit's two earlier raids; the first being on Guernsey in July 1940, called Operation Ambassador

– a raid that ended up with no military gain but had proved useful for its planning and operational experience – and the second being Operation Claymore. His raiding force for Archery was to be augmented by two troops from 2 Commando and a small detachment from each of 4 Commando (to provide medical support) and the Norwegian Independent Company 1, led by Captain Martin Linge.

Amongst the many objectives of Archery were the destruction of a coastal battery and enemy barracks, the elimination of the enemy at their strongpoint at Hollevik and in the town of South Vaagso and on Maaloy, and to engage any enemy reinforcements. The raiders would also destroy the fish-oil factories and stores to prevent the German manufacture of high explosives, and destroy any enemy shipping at anchorage in Vaagsfjord. It was also hoped the commandos would bring back some enemy prisoners and Quislings (members of the Norwegian collaborationist government under the German occupation and named after the leader Vidkun Quisling) and provide passage to Britain for any Norwegian volunteers wishing to join the Norwegian Army of Liberation. Furthermore, it was hoped that a large raid of this type would result in the enemy having to maintain, or even increase, its forces in the area; forces that might otherwise be deployed to the Eastern Front.

With a total force of some 570 commandos, Durnford-Slater divided his men into five main groups. The plan was for the first group to land to the north of the town of South Vaagso and to prevent any reinforcements from reaching the town once the attack was underway. The second group would land to the south of the town at Hollevik and deal with the battery and enemy strongpoint known to be there. The two main assault groups were Groups Three and Four. Durnford-Slater would lead Group Four, consisting of four troops of commandos, a total of 200 men, with the task of carrying out all the objectives in South Vaagso. His second-in-command, Major 'Mad Jack' Churchill, would lead Group Three with two troops under his command, a hundred men, tasked with attacking the enemy gun battery, barracks and ammunition store on the neighbouring island of Maaloy. A fifth group would be held back on the troop transports as a reserve.

The commandos left their base at Largs in mid-December. On arrival at Gourock on the Clyde they boarded their two troop transport ships, the converted Belgian ferries HMS *Charles* and HMS *Leopold*. They then sailed to Scapa Flow to begin planning for the raid, although the exact location of the target was kept from the men before they left for their setting-off post in the Shetlands on Christmas Eve. Then, having enjoyed Christmas Day on board, the two troop transports left the Shetlands with their naval escort the following evening.

Meanwhile, 12 Commando was carrying out a diversionary raid against the Lofoten Islands, called Operation Anklet, and just before dawn on 27 December the troop transports carrying Durnford-Slater's men approached the western coast of Norway. Having picked up the guiding light marking the approach to the Vaagsfjord, which had been provided by the submarine HMS *Tuna*, the ships sailed on towards their drop-off point.

As daylight started to break, Hampden light bombers of RAF Bomber Command carried out an attack on the coastal battery and anti-aircraft gun positions, while six Blenheims attacked shipping off the Norwegian coast to draw off any enemy fighters, and a dozen more Blenheims carried out a low-level raid against a German fighter airfield nearby.

By now the commandos had boarded their landing craft and were running in towards their targets. The Hampdens now lay a smokescreen for protection while star shells fired from the naval ships illuminated the area as the commandos approached the shore, just at the point when the final shells of the naval bombardment crashed into the enemy's defences. Then, when the landing craft were just a minute or so from landing, the red Verey lights fired by Durnford-Slater instructed the naval bombardment to cease.

The commando landings that followed went much as planned. Being winter and quite far north, the short hours of daylight meant that the attack could not start too early and so it was already past 9.00 am. Furthermore, it would get dark again around mid-afternoon, so there was not much time.

On the tiny island of Maaloy, Churchill, already a holder of the Military Cross from his days at Dunkirk, lived up to his name of 'Mad Jack' as he led his men ashore playing the bagpipes as he went. The naval barrage had been so effective that Churchill's group met little resistance. Less than fifteen minutes later the fighting was over, and within an hour of landing on the island the last of the enemy had been rounded up. The raiders had taken their objectives without suffering any casualties or losses.

Unfortunately for Durnford-Slater's group, it had not been quite so straightforward. The barrage had done its job and the landing had been unopposed, but the soft snow, sometimes deep in parts, and the extreme cold had meant that it was not easy going. As Durnford-Slater led his men down the main street into the town they came across fierce opposition. The commandos had come under heavy machine-gun fire, as well as fire from snipers who had positioned themselves amongst the houses. Unfortunately for the commandos, the timing of their raid had coincided with an experienced German mountain unit enjoying a period of leave from the Eastern Front in the town.

The fighting soon deteriorated into congested street fighting and sniping. Durnford-Slater decided to signal the ships to send in the fifth group of commandos that had remained on board as reserves. He also called for reinforcements from Churchill's group on Maaloy, where the fighting was already over.

Churchill sent the troop led by Captain Peter Young, a veteran of Dunkirk and now taking part in his third operation with the commandos. Young's troop arrived in the town to find Durnford-Slater's group pinned down and having suffered serious casualties. Two of the group's four troop leaders were dead. Captain Herbert Forrester, a giant of a man and a great rugby player and heavyweight boxer, was killed while storming a heavily defended hotel being used by the enemy as its headquarters, and 23-year-old Captain Johnny Giles fell when a burst of machine-gun fire cut him down as he was clearing houses. Furthermore, the commander of the Norwegian Independent Company attached to one of the troops, Martin Linge, was also dead; he had been killed during the same attack against the hotel as Forrester. Three more officers had been badly wounded.

There was little or no space for the commandos to try and outflank the enemy positions. Snow-covered hilly terrain to one side of the town and the fjord on the other meant the enemy were well protected on their flanks and had now got into firmly established defensive positions. It was now, more than ever, that Durnford-Slater demonstrated his strong leadership. With so many of his officers down, the attack was in great danger of stalling but he succeeded in rallying his men, superbly assisted by his very capable non-commissioned officers, many of whom had now taken over command of their men.

Showing great personal courage and complete coolness under heavy enemy fire, Durnford-Slater led his men forward. They had now been boosted by the arrival of reinforcements and were ably assisted by the local Norwegians, who carried ammunition for the raiders and helped with the wounded.

The commandos slowly made their way up the main street and through warehouses along the wharf. Peter Young and another junior officer, Lieutenant Denis O'Flaherty, led their men with great courage and determination as the commandos moved from building to building and house to house. The combination of intense enemy fire from both sides and the wooden construction of the buildings meant that many fires had broken out. Flames raged through houses and buildings where enemy snipers had been dug-in. They had held up the commandos for some considerable time but were now gradually removed one by one as buildings burnt to the ground. Finally, having destroyed four fish factories in the northern part of the town and a herring-oil factory on the far edge of the town, as well as enemy ammunition and fuel stores, and the telephone exchange, Durnford-Slater's men linked up with the first group that had landed further to the north and had now made their way to the edge of the town.

It had taken Durnford-Slater's group into the early hours of the afternoon to reach the northern part of the town. Then, having swept through the area, he knew that it was time to start withdrawing south again to where the landing craft would be waiting to take them back to the ships. With less than six hours ashore it was only ever meant to be a hit-and-run raid, although enemy resistance had turned out to be far heavier than anticipated. As the commandos made their way back towards the landing craft they still came across areas of resistance, which had to be dealt with before they could leave.

While the main action had been going on ashore, the naval assault force of HMS *Kenya* and four destroyers had sunk ten enemy vessels in the fjord. Royal Navy boarding parties had also managed to secure some important documents, including enemy codes. No Royal Navy ships were lost, but four naval men had been killed and four more wounded. The Hampdens and Blenheims of Bomber Command had remained active overhead, attacking several targets of opportunity outside of the town to support the raid, but the RAF had also suffered losses. Eight of the twenty-nine aircraft dispatched were lost.

By mid-afternoon the commandos were back on board the landing craft with nearly a hundred prisoners and four Quislings, plus more than seventy new recruits for the Norwegian Army of Liberation. The voyage back to

Britain soon passed and the commandos were welcomed back as heroes; news of the successful raid had already been given huge publicity back home.

The raid was considered a great success, particularly the combined aspects where, for the first time, all three Services had planned and operated together to achieve the same aim. Many factories, stores and buildings had been destroyed, as well as the ten vessels sunk in the fjord, and an estimated 150 of the enemy had been killed. The commandos had also taken back enemy prisoners and Quislings, plus Norwegian volunteers, and the valuable enemy codes that had been captured. But it had cost the commandos dear, with seventeen men killed and more than fifty wounded. There had also been the loss of Martin Linge, the leader of the Norwegian Independent Company attached to the commandos for the raid, a loss that was particularly devastating for the Norwegians, while both the Royal Navy and RAF had suffered a number of casualties.

For his leadership of the raid, John Durnford-Slater was awarded the DSO. He had demonstrated personal courage, complete coolness and a quick grasp of the situation while inspiring his men and ensuring that all the objectives were achieved. Amongst other awards for the raid were a DSO to Denis O'Flaherty, who had been wounded during the action, a bar to his MC for 'Mad Jack' Churchill and an MC to Peter Young.

In the aftermath of the raid the Germans were concerned that Britain might try and mount a full-scale invasion of Norway and so diverted an estimated 30,000 troops to the region and increased their coastal defences. Archery had, indeed, been a great success.

Chapter Nine

Postmaster

14 January 1942

W hile many daring raids carried out during the Second World War became legendary tales in the post-war era, through book or film, others remained unheard of. One probably falling into this latter category was carried out in January 1942 by a small group of men working for the SOE. The mission, called Operation Postmaster, was one of SOE's classic operations of the war and took place in the neutral port of Santa Isabel on the Spanish island of Fernando Po (now known as Bioko) off the west coast of Africa. The aim was to board Italian and German ships in the harbour and then sail them to Nigeria. It was a raid that boosted SOE's reputation at a critical time and demonstrated its ability to plan and conduct secret operations no matter what the political consequences.

Under the command of Major Gus March-Phillipps, the raiders left Britain bound for West Africa during August 1941 in a Brixham trawler called the *Maid Honor*. The 60-feet ketch-rigged *Maid*'s non-naval appearance made it ideal for operations, and for the next few months she posed as a neutral Swedish yacht operating out of Freetown, from where the crew could reconnoitre the coastline, as it was believed German submarines were sheltering there and using the river deltas in Vichy West Africa as refuelling depots for their Atlantic operations.

The *Maid* was only big enough for a total of eleven on board and so March-Phillipps had chosen his men carefully. His second-in-command was his trusted friend Captain Geoffrey Appleyard, already a holder of the MC awarded for an earlier SOE operation. The two had first met in 1940 amongst the sand dunes of Dunkirk while waiting to be evacuated off the beaches. At the time March-Phillipps was an artillery officer and Appleyard was serving with the Royal Army Service Corps, but when the Commandos formed soon after both men had been amongst the first to volunteer. While serving with 7 Commando they were both recruited by the SOE in early 1941, after which March-Phillipps had been instructed to form a Special Service Unit, with Appleyard as his deputy, to train for specialist amphibious operations. Now the training was over and this was the unit's first opportunity to prove its value on operations.

Also on board the *Maid* was Captain Graham Hayes, a boyhood friend of Appleyard's and from the same Yorkshire village. Before the war Hayes had served as an apprentice seaman on a Finnish four-mast barque sailing from England to Australia, and later as a craftsman with a furniture company in London. The outbreak of war had brought an end to his furniture-making career. He joined the army and then volunteered for the paras before he was reunited with Appleyard and asked to join the West African adventure. The others on board were all trained commandos, but now posing as a civilian crew. There was 22-year-old Denis Tottenham, Frank Perkins, only just 18 and the youngest member of the crew, a sergeant from the paras called Tom Winter, cook Ernest Evison, March-Phillipps's batman Jock Taylor, the quartermaster Leslie Prout, a Free Frenchman called André Desgranges, and a tall, blonde Dane called Anders Lassen, who had travelled to England with the Danish Merchant Navy to volunteer for the Commandos.

The SOE always maintained a presence in West Africa from where it could observe the Vichy French, Spanish and Portuguese territories in order to identify and hinder any activities threatening the British interest. While the crew of the *Maid Honor* had been searching for submarine bases during the last weeks of 1941, SOE agents had become aware of three vessels in the port of Santa Isabel on the Spanish island of Fernando Po, 20 miles offshore in the Gulf of Guinea, the nearest island to the mainland and not far from the coast of Nigeria.

The three ships identified were an 8,500 ton Italian merchant ship called the *Duchessa d'Aosta*, a large German tugboat called the *Likomba* and a barge called the *Burundi*. The *Duchessa d'Aosta*, in particular, was of great interest. She was carrying a large load, but exactly what was on board was uncertain. Although she was supposedly carrying wool, hides and skins, as well as copra, asbestos fibre and ingots of electrolytic copper, her captain had failed to declare the full load and so it was assumed she was also carrying arms and ammunition.

To seize ships in a neutral harbour was considered extremely controversial, so British authorities in the area refused to support the raid, but permission was eventually given by London for it to go ahead. The raid was planned for late in the evening of 14 January 1942, the darkest night of the period, with no moon, and while the ships' officers would be ashore attending a dinner party arranged by an SOE agent, Richard Lippett.

Lippett had managed to get work with a shipping company that had business offices on the island. From there he had been able to make preparations for the raid and was very much aware just how sociable the crew of the *Duchessa d'Aosta* were known to be. They were only too happy to accept the hospitality of the locals ashore, as well as hosting parties aboard, and it was during one such party on board the *Duchessa* that Lippett had first been able to glean valuable information about the ship and crew.

Even though permission had been given for the raid to go ahead, the British Foreign Office remained concerned that seizing the ships in a neutral port would be seen as an act of piracy and so a Royal Navy corvette, HMS *Violet*, was sent to the area; this would support the cover story that the enemy ships had been intercepted at sea while trying to make their way to Europe. There was also concern at the British Embassy in Madrid, as it was unclear exactly how the Spanish government would react, and so the political consequences of such a raid were considered to be potentially severe.

While suspicion of British involvement would be inevitable, tangible proof had to be avoided. To seize the ships March-Phillipps would have a raiding force of thirty-two men, including the crew of the *Maid Honor*, with the rest made up of four SOE agents and seventeen volunteers from local army units. To tow the enemy ships, two tugs were provided by the Governor of Nigeria and crewed by Africans.

Early on the morning of 11 January 1942 the tugs left Lagos. On board the larger tug, the *Vulcan*, were March-Phillipps and his raiding party of Appleyard, Lassen, Tottenham, Evison, Desgranges, Taylor and Prout, with over half of the volunteers. Hayes, aided by Winter and Perkins, was leading the second raiding party from the smaller of the two tugs, the *Nuneaton*. For the next couple of days the men practised lowering Folbot canoes and boarding a ship at sea, but the *Nuneaton* was already experiencing problems with her engines. However, there was no choice other than to press on, so March-Phillipps finalized his plan.

The plan was simple and straightforward, and would hopefully be carried out without a single shot being fired. The two tugs would enter the harbour and make their way independently alongside their respective targets. The raiding parties would then board the enemy ships and make fast the towing cables, while the others were to overcome any resistance encountered and place cutting charges on the anchor and stern cables. The tugs were then to steam slowly ahead to enable the strain on the cables to spring the ships from their moorings after the cables had been cut. Once this task was complete, March-Phillipps would signal the blowing of the cables by a single blast on his whistle and the tugs would then steam full ahead and tow their prizes out of the harbour.

Late in the evening of 14 January, and with the three target vessels' officers ashore and well out of the way, the raiding party entered the port. The *Vulcan* headed straight for the *Duchessa d'Aosta*. March-Phillipps could see some of the crew on board, but they paid no attention to the tug as it approached the merchantman from its starboard side.

Meanwhile, Hayes and Winter had left the *Nuneaton* in Folbots and were now paddling towards the *Likomba* and *Burundi*, which were moored together in the harbour. Although they were challenged on approaching the *Burundi*, the watchman initially believed it was the captain returning to the ship before he suddenly realized it was a raid and promptly jumped overboard to swim towards the shore. Then, as the raiders stormed the barge, another watchman jumped overboard. Having then planted explosive charges on the anchor chain, the *Nuneaton* pulled alongside the *Likomba*, ready to take her and the *Burundi* in tow.

Back at the *Duchessa d'Aosta*, the *Vulcan* had managed to get alongside without any problems. The first to board were March-Phillipps and Lassen, before the rest of the raiders stormed the ship, taking those on board completely by surprise. While one group set the charges on the anchor chain, another searched the decks for the crew, who seemed happy to surrender without a fight. They had, in fact, little choice.

All three ships had been seized in a matter of minutes and without suffering any casualties. With nearly thirty prisoners on board, and with the raiders ready to depart, the charges were blown. The tugs struggled to gather any momentum. On board the *Vulcan*, March-Phillipps was concerned when there was no forward movement, despite the best efforts of the powerful tug. One of the charges had not blown and so Appleyard quickly set another. With no time to set a lengthy delay on the fuse, Appleyard then took cover as the explosion filled the air. Once again full power was applied to the *Vulcan*'s engines and, after a few jerky movements, the *Duchessa* slowly, but steadily, started to move.

On the *Nuneaton*, Hayes had already blown the charges. Having had problems with the tug's engines on the way to Santa Isabel, he could expect further problems on the way out of the harbour, particularly under the strain of towing two vessels, and did not want to waste any time getting away. He could hear the explosions nearby and then saw the silhouetted shape of the *Duchessa* ahead of him, slowly making its way out of the harbour. Both the breeze and the current were against them, but slowly the *Nuneaton*, with its prizes under tow, crept forward against the strong tide.

As the raiders made their way out to sea, they could hear the pandemonium behind them. It had been the sound of the charges exploding in the harbour that had suddenly alerted those ashore. Many had gathered around the harbour to see what was going on, but no attempt was made to stop the ships from leaving, although some of the anti-aircraft guns opened up as the gunners believed the harbour was under air attack. The raid had taken everyone completely by surprise and it was not until several hours later that they realized the ships had gone.

Once out at sea, March-Phillipps was able to organize his men into different watches on the *Duchessa* as things were going to plan. On board the *Nuneaton*, however, it was much harder work. When daylight broke the following morning, Hayes could still see the harbour. It was hardly a quick getaway. The combination of the trouble with the tug's engines and the difficulty of towing two vessels at the same time meant the *Nuneaton* was now sheering alarmingly in the swell of the sea. She was barely able to make 2 knots.

The *Vulcan* eased ahead and the rendezvous with HMS *Violet* went as planned. The *Duchessa d'Aosta* had supposedly been captured at sea. Escorted by the *Violet*, the *Duchessa* and *Vulcan* later made a triumphant entrance into Lagos, where they were greeted by a large crowd. Meanwhile, on board the *Nuneaton*, Hayes knew there was no chance of making it all the way to Lagos. Fortunately, the crew was able to establish contact with the Nigerians and arranged for a ship to be dispatched from Lagos to tow them into port.

Back in London, details of the raid were initially kept secret from the British chiefs of staff, although Prime Minister Winston Churchill was kept fully aware. The chiefs were eventually informed of the capture of the *Duchessa d'Aosta* a few days later; they were told that she had been intercepted more than 200 miles offshore and was being taken to Lagos.

As expected, the Spanish government was outraged by the raid and saw it as a breach of the country's neutrality and an intolerable attack on Spain's sovereignty. German reports that naval forces had entered the harbour were simply denied by the British Admiralty and countered by a British Naval Intelligence communiqué stating that no British, or even Allied, ships had been in the vicinity at the time.

Back on the island of Fernando Po, Richard Lippett was taken in for questioning by the Spanish authorities, but he managed to persuade them he had nothing to do with the departure of the ships. He was later released, but was refused permission to leave the island, although he later left secretly by canoe and made it to British territory a few weeks later.

In the aftermath of the operation, the *Duchessa d'Aosta* was sailed to Greenock and then used by the Canadians as part of the Allied war effort. The *Maid Honor*, meanwhile, was left in Lagos and was eventually sold to the government of Sierra Leone. For their part in the West African adventure, particularly for Postmaster, which had been brilliantly planned and expertly carried out, Gus March-Phillipps was awarded the DSO, while Graham Hayes and Anders Lassen were both awarded the MC, and Geoffrey Appleyard received a bar to his MC.

Chapter Ten

Channel Dash

12 February 1942

Would it be possible for the German Navy's three mighty warships – the *Scharnhorst*, *Gneisenau* and *Prinz Eugen* – to return from the Atlantic to their bases in Germany by passing through the English Channel, right under the noses of the Royal Navy and RAF? Surely not. But that is exactly what the Germans intended to do, and besides, who could try and stop them? The answer was the good Old Stringbags of the Fleet Air Arm.

With the *Bismarck* having been sunk in May 1941, the *Prinz Eugen* had then been forced to abandon its Atlantic patrol due to engine problems, and she arrived in Brest on 1 June to undergo repairs alongside the *Scharnhorst* and *Gneisenau*. As the three powerful warships had been subject to a number of air attacks ever since, the German Naval Command made the decision in January 1942 to return them to Germany so that they could intercept Allied convoys heading for the Soviet Union.

Under Operation Cerberus, the plan was for the *Scharnhorst*, *Gneisenau* and *Prinz Eugen*, along with their escorts, to return to their bases in Germany via the short passage of the English Channel, rather than take the longer route through the Denmark Strait. It was an extremely risky plan as the ships would have to pass right under the noses of the British, and would have to run the gauntlet of both the Royal Navy and the RAF as they made their dash for the relative safety of the North Sea.

The idea would not have come as a complete surprise to the British. For several months the Admiralty had worked on the possibility that the ships might risk a Channel dash and had put into place Operation Fuller, with aircraft of RAF Coastal Command continuously monitoring the location of the ships. However, the British assumption had always been that if the Germans were to attempt such a plan, then the warships would pass through the Strait of Dover, the narrowest part of the passage, at night, and this would mean the ships would have to leave Brest during the hours of daylight.

It was an assumption that would prove to be wrong. No one seemingly contemplated the ships trying anything else, but, during the evening of 11 February, and under the cover of darkness, the German battle group of *Scharnhorst*, *Gneisenau* and *Prinz Eugen*, with their escort of around thirty ships, slipped out of Brest unnoticed. Hugging the French coastline and passing the Cherbourg Peninsula before daybreak, the main warships were joined by a flotilla of torpedo boats and patrolling fighters of the Luftwaffe, flying at very low level to avoid detection from the British radar sites along the south coast of England, as the battle group sailed unnoticed through the English Channel. By midday the group was entering the Strait of Dover.

It was the first time since the Spanish Armada more than 350 years earlier that an enemy fleet had sailed unopposed through the English Channel. The Germans had planned the breakout exceedingly well, having built up their own forces in the region over several days and making best use of predicted murky weather conditions in the Channel. By the time the *Scharnhorst*, *Gneisenau* and *Prinz Eugen* were in the Strait of Dover, the total number of German ships in the Channel totalled around 60, while some 250 Luftwaffe fighters had been made available to provide day and night cover for the battle group.

The murky weather conditions almost provided the ships with a trouble-free passage, but eventually the British realized what was happening and it was approaching midday when Lieutenant Commander Eugene Esmonde, the commanding officer of 825 Squadron, received news of a possible target for his squadron.

Esmonde had been to Buckingham Palace the day before to receive the DSO for his leadership of the Swordfish attack on the *Bismarck* the previous May. Since then much had happened. His squadron had been transferred to the *Ark Royal* and he had been serving on board the carrier when it was torpedoed by a German U-boat and sank the following day. Esmonde had managed to fly off the carrier before it sank, but the loss of the *Ark*, with its aircraft, equipment and personnel, had meant the squadron had been temporarily disbanded. Esmonde had then reformed it at Lee-on-Solent just a few weeks before, and he then found himself, with just six aircraft and crews, detached to Manston in Kent, where they had spent the past few days flying around the area in poor weather in preparation for a possible dash up the Channel by the German warships.

News that there might be a target for his squadron came as something of a surprise as he stared out across the snow-covered airfield into conditions that were far from ideal, with a mix of occasional sleet and slight drizzle; however, he ordered his crews to get ready to go. As the crews prepared, enough snow was cleared off the grass runway to allow the Swordfish to take off just as the Admiralty received confirmation that the German warships had been identified.

Esmonde waited for further orders. Then, with no time to spare, and no time to wait for any other aircraft to reach the area, the squadron's six Swordfish were ordered to take off at 12.20 pm and to attack the battle group fifteen minutes later. This was supposedly timed to coincide with other attacks from different air and surface units, while fighter cover would be provided by the RAF fighter wing at nearby Biggin Hill.

The German warships were estimated to be passing through the Strait some 10 miles to the north of Calais at nearly 30 knots and just fifteen minutes flying time from the south of Manston. There was no time for a detailed briefing or to plan rendezvous points. The British had been caught totally by surprise and it is no wonder a plan did not materialize. The reality was that the Swordfish of 825 Squadron were the only air or surface assets in a position to make an attack, and Esmonde would not receive the protection of a fighter wing that he had been told to expect.

The six Swordfish, each carrying a single torpedo, took off and circled Manston to see what fighter protection they would get, but just ten Spitfires showed up before the Swordfish headed straight for the might of the German battle group. Even with a complete fighter wing to offer some protection it would have been difficult, but, as things stood, Esmonde was now faced with an impossible task. The six ageing biplanes would be no match for the firepower of the German warships and the might of the Luftwaffe, but he had been given no option. Whatever he was feeling inwardly, Esmonde put his personal thoughts and concerns to one side as, seemingly undismayed, he bravely led his depleted squadron into action. He knew that he must at least try to slow down the battle group and simply briefed his crews to attack any one of the three major ships in whatever way they could. From the brief plan he had put together, the Swordfish were to attack in two flights, each of three aircraft in a standard line astern formation to minimize as much as possible the width of the attack.

Esmonde led the Swordfish out over Ramsgate, taking one final look to see if any more of the promised fighter escort had turned up before he headed out into the Channel. Conditions were every bit as bad as he had expected, with low cloud and poor visibility, but as they coasted out at a height of not much more than 100 feet the Swordfish were spotted by the patrolling German fighters, a mix of Messerschmitt Bf 109s and Focke-Wulf FW 190s. As the Spitfires engaged the attackers as best they could, the Swordfish descended even lower as Esmonde could now make out the vast armada appearing out of the gloom ahead of him.

It was just after 12.40 pm when the Swordfish commenced their attack. They had already been spotted by the enemy naval gunners and immediately came under a huge barrage of anti-aircraft fire, causing clouds of spray from the sea as the heavy shells exploded in front of them. Remaining calm and resolute as he led the first flight into attack, Esmonde ran in from the south-west at a height of just 50 feet. The *Scharnhorst* soon appeared out of the murky conditions ahead of him, but Esmonde had not long started his run-in when his aircraft was hit, a shell ripping through the surface of the lower port wing and causing the outer part to break away. Wrestling with the controls, Esmonde temporarily brought his aircraft under control and pressed on courageously towards the *Scharnhorst*. It was then the turn of the Luftwaffe as the naval gunners ceased firing for fear of hitting their own aircraft.

Hopelessly outnumbered, and before they could get any closer to the battle group, the Swordfish came under heavy attack from the patrolling Luftwaffe fighters. With a top speed of little more than 100mph, the Swordfish crews stood no chance against the dozens of Bf 109s that now swooped on their prey from the rear of the formation. Just as Esmonde was launching his torpedo, an FW 190, sensing an easy kill, pounced on the stricken aircraft, hitting it again and again, killing Esmonde instantly as cannon shells rained from behind, before the Swordfish burst into flames and plunged in a curving dive into the sea, taking the crew to their deaths.

Having seen the fate of their leader, and under considerable attack themselves, the two Swordfish flown by Sub-Lieutenants Pat Kingsmill and

Brian Rose pressed on regardless. The first of the two to attack was Rose. Lining up on the *Scharnhorst*, he soon found he was also in a desperate situation. His aircraft had been hit and was losing fuel, and his air gunner, Petty Officer Airman Ambrose Lawrence 'Ginger' Johnson, who had been awarded the DSM for the attack on the *Bismarck* the previous year, was dead. Rose had also been hit in the back and knew that he did not have enough fuel to complete his attack and return to base, but ignoring the option to break off and try to return to base, he elected instead to press on towards the ships.

Hugging the sea as close as he dared, and with each second taking the Swordfish closer to the battle group, Rose pushed on through the relentless fire. Finding that it was now impossible to continue his attack against the *Scharnhorst*, he turned towards the *Prinz Eugen* to line up on his target. Passing the outer screen of destroyers, Rose took the Swordfish closer and closer, finally releasing his torpedo at a range of around 1,200 yards before turning away.

Having already lost so much fuel, Rose was never going to be able to make it back to land; he barely made it outside the protective screen of German destroyers before ditching his aircraft in the bitterly cold sea. As the Swordfish started to sink, the observer, Sub-Lieutenant Edgar Lee, was able to assist Rose out of the aircraft, but Ginger Johnson, already dead and jammed in the cockpit, could not be released. Both Rose and Lee would spend nearly two hours in their dinghy before a British patrol boat arrived to rescue them. They had been fortunate because one of the Spitfires had seen the Swordfish come down and had reported its position, but the body of Ambrose Lawrence Johnson was never recovered; he was just 22 years old.

The third aircraft of the lead flight, flown by Kingsmill, had also run the gauntlet of fighters and intense anti-aircraft fire as the crew pressed on towards the *Scharnhorst*. The Swordfish had been hit several times in the engine compartment, but remarkably, the Pegasus radial engine kept turning enough for Kingsmill to continue his run-in towards the ship. The air gunner, Leading Airman Donald Bunce, even claimed to have shot down a German fighter despite the fact the Swordfish had been under continuous attack as it bravely limped on.

The Swordfish was then hit yet again, causing a fire in the wing and forcing Kingsmill to change his direction of attack. Kingsmill and his observer, Sub-Lieutenant Mac Samples, had both been hit during the attack and they now also elected to head for the *Prinz Eugen* instead, Kingsmill closing to a range of around 1,400 yards before he released his torpedo and turned away. Still on fire and unable to make it any further, the Swordfish came down just a few moments later, no further than a mile away from the German battle group; fortunately for the crew, they were later rescued by a nearby British trawler.

The second flight of three aircraft, led by Lieutenant John Thompson, was seen to approach the German battle group. For some unknown reason the two other Swordfish of Thompson's formation, those flown by Sub-Lieutenants Cecil Wood and Peter Bligh, were not flying in line astern as had been briefed. They were last seen passing over the escorting German destroyers as the three Swordfish bravely ran the gauntlet of Luftwaffe fighters and the intense barrage of flak from the battle group; none of the three Swordfish survived and all nine crew members were killed.

None of the six Swordfish that had set off from Manston only minutes before returned, although five of the eighteen airmen were fortunate to survive. Further attempts were made against the German battle group, and some damage was achieved, but the opportunity to cause significant damage to the might of the German Navy had been lost. The *Gneisenau* reached Kiel but suffered extensive damage later in the month during a bombing raid and took no further part in the war. The *Scharnhorst* would later join the *Bismarck*'s sister ship, the *Tirpitz*, in Norway to intercept Allied shipping heading for the Soviet Union, but was later sunk by the Royal Navy in December 1943. After the Channel dash, the *Prinz Eugen* arrived in Brunsbüttel and joined up with the heavy cruiser *Admiral Scheer* to operate in Norwegian waters, where she was hit by a torpedo. Following repairs in Germany she later operated in the Baltic before being surrendered to the Allies at the end of the war.

The extraordinary courage of the crews of 825 Squadron against the German battle group epitomizes the bravery of those who went to war in the Old Stringbag, and the raid was later described as one of the finest exhibitions of self-sacrifice and devotion to duty yet witnessed during the war. The four surviving officers of the raid – Pat Kingsmill, Edgar Lee, Brian Rose and Mac Samples – were each awarded the DSO, while the only surviving air gunner, Donald Bunce, was awarded the CGM. Those who were killed during the raid were awarded a Mention in Despatches.

Finally, for his extreme bravery and leadership of the six Swordfish against such overwhelming odds, Eugene Esmonde was awarded a posthumous Victoria Cross; the first to a member of the Fleet Air Arm. His citation in the *London Gazette* includes:

> *He flew on, cool and resolute, serenely challenging hopeless odds, to encounter the deadly fire of the Battle-Cruisers and their Escort, which shattered the port wing of his aircraft. Undismayed, he led his Squadron on, straight through this inferno of fire, in steady flight towards their target. Almost at once he was shot down: but his Squadron went on to launch a gallant attack, in which at least one torpedo is believed to have struck the German Battle-Cruisers, and from which not one of the six aircraft returned. His high courage and splendid resolution will live in the traditions of the Royal Navy, and remain for many generations a fine and stirring memory.*

Esmonde's body was later discovered at the entrance to the River Medway and he was buried at the Woodlands Cemetery in Gillingham, Kent, with full naval honours. Not only did Esmonde and the Swordfish crews of 825 Squadron receive the highest praise from their own senior officers for the gallantry displayed during the Channel dash, their courage and bravery did not go unnoticed by German observers on board the ships of the battle group. The most notable comments came from the senior commanders on board the *Scharnhorst*, one of which was from the commander of Operation Cerberus, Vice Admiral Otto Ciliax, who flew his flag on board the *Scharnhorst* and commented on the '*attack of a handful of ancient planes piloted by men whose bravery surpasses any other action by either side that day.*' There was also praise from the captain of the *Scharnhorst*, Kurt-Caesar Hoffmann, who exclaimed '*poor fellows, they are so very low, it is nothing but suicide for them to fly against these big ships.*'

Chapter Eleven

Bruneval

27/28 February 1942

Today the Parachute Regiment forms an elite and vital airborne element of the British Army. Trained to conduct a range of missions and ready to form the spearhead for rapid intervention, it is light by design as its operations are usually based on speed. The paras formed during the Second World War, and an early raid to capture an enemy radar site at night, and then dismantle it so that parts could be taken back to Britain for expert evaluation, sounds more like a tale of fiction rather than fact. But that was exactly the task that was given to paratroopers on the night of 27/28 February 1942, and the raid on Bruneval must surely be one of the most audacious of the war.

The development of radar was vital to both sides during the Second World War, and each wished to retain a technical edge over the other. This meant finding out what the other side was doing – and there was no better way for the British to know how German radar had evolved than to analyse its components.

The low-UHF band Würzburg radar was Germany's primary ground-based gun-laying radar during the war, having entered service during 1940. Reconnaissance flights carried out by the RAF's Photographic Reconnaissance Unit during late 1941 had identified installations along the northern coastline of France but their purpose had initially remained unknown. Some were convinced that the installations coincided with increasing RAF Bomber Command losses and British intelligence had concluded that Germany had significantly developed its radar techniques. And so a request was made to the headquarters of Combined Operations for one of the installations to be raided, with a view to identifying and understanding the German technology and, better still, capturing equipment and returning it to Britain for further examination. This would enable the

British to effectively neutralize the system through the development of suitable countermeasures.

One installation in particular was considered accessible and, therefore, suitable for a raid. It was at Bruneval, just over 10 miles to the north of Le Havre, with the radar installation being located on a clifftop to the north of the village. Extensive German defences along the coastline would make a commando raid from the sea difficult. Not only might it prove costly in terms of lives lost, but any advanced warning that a raid was in progress would allow the German garrison located at the installation to destroy any secret equipment rather than risk it being captured. It was, therefore, decided that an airborne raid would take place to seize the technical equipment intact, after which evacuation of the equipment would be carried out by sea.

At that time, airborne operations were still in their early days. The first carried out by the British, called Operation Colossus, had taken place in February 1941 with mixed results. It had been undertaken to test the concept of conducting an airborne assault and to assess the RAF's ability to deliver such a force. The target chosen was an aqueduct near Calitri in southern Italy, which supplied water to several ports used by the Italian military, and its destruction would hamper Italian operations in North Africa and Albania. The raid was carried out by thirty-eight members of X Troop, part of a new unit called 11 Special Air Service Battalion, which had been formed from 2 Commando. Although the aqueduct had been damaged, the raiders were captured and the aqueduct soon repaired, and so enemy operations had not been hampered for long, if at all. Nonetheless, the concept had been tried and valuable lessons learned. The raid was considered successful enough to expand British airborne forces and so, in September 1941, the battalion became the 1st Parachute Battalion and was assigned to the 1st Parachute Brigade. A call for further volunteers led to the 2nd Battalion being formed, with the Parachute Brigade becoming part of the newly formed 1st Airborne Division.

The idea of an airborne assault against the Würzburg installation at Bruneval was first put to the headquarters of the 1st Airborne Division during the early days of 1942. Its commander, Major General Frederick Browning, was full of enthusiasm, as it offered a chance to boost the morale of his new organization and an opportunity to instantly make its name. At the time only the 1st Battalion was fully trained, but Browning wished to retain this intact for any larger-scale operation that might be required in the near future, and so he gave the task to C Company of the 2nd Battalion, a unit largely made up of men drawn from Scottish units.

The raid was given the codename Operation Biting. The plan, using an assault force of 120 paratroopers to capture and then hold the radar installation and its surrounds while vital parts of the radar were dismantled and evacuated back to England, was to be based on total surprise. Chosen to lead the raid was the commander of C Company, Major John Frost.

Bruneval would be the first major British airborne raid of the war and so training would require close co-ordination between airborne troops and aircrew. The RAF element of the task was given to the Whitleys of 51 Squadron under the command of Wing Commander Charles 'Pick' Pickard, a holder of the DSO and the DFC and already known to the British public, having starred in the 1941 wartime propaganda film *Target for Tonight*, in which he featured as a Wellington pilot of '*F for Freddie*'.

There was little time for much training, as Biting had to be completed by the end of February, when the combination of the moon, a rising tide and the general weather conditions were likely to be suitable for the raid to take place. However, the training was as thorough as possible. It was mainly conducted from Tilshead in Wiltshire and involved much time on Salisbury Plain, including a parachute drop with 51 Squadron. The paras also spent time in Scotland, where they practised night embarkations on landing craft from the Combined Operations training base at Inverary in order to prepare the men for the evacuation by sea once the radar had been dismantled, when they would be using six landing craft from the landing ship HMS *Prince Albert*.

The naval part of the operation was to be led by an Australian, Commander Frederick Cook, and was dependent on suitable sea conditions on the night. Although the *Prince Albert* would be protected by a group of motor gunboats (MGBs), the lowering of landing craft in a high swell was never easy and finding a specific part of the French coastline at night in less than ideal conditions would be a challenge. Cook would transfer to one of the lead landing craft for the final run ashore, and also on board one of the craft would be Donald Priest, a scientist and radar engineer from the Telecommunications Research Establishment, who would only land if the entire area around the radar installation was considered totally secure. If so, Priest's task would be to assist in the dismantling of the radar and to make a brief technical assessment of the equipment. If, however, there was any doubt about the security of the area then Priest was not to go ashore and under no account was he to fall into enemy hands; he would, therefore, have two soldiers to protect him. The evacuation plan was for the landing craft to beach two at a time to collect the paras and radar equipment. Although each landing craft was to be armed by a Bren light machine-gun team, another two support landing craft, carrying thirty-two men of 12 Commando, would provide additional firepower to cover the raiders as they withdrew from the beach. Once the paras had been evacuated they were to be transferred to the faster MGBs for the run back to the south coast of England while RAF fighters provided air cover over the Channel as first light broke.

As the men arrived back at Tilshead they were still unaware of what their actual target was to be. Given the time available, and the fact that this kind of operation was new, training had gone very well. Information about the radar site had been gathered from every source available, including observations from members of the French Resistance on the ground, which included valuable details about the German garrison at the site. Furthermore, a model of the installation and surrounding buildings had been built using the aerial reconnaissance photos taken by the RAF, which all helped provide the men with an understanding of the task they faced. The men were then given more information and carried out their final training along the Dorset coast, although they were still unaware of exactly where their target was to be.

The radar installation at Bruneval was located on a reasonably flat plateau and was essentially made up of two main areas: the radar station, contained in a building a hundred yards from the edge of the cliff and manned by signallers, and an enclosure of smaller buildings housing a garrison of enemy troops, believed to be about a hundred in strength, and another shift of signallers. The compound was surrounded by guard posts with an estimated thirty guards on shift at any one time. There was a further detachment of soldiers to the north with responsibility for manning coastal defences in the area. These included a strong defensive point near the intended evacuation beach, and pillboxes and other defensive positions along the top of the cliff, which included a number of machine-gun nests overlooking the beach. The only good news was that the pebble beach, some 300 yards long, was believed to be free of mines, with the only known hazard being barbed wire along its stretch. However, regular enemy patrols were known to be active and the mobile reserve, although garrisoned further inland, could be in the area within an hour.

Based on all the intelligence he had, Frost decided to divide his force into five teams, operating as three main groups each of forty men, and given the names Drake, Hardy, Jellicoe, Nelson and Rodney. Three groups – Drake, Hardy and Jellicoe – would capture the radar site and a nearby building housing the technicians and guards, while Nelson would secure the area of the evacuation beach and Rodney would provide protection for the three main assault groups by taking up a position between the radar installation and the direction of enemy approach.

Frost was to lead the twenty men of Hardy and capture the villa housing the radar operators while 22-year-old Lieutenant Peter Young would lead the ten men of Jellicoe to capture the radar. The other group, the ten men of Drake, would be led by Lieutenant Peter Naumoff. They were to deal with the other buildings at the farm at La Presbytère, where up to sixty enemy troops were believed to be housed, and to divert any enemy fire away from the other two assault groups.

After capturing the installation and the garrison, the task of photographing the radar set and then dismantling it would fall to Flight Sergeant Charles Cox, a radar technician from the RAF who had volunteered to take part in the raid. Cox would be attached to Hardy, but time would not be on his side and so it was crucial for him to remove specific parts that had been briefed to him prior to the raid. These parts would then be loaded onto a hand trolley and taken with the men down a gulley to the beach for evacuation.

While the three main assault groups had the challenge of capturing the radar installation and its surrounds, the task faced by the forty men of Nelson was also crucial. Half the men were to be led by the youngest officer taking part in the raid, Second Lieutenant Euan Charteris, the son of a brigadier and just 20 years old. His group was to secure the beach and take out the two enemy machine-gun posts known to be in the area. When it was time to evacuate the beach they would then signal the flotilla of landing craft to come ashore to pick them up. The rest of Nelson, led by 21-year-old Captain John Ross, the second-in-command of C Company, were to protect the beach by holding the road leading from Bruneval village. Ross's group would then cover the evacuation and be the last to leave the beach. The forty men making up Rodney were to be led by Lieutenant John Timothy. His group would be last to drop, with the task of protecting the eastern flank, as this was the direction from which the main threat of reinforcements could be expected, particularly from La Presbytère.

As the training neared an end, the date of the raid was narrowed to a four-day period starting on 24 February. The day before, a final rehearsal took place but, despite all conditions seemingly favouring the raiders, it proved to be a drastic failure when the landing craft for evacuating the raiders became grounded several yards offshore.

The men were now fully aware of their mission and the target but their training never seemed to go exactly to plan. Then, with poor weather over the next few days, there were concerns that the raid might not take place at all. On two consecutive days the men had packed their equipment and prepared to move, only to be told the mission had been postponed. It was mentally draining as well as totally frustrating.

The three nights considered suitable for the raid came and went and it now looked like the opportunity had been missed. Then, on the morning of 27 February, the men woke to find a bright, clear sky. It was bitterly cold, but the wind had gone and visibility was good. Frost received word that headquarters had extended the period for the op to be carried out by twenty-four hours, and so the men were told to prepare once more. Then finally, soon after midday, Frost received the word that the mission was on. The weather conditions were going to be near perfect, with clear skies, a full moon and good visibility, but then came the news that Bruneval and its surrounding area were covered by snow.

The likelihood of snow had seemingly not really featured in the planning. None of the combat clothing or equipment was for winter warfare, but it was too late to do anything about that now. The naval evacuation force left southern England during the afternoon to take up its position about 15 miles off the coast, then it was the turn of the men of C Company to leave Tilshead for the short journey to the airfield at Thruxton.

Soon after 9.30 pm they boarded their aircraft to the sound of pipes, to stir the men and send them into battle. An hour later the twelve RAF Whitleys were airborne, each carrying ten men and equipment, and heading for the south coast of England, where they joined up before heading out across the Channel. On board the conditions were dark, cold and cramped. The men sat on the floor and huddled together along the sides of the fuselage, with sleeping bags and blankets to keep them warm.

Diversionary air raids had been planned for the night to keep the Luftwaffe and anti-aircraft flak batteries occupied and these were already in full operation. The Whitleys crossed the Channel at low altitude to avoid being detected by enemy radar. The clear visibility meant that navigation was not a problem and so the aircrew had little trouble locating the drop zones. Then, descending to below 500 feet, the Whitleys made their final run-in towards their drop zones.

On the ground there was little for the Germans at Bruneval to be concerned about. It had been a perfectly normal evening and although they were aware of RAF bombers approaching Le Havre, this was not unusual. The diversionary raids had done their job. The Germans suspected nothing.

The Whitleys initially paralleled the French coastline towards Le Havre and then turned towards Bruneval. It was now just after midnight and they were only minutes from the first drop. Their track took them about half a mile inland and they were now in their required order for the final run-in for the drop, with Pickard's aircraft leading.

Inside Pickard's aircraft was Charteris. He was the first to jump. Seconds later he was on the ground, but as he looked around and surveyed the scene, nothing was recognizable to him. Within minutes the other members of his group from the two lead aircraft, the men making up half of Nelson, were assembled with their equipment and ready to move, but there was no sign of Ross and the other half of the team. Unbeknown to Charteris at that time, Ross and his half of Nelson had been dropped in the correct place, but Charteris's team had been dropped more than 2 miles short. The problem now was for him to decide in which direction they should go. Charteris had to take a chance and so he led his men off in a northerly direction, believing that to be correct. Ross, meanwhile, having waited a few minutes to see if Charteris and the men would turn up, had decided to move off regardless.

Frost and his main assault group arrived over their drop zone just five minutes after the lead element. The forty men of Drake, Hardy and Jellicoe then jumped and, five minutes later, the four aircraft carrying Timothy's group, Rodney, arrived. They, too, then started to jump.

For Frost and the men of Drake, Hardy and Jellicoe the drop went as planned. They came down in the centre of their drop zone, and just twenty minutes later were in position and ready to commence their attack. For Timothy, however, the men of Rodney had initially become separated after a couple of wayward drops and one aircraft had to circle round for a second time. Nonetheless, Timothy had managed to get most of his men into position to provide protection for the main assault.

With his men ready, Frost gave a long, hard blast on his whistle as the order to open fire. Grenades and automatic fire rained down on the villa. The paras had taken the Germans completely by surprise, but what had come as a surprise to the raiders was that only one German had been encountered in the building; he stood no chance. Meanwhile, the assault on the radar by Young and the men of Jellicoe was fully underway. Frost and his men could hear the battle raging just a hundred yards or so away but it soon fell silent. A number of Germans lay dead and one radar technician was taken prisoner. Young's group was still fully intact.

Everything had, so far, gone according to plan. Now it was Charlie Cox's turn to do his bit. He had been in Frost's group since leaving Tilshead but had to remain in the rear while the fighting had taken place. It was now time for him to set about his task. He quickly moved up to the radar and familiarized himself with the major components before dismantling what he could and placing the pieces of equipment on the trolleys ready for evacuation.

The German troops nearby were now fully alive to what was going on. The low-flying Whitleys, followed by the sound of explosions and gunfire, had initially caused confusion amongst the troops at La Presbytère as to what the target was likely to be. There was a much larger Freya radar installation nearby but they had now worked out that it was the Würzburg that was under attack. Having quickly made their way to the area, they could see the paras a few hundred yards away and were now in a position to counter-attack.

The rapid fire that suddenly came down on the paras from the area known as the Rectangle did not exactly come as a surprise. It had, indeed, been anticipated and planned for, but the speed at which the Germans had got to a strong position was a major concern. The incoming fire was fierce and accurate and the paras soon suffered their first casualty.

While Cox continued to dismantle the radar, Frost reacted by ordering Naumoff to take Drake to counter the threat coming from the Rectangle. The enemy troops were now getting stronger but the men of Drake continued to hold them at bay, each minute helping towards the mission's success.

Frost was now aware that Nelson had become split during the drop and, as yet, had been unable to secure the evacuation route and the beach. He was having further difficulties with communicating with his groups because two radio operators were missing. They had been on board the aircraft that had been forced to go round again to make a second drop, but there was a further problem as some of the radio sets did not seem to work.

Ross, with only half the men available to him, had split them into three small groups, with two of his sergeants leading a group each: one went to the beach and the other to attack an enemy position on the cliff. Ross, meanwhile, took his small group to clear a network of enemy defensive positions. At first everything had gone well, but one of the small groups had been spotted and a heavy firefight had soon broken out. The sound of heavy machine-gun and semi-automatic fire could be heard for miles around. The flashes of weapons firing around the cliffs and down towards the beach had lit up the darkness of the night sky. The Germans seemed to be firing down on one group of paras while another group had gained a height advantage further up the cliff and were now firing down on the German emplacement. The defenders were well dug-in but rather static in their positions, whereas the paras were able to move and fire from different directions; also, the German defenders simply had no idea of the strength they were up against.

It had now turned into a full-scale battle and Frost could clearly hear just how ferocious the fight had become, but with no radio contact with Nelson he was unable to determine who was where. With casualties likely to mount he ordered Young to take Jellicoe down to the beach and to provide Ross with whatever support he could. It would not be any easier for Young to determine who was where either and so the men of Jellicoe proceeded as quickly, but as cautiously as they could. Meanwhile, Frost had instructed Timothy to send some men of Rodney towards the beach to add weight to the assault on the German positions that were dug-in, while using the rest of his group to counter the enemy approaching from the direction of La Presbytère.

The paras had now been on enemy soil for an hour, but to the men trying to get away it was starting to feel as if it had been much longer. Cox was still working as best he could to dismantle the radar but it was clear he was not going to be allowed much more time to do so. The situation was starting to become desperate as the enemy were getting more of a foothold in the surrounding area. Finally, having secured as much equipment as they could, and still under heavy fire, the raiders were ordered by Frost to withdraw to the beach. He knew the escape route had still not been cleared but he felt that it would be better for the men to try and fight their way to the beach rather than to stay where they were. But pulling fully laden trolleys across the snow-covered rugged ground proved hard work. As the paras made their way to the beach, a burst of heavy machine-gun fire made it obvious the evacuation area had still not been cleared.

Meanwhile, having been dropped some way short of their intended drop zone, Charteris and the rest of Nelson had made their way quickly to the scene. Charteris's initial heading from their drop point had been good and he had soon been able to establish where they were. There had been the odd skirmish on the way to the beach but nothing his men could not handle. It had taken them well over an hour to reach the scene and when he arrived the battle had reached something of a stalemate. Moving quickly across unfamiliar terrain at night, and carrying equipment, some of it quite heavy, had meant that his group had now split into smaller units. So, having reached the cliff overlooking the beach, Charteris gathered what men he could as he assessed the situation as well as possible given the dark and the confusion, before leading them quietly down the slope of the cliff towards a villa on the beach that was occupied by enemy troops.

Charteris could wait no longer and, with his small group of men, stormed into the fight. They announced their arrival by lobbing grenades at the villa while some kept up constant fire on German positions overlooking the beach. The paras were now at their most vulnerable as they charged down the road towards the villa. It was a moment of outstanding bravery and swung the momentum of the battle in favour of the paras. Charteris was the first to reach the villa, along with one of his sergeants, David Grieve. They stormed the building with grenades and Sten machine guns firing, only to find just one startled German soldier inside; the rest had escaped. With the villa captured, Ross appeared; his men having cleared out the last of the defenders as others had fled to safety. At last the beach was in British hands. It was nearly 2.30 am.

Back up on the cliffs the enemy had reoccupied the villa that had housed the radar operators and guards. Frost, fully aware of the threat now posed from the rear, decided this would have to be dealt with. He could not afford to have more enemy troops firing on them from so close behind as his men tried to make their way down the cliffs. Rounding up what men and equipment he could, he led his men back across the plateau towards the villa. As they got closer they charged the building with all guns blazing. The sight of paras charging back to the villa came as an unwelcome surprise to those inside. The villa had been reoccupied, but not in sufficient strength to prevent the paras from regaining the building. With the Germans retreating back to safety, Frost returned towards the clifftops and gave the order for his men to make their way down towards the beach.

Once again, the trolleys laden with pieces of radar equipment were dragged down the gulley. With them was the German radar technician who had been taken prisoner. Down on the beach the scene was one of devastation. A handful of German prisoners stood under guard, their hands held high, but there was no sign of the evacuation flotilla of landing craft. Unbeknown to Frost, the flotilla had received no signals from the raiding party and had spent much of the time avoiding an enemy patrolling vessel that had nearly discovered them.

With Nelson left to protect the beach from any counter-attack from inland, flares were fired as a last desperate attempt to signal the flotilla. It was just what Cook and his men on board the landing craft had been waiting for. Finding a small beach at night along an extensive coastline, with all beaches and cliffs looking much the same, was never going to be easy, but Cook had managed to position the flotilla perfectly. They had been little more than a mile offshore and had witnessed the assault and the raging battle that followed, but Cook could not risk sending the landing craft ashore until the beach was secure.

Now it was time to begin the evacuation. The landing craft moved in quickly. The sight of the cavalry, in the form of landing craft, approaching the beach was a most welcome sight for the raiders, but suddenly machine-gun fire rattled down from the cliffs above. The landing craft had been spotted. With German troops firing on the paras from the cliffs above, and with the landing craft also coming under enemy fire, there was no time to land two by two and so, as the commandos on board returned fire on the German positions on top of the cliffs, all six craft came ashore at the same time.

For several minutes there was confusion and chaos on the beach. There was a further problem when a number of German troops came out of hiding in the cliffs and started to open fire on the landing craft below. The paras piled on board any landing craft they could find but the evacuation was now taking place later than planned, which meant the tide had changed and was now on its way out. Some landing craft got stuck on the pebbles and some left the beach completely overcrowded, while others left only partially loaded. Fortunately, though, the radar equipment was quickly evacuated, as were the German prisoners. Somehow, the raiding force was evacuated off the beach with Frost being the last to leave.

Having reached the safety of mid-Channel the paras were transferred to the faster MGBs to complete their transit back home. The journey back across the Channel passed uneventfully as the MGBs were escorted by four naval destroyers while air cover was provided by RAF Spitfires.

The raid on Bruneval was undoubtedly a success. It had cost the lives of just two men: 28-year-old Private Hugh McIntyre, who had been killed at the radar installation during the German counter-attack, and 24-year-old Private Alan Scott, who was killed on the cliffs during the evacuation. Eight others had been wounded and half a dozen had been left behind and were subsequently taken as prisoners of war; one had been wounded and five never made it to the landing craft during the rush and chaos of the evacuation.

The raid was made public when it was given great coverage by the media. It had come at a time when hitting back at the enemy was essential and was seen as a great morale boost, not only for the men of Combined Operations, but also for the British public at large. Prime Minister Winston Churchill had taken great interest in the raid; after all, it was exactly what units such as the paras and commandos had been formed to do.

Ten gallantry awards followed the success of the operation and were announced in the *London Gazette* on 15 May. For leading the raid John Frost was awarded the Military Cross, as was Euan Charteris, and there was a Distinguished Service Cross, one of three awarded for the raid, for Frederick Cook, while two other members of the evacuation party received the Distinguished Service Medal. There was also a Military Medal for Charlie Cox, the RAF radio technician who had volunteered to take part in the raid. His was one of three MMs awarded for the raid; the others were to Sergeant David Grieve, who had stormed the villa on the beach with Charteris, and Sergeant Gregor McKenzie, known as 'Mac the Knife', who had fought in the same decisive action. Nine others were awarded a Mention in Despatches. There was also subsequent recognition of Pick Pickard's leadership of the Whitleys that had dropped the paras at Bruneval; Pickard received a bar to his DSO.

The success of the raid also ensured the expansion of British airborne forces and resulted in more airborne battalions later in the year. But it was the technical knowledge gained by British scientists that was the most important aspect of the raid. Examination of the Würzburg equipment showed the radar was vulnerable to new jamming techniques being considered at the time and this led to the development of Window, which were aluminium strips dropped in bundles as an effective countermeasure against German radars. It was a development that would save countless lives throughout the rest of the war.

Chapter Twelve

St Nazaire

28 March 1942

Often described as the most daring raid of them all, the attack on the port of St Nazaire by the Royal Navy and Army Commandos during March 1942 resulted in the award of five VCs, the most for a single action of the Second World War.

The major port of St Nazaire lies on the Atlantic coastline of western France and on the northern bank of the River Loire estuary. Its outer harbour, the *avant-port*, juts out into the Atlantic and leads to two lock gates, before the Bassin de St Nazaire, that control the water level in the basin so that it is not affected by the tide; beyond these is located the larger inner dock. In 1942 the port, some 300 miles from the nearest British naval base, was under German occupation, and was the only port on the Atlantic coast that could accommodate the largest German warships. Its Normandie dry dock, built in the 1930s to house the French cruise liner SS *Normandie*, was the largest dry dock in the world and the only one capable of accommodating such ships.

The threat of the great German warships to British convoys in the Atlantic was simply too great to be ignored, and so a British commando raid against the dock was proposed late in 1941. Combined Operations considered a number of options for the destruction of the dock. One was to carry out aerial bombing, but it was debatable whether resources should be made available for such a raid, also, bombing techniques at that stage of the war were considered inaccurate. Furthermore, an air raid would probably result in civilian casualties, which Britain was not prepared to risk. Another option was to ask the SOE if its agents could conduct a raid, but any raid of such a size was beyond the SOE's capability. A further option of a naval frontal attack was also ruled out because the port was situated 5 miles up the river estuary.

Having dismissed a number of options, the planners examined the feasibility of a commando raid taking place in early 1942. The estuary was well defended, as would be expected, but an unusually high tide scheduled for March would allow any lightened ships, from which a raid could be mounted, to approach the docks. The planners pieced together the elements of a raid with three main objectives: to destroy the Normandie dry dock; destroy the gates into the Bassin de St Nazaire, together with the pumping station and any other installations; and to destroy any U-boats or other shipping that happened to be in and around the docks at the time. It was estimated there was an array of heavy guns protecting the port and some five thousand German troops in St Nazaire. There were also a number of German ships in and around the estuary at any one time, including a destroyer and a minesweeper designated as a guard for the port, while St Nazaire was also home to two U-boat flotillas.

The plan finally put together for the raid, called Operation Chariot, was an extremely audacious one. The planners elected to use two lightened destroyers for the raid. One would be packed with explosives and rammed into the dry dock, from which commandos could quickly disembark to mount the raid and use demolition charges to destroy any installations or gun emplacements. The destroyer would then be blown up to prevent the dry dock from being used again, while the second ship would be used to evacuate the first ship's crew and the commandos that had carried out the raid. Meanwhile, the RAF would carry out diversionary air raids in the area.

It was a daring plan but, with the certain loss of at least one destroyer, it was not supported by the Admiralty, who believed the raid would be better conducted using an old French ship to destroy the dock and a flotilla of motor launches to land the commandos. The idea also had no support from the RAF senior command who believed it to be an unwelcome drain on its resources. Churchill was sympathetic to the RAF's concerns as he also felt that bombing should only be used if specific targets had first been identified, thus avoiding unnecessary collateral damage.

The planners at Combined Operations did not agree. The use of a French ship would require more people being made aware of the raid, thereby compromising it, but the revised plan included the use of just one obsolete Royal Navy ship, HMS *Campbeltown*, a former First World War American destroyer, to ram the dock gates, and several smaller craft to transport the commandos.

The *Campbeltown* required conversion for the raid and this took several days to complete. It included lightening the ship as much as possible to get it over the sandbanks by removing her torpedoes, depth charges and three main 4-inch guns; the forward gun being replaced by a lighter and quick-firing 12-pounder. The bow was packed with more than four tons of high explosives set in concrete and timed to explode after the raiders had left the port, and the ship's seacocks would be opened after she had rammed the dock so that she could not be towed away. To enable her to approach St Nazaire without being identified, two of her funnels were removed and the other two modified to give the appearance of a German vessel, and extra armour plating was fitted to the bridge and sides to offer the crew and commandos more protection. In the event anything should go wrong during the attack, four motor launches were fitted to allow the men on board to escape.

In addition to the *Campbeltown*, a motor gunboat, MGB 314, commanded by Lieutenant Dunstan Curtis, was allocated for the raid as the attacking force's headquarters. On board would be Commander Robert 'Red' Ryder, the senior naval officer with overall responsibility for the raid, and Lieutenant Colonel Charles Newman, the leader of the commando force; his unit, 2 Commando, would provide 170 men for the raid with a further 100 commandos being drawn from other units.

There was also a motor torpedo boat allocated for the raid and commanded by 24-year-old Sub-Lieutenant Michael Wynn, the eldest son of the 6th Baron Newborough. Wynn's MTB 74 had initially been involved in a plan to attack the German warships *Scharnhorst* and *Gneisenau* in Brest harbour, but both ships had suddenly escaped the Allies in February's Channel dash, and so, having been left without a mission, MTB 74 was assigned to the raid on St Nazaire instead. Wynn's mission was to perform one of two tasks. If the outer Normandie gates were found to be closed his MTB was to torpedo the gates at the old entrance to the Bassin de St Nazaire. If, however, the gates were found to be open, then he was to torpedo the inner dock gates instead.

To assist in transporting the commandos, twelve motor launches, each fitted with an auxiliary fuel tank to increase their range, were assigned to the raid. An additional four motor launches would accompany the flotilla and attack any enemy shipping found in the estuary. The submarine HMS

Sturgeon would also provide assistance by marking the entrance to the estuary.

The commandos were split into three groups; two groups were to be transported on the motor launches while the third group would be on board the *Campbeltown*. The first group was to be led by 23-year-old Captain Eric Hodgson, known to his friends as Bertie, with the task of securing the area known as the Old Mole and destroying the anti-aircraft installations around the southern quay. The men would then make their way into the old town and destroy a power station, bridges and locks. The second group was to be led by Captain Micky Burn. Their task was to land at the old entrance to the Bassin de St Nazaire and take out the enemy's headquarters as well as destroying anti-aircraft guns, bridges and locks. The third group on board the *Campbeltown* was to be led by Major Bill Copland, Newman's second-in-command for the raid. Once ashore, they would secure the area around the *Campbeltown* and then destroy the dock's water pump installation, gate machinery and underground fuel tanks. All three groups were further subdivided into teams to carry out specific tasks. Assault teams would be the first into action to clear the way ahead, followed by heavily laden demolition teams carrying the explosive charges and more heavily armed protection teams to protect the demolition teams as they carried out their tasks.

It was mid-afternoon on 26 March when the armada of three destroyers and sixteen small motor launches slipped away from their moorings at Falmouth in Cornwall to form up in a convoy of three lanes. Without the range to reach St Nazaire unaided, the MGB, with Ryder and Newman on board, and Wynn's MTB, were towed by *Campbeltown* and the destroyer HMS *Atherstone*. With the threat of German torpedo boats in their path, two more destroyers were dispatched to help protect the convoy.

By the following evening the convoy had reached a position 70 miles from St Nazaire. The command MGB, flanked by two motor launches, now positioned itself out in front of the convoy, with *Campbeltown* behind. The remaining motor launches took up their positions in two columns abeam and astern the destroyer, with Wynn's MTB at the rear, as the flotilla took up its final formation to commence the attack. Later that evening RAF bombers passed over St Nazaire, but cloud cover over the port limited the raid and only a handful of bombers were able to identify their targets in order to release their bombs; nevertheless, it was enough to occupy the German defences for nearly an hour.

It was half past midnight, an hour before the attack was due to commence, when the convoy entered the Loire estuary. The *Campbeltown*'s skipper, Lieutenant Commander Stephen Beattie, known as Sam, had already ordered the German naval ensign, the Reichskriegsflagge, to be raised in an attempt to further deceive the enemy defences. It proved to be a good idea. Just minutes before the convoy was due to attack, searchlights from both banks of the estuary suddenly illuminated the flotilla. As a shore battery fired a few warning shots, a signal lamp demanded the convoy identify itself. The MGB responded in a coded message, stating they were coming under fire from friendly forces. The firing stopped and bought the convoy some valuable time as they were now just five minutes away from the port.

But then the firing started again, only this time it was aimed at the convoy and was far more intense as the enemy defences opened up with everything they had. Now, with less than a mile to go, Beattie ordered the Reichskriegsflagge to be replaced by the Royal Navy's white ensign. The attack had begun. All the ships in the convoy responded as the night sky lit up, now running at full speed towards their target.

Trapped by the illuminated cone, those on board the *Campbeltown* were dazzled by the brilliance of the searchlights. Under intense fire directed at the bridge from near point-blank range, and in the face of the blinding glare of many searchlights, Beattie commanded the destroyer with complete valour and total disregard for his own safety. The commandos were split between being on deck amidships, where they took shelter behind low armoured screens, and in the wardroom below. As the destroyer ran in towards the dock gates at full speed, approaching 20 knots, she was hit several times. Cutting through anti-torpedo nets, the *Campbeltown* rammed into her target, the outer caisson of the Normandie dock, as the force propelled the old destroyer's bow over the massive structure of the caisson, wedging the destroyer firmly on top of the dock gates, her bow crumpled by the force of the impact.

Using scaling ladders the two assault teams quickly disembarked, with Copland, standing at the base of the bridge, directing each team port and starboard as they raced off the ship. First off on the port side of the bow was the fifteen-man assault team led by the kilted Captain Donald Roy, wearing the tartan of the Liverpool Scots, with the task of destroying the two enemy gun positions on top of the pumping station. On the other side of the bow, Lieutenant Johnny Roderick led his assault team to tackle the guns on the starboard side of the ship. They were followed by the five demolition teams, accompanied by their protection teams.

On board the MGB, Ryder continued to command the small flotilla of launches while under intense fire from the shore. Newman also stood coolly and calmly on the bridge throughout the attack. Although the convoy had been caught in the enemy searchlights and a murderous crossfire from both banks, causing heavy casualties, Newman did not flinch. Empowered to call off the assault at any stage, he was determined to press on and to succeed in the important task assigned to him. Having reached the point of assault, he had not been required to go ashore but he was one of the first to do so, quickly disembarking from the MGB and immediately directing mortar fire onto enemy gun positions on top of a U-boat pen that had already started causing casualties among the attackers until the enemy positions were taken out. Still fully exposed, he then brought machine-gun fire to bear on an armed trawler in the harbour, compelling it to withdraw and thus preventing many casualties in the main demolition area.

The enemy defences were startled by what had happened. The seemingly impenetrable estuary had been penetrated, but while the initial assault had gone almost to plan for the commandos on board the *Campbeltown* the same was not the case for the other two groups on the motor launches.

Most of the motor launches were destroyed during the run-in and were now left burning. Only one launch from the port column, ML 457, which had been second in line, had managed to land its commandos on the Old Mole. The lead launch, commanded by Lieutenant Tom Collier, had come under heavy fire, and, following a direct hit, had been set ablaze. Behind ML 457 the third launch had abandoned its attempt to land because of significant damage and heavy casualties. The launch next in line had suffered severe damage and casualties and had to withdraw.

On board the fifth launch, ML 306, commanded by Lieutenant Ian Henderson, the situation had become desperate. During its run up the River Loire towards the port, it had repeatedly come under heavy fire from the shore. One of the commandos on board, 23-year-old Sergeant Thomas Durrant, was in charge of a Lewis gun aft of the bridge where there was no cover or protection. As the launch ran the gauntlet of enemy fire, Durrant continuously engaged the enemy gun positions and searchlights along the shore. He had been hit in the arm but refused to leave his post. As ML 306 continued down the river it was then attacked by a German destroyer from very close range. As the destroyer closed in on its victim, illuminating the launch with its searchlight, and now within a hundred yards, Durrant continued to fire at the destroyer's bridge with great coolness and with complete disregard of the enemy's fire. Wounded yet again, this time in many places, Durrant remained at his post, exposed to continuous enemy fire and still firing his gun, with empty drums of ammunition now lining the deck alongside. He was now barely able to support himself and had become very weak. An initial attempt by the destroyer's captain to get the motor launch to surrender had failed – in fact it had been greeted by further bursts of fire from Durrant – but eventually a renewed attack by the destroyer brought an end to the gallant resistance of those on board the launch.

The destroyer then went alongside the launch and those that were still alive were taken prisoner. The gallant Durrant died soon after from the many wounds he had sustained during his heroic action. His gallant fight was later commended by the German officers who had boarded the motor launch, and when they brought the young commando's heroic action to the attention of the British, it was announced that Thomas Durrant was to be recognized for his action with the posthumous award of the Victoria Cross.

The last launch of the port column, with Bertie Hodgson on board (having transferred earlier from another launch due to mechanical problems), overshot the Old Mole and immediately came under heavy fire. Amongst those killed was Hodgson and, as any further attempt to land would have been futile, the launch withdrew.

It had been a similar story for the launches of the starboard column that were due to land on the quayside of the old entrance to the basin. The lead launch of the column, with Micky Burn on board, had been hit even before the *Campbeltown* had rammed the dock. There were many casualties, but Burn was determined to press on with his mission and made his own way ashore. The two launches following had overshot their landing point, although they would later return. The fourth had been hit and blown up before reaching its objective and the fifth had to withdraw back up the river because of its sustained damage. Only one, ML 177, commanded by Sub-Lieutenant Mark

Rodier, and the last launch of the column, had managed to reach the gates; the blazing wrecks of earlier attempts marking the point of disembarkation for Rodier and the assaulting group of commandos.

Meanwhile, the crew on board the *Campbeltown* had set the charges and were now waiting to be evacuated from the ship. ML 177, being the only vessel in a position to do so, managed to get alongside to take on board thirty men from the destroyer, including Beattie, although it would later be sunk on its way out of the estuary. Sam Beattie, however, would survive and was taken as a prisoner of war. He was later awarded the Victoria Cross, not only in recognition of his own valour, but also that of his officers and men of a very gallant ship's company, many of whom did not return.

With Newman ashore, Ryder remained on the spot conducting operations, evacuating men from the *Campbeltown* and dealing with strongpoints and close-range weapons while exposed to heavy fire for more than an hour. He did not consider withdrawing until it was certain that his MGB could be of no use in rescuing any of the commandos who were still ashore. Throughout the engagement, the MGB's gun-layer of the pom-pom, Able Seaman William Savage, had continued to engage positions ashore with cool and steady accuracy despite being completely exposed and under heavy fire.

With his MGB full of dead and wounded, Ryder realized there was nothing more they could do. It was approaching 3.00 am when he eventually gave the order to leave. Through an intense barrage of close-range fire, the little MGB headed out to sea; Savage keeping up the same vigorous and accurate fire throughout. Continuously illuminated by searchlights and hit several times, the boat made its escape alongside ML 270 and the cover of smoke.

Even when out of range of smaller weapons, the MGBs came under continuous fire from the longer-range artillery. It was then that the little MGB was hit for the last time, killing Savage, who was still manning his gun. His exceptional courage displayed throughout would earn him a posthumous Victoria Cross and would represent the valour of many others in the motor launches, motor gunboats and torpedo boats who had gallantly carried out their duty in entirely exposed positions and against relentless enemy fire at very close range. Ryder would also be awarded the VC, his citation stating it was almost a miracle that his MGB survived and was able to withdraw through an intense barrage of close-range fire.

Back in the port area German reinforcements had been quick to arrive. With no motor launches available to conduct an evacuation, Newman could see the situation was becoming desperate. There were still more than a hundred commandos ashore and during the hours of bitter fighting that followed he led his men from the front, personally entering several houses and shooting the enemy while supervising operations in the town; utterly regardless of his own safety he never wavered in his resolution to carry through the operation upon which so much depended.

Under Newman's exceptional leadership his men fought magnificently and held vastly superior forces at bay until the demolition groups had successfully completed their work. With evacuation by sea no longer possible, Newman was determined to fight his way out into open country and so give all his surviving commandos a chance to escape, but the only escape route from the harbour was across a narrow iron bridge covered by enemy machine guns.

Severely shaken by a hand grenade, which had burst at his feet, Newman, with Copland at his side, led the charge to storm the position. Under his inspiring leadership the small force fought its way through the streets to a point near the open country but, with all ammunition expended, he and his men were finally overpowered by the enemy. Incredibly, five of his men managed to avoid capture and eventually made it back to England via neutral Spain. For his outstanding gallantry, exceptional leadership and initiative, which were largely responsible for the success of this perilous operation and resulted in heavy damage to St Nazaire, Charles Newman was awarded the Victoria Cross.

As daylight came on the morning of 28 March, senior German officers arrived at St Nazaire to inspect the damage. They observed the wreck of the *Campbeltown* but, as they were doing so, five tons of ammanol in her bows detonated. Many Germans were killed in the blast, as were two commando officers, who had been captured and taken back to the ship; they had bravely remained silent about the explosives on board.

The main objective had been met. The Normandie dry dock had been rendered completely useless and it would remain so until long into 1944, denying the German Navy, and, most significantly, the mighty battleship *Tirpitz*, its use for the rest of the war. However, success had come at an enormous cost. Only four of the eighteen vessels that had taken part in the raid returned. More than 600 men had entered the Loire estuary, including 265 commandos, but just over a third returned to England: 169 were killed (more than 100 naval personnel and 64 commandos) and 215 had been captured and taken as prisoners of war.

The courage and bravery of those taking part was recognized by the award of many decorations for gallantry. In addition to the five VCs to Beattie, Durrant, Newman, Ryder and Savage, there were four awards of the DSO, including to Copland and Roy, as well as awards to Lieutenants Tom Boyd (ML 160) and T. D. L. Platt (ML 447). There were also seventeen DSCs awarded, including to Curtis (MGB 314) and Wynn (MTB 74), eleven MCs, including awards to Burn and Roderick, four CGMs, five DCMs, twenty-four DSMs and fifteen MMs. Fifty-one were Mentioned in Despatches, twenty-two of them posthumously. St Nazaire had surely been the greatest raid of them all.

Chapter Thirteen

Boulogne Harbour

11/12 April 1942

Britain's armed forces today can boast some of the best Special Forces in the world. Like its sister elite unit the Special Air Service, the Special Boat Service, simply known as the SBS, can trace its origins back to the Second World War when Captain Roger Courtney first demonstrated the potential of using canoes to carry out special operations on the lochs of Scotland during commando training in 1940. Courtney's belief that folding kayaks could be used for raids was initially rebuffed by his senior commanders but, not satisfied with their reaction, he simply decided to prove his point. He did so by paddling up to a commando landing ship, HMS *Glengyle*, at the time anchored in the Clyde, and then climbed aboard undetected to write his initials on the captain's door before stealing a deck gun cover from the ship. He then took the cover to a nearby hotel and presented it to a group of senior naval officers.

Courtney's audacity led to him being given permission to form his own specialist unit, initially called the Folbot Troop (named after the type of canoe) but later to become 1 Special Boat Section and ultimately the SBS. Courtney had also won many admirers from elsewhere. His early vision of using canoes would later lead to the legendary raid by Royal Marines on the French port of Bordeaux, a raid that was to become immortalized as the Cockleshell Heroes, but eight months before that there was a similar, but seemingly unheard of raid, carried out by two men of a specialist troop of 6 Commando.

The specialist troop, called 101 Troop, was formed to carry out reconnaissance missions and attacks on enemy shipping. Leading the troop was 25-year-old Captain Gerald Montanaro. Born in Kent, but from a Maltese background, Montanaro had studied engineering before the war and had naturally been commissioned into the Royal Engineers.

Following the outbreak of war he had served as an engineer with the British Expeditionary Force in France before volunteering for the commandos. Although Montanaro clearly believed in the concept of using canoes to carry out special operations, not everyone was convinced by the idea.

By the end of 1941 the troop had carried out only a few beach reconnaissance missions, but it now needed a bigger challenge if it was to survive. Montanaro knew that shipping anchored in harbour was always vulnerable to attack and so he pushed forward a simple but daring plan to lead a raid against two large tankers, each believed to be carrying thousands of tons of copper, known to be anchored in the outer harbour at Boulogne. His plan was for two canoe teams, each of two men, to cross the Channel in a Royal Navy motor launch under the cover of darkness and, having been dropped off just a few miles from the shore, to then paddle into the harbour and plant limpet mines on the tankers before making their escape.

The plan, called Operation JV, was given the go-ahead by the Admiralty and planned for the night of 11/12 April 1942. However, permission to carry out the raid was only given on the understanding that only one canoe took part. To send two canoes was considered too risky and so only one tanker could be attacked. Naturally, Montanaro was to go on the raid and he chose Trooper Fred Preece to accompany him.

The launch allocated to take the canoe and its two men across the Channel was ML 102 commanded by Sub-Lieutenant Trevor Mathias. Although it was still only April, the weather was good and the sea conditions fine for the crossing, and soon after midnight the motor launch was on the other side of the Channel and positioned off the port of Boulogne.

Having lowered their canoe into the water, Montanaro and Preece paddled towards the harbour. The moonlight meant they could clearly see vessels in and around the harbour, but the strength of the tide and a stiffening breeze was making paddling incredibly hard work. Furthermore, to enter the harbour meant passing close to two historic fortifications, and a lighthouse on the breakwater meant there was a possibility they would be illuminated against the water.

The two men pressed on towards the harbour and then eased their way as quietly as they could past the fortifications. They could now see the threatening shape of an enemy E-boat moored alongside, but still they pressed on. They could even hear people coming out of a building close by as they paddled and then glided slowly into the harbour, keeping as low as they could in their canoe. Then, their hearts missed several beats as they heard the sound of E-boats approaching and then passing them on their way out of the inner harbour and into the Channel at the start of a patrol. Although Montanaro and Preece had felt the full force of the wake caused by the E-boats as they passed through the outer harbour, the canoe had remained unseen in the darkness of the shadows of the harbour wall.

With the E-boats out of the way, Montanaro surveyed the scene as he looked for their target. He could make out the silhouette of the tanker but the team hit more problems as the front of the canoe became grounded on rocks. The two men tried to free the canoe by rocking it backwards and forwards as quietly as they could in the shallow water, but all they managed to achieve was to puncture the hull to the point that the canoe started taking on water. Undeterred, they temporarily plugged the hole as best they could, set the timers on their charges and headed back out into the harbour towards the tanker to make their attack.

They quickly and quietly made their way to the tanker, eventually positioning themselves up against the stern. While Preece held the canoe as steady as possible, Montanaro set the charges. The limpet mines had to be positioned a couple of feet or so below the waterline, but the shape of the hull, and the barnacles covering its surface, meant it was a difficult task. Montanaro scraped away as best he could before fixing the mines. The two men then slowly worked their way along the hull and then back up the other side until all eight charges were set.

Time was now getting short. It had been two hours since they had left the launch and they had already been inside the harbour for nearly an hour. They were cold and getting very tired, and so it was time to make their escape, otherwise they would miss their rendezvous with the launch.

Again keeping as low to the canoe as they could, they paddled slowly and quietly away. The breeze had increased and so had the swell. It took the two men nearly an hour to make their way back out of the harbour and into the Channel. But now the canoe was taking on more and more water. While one man paddled, the other mopped up the water using whatever clothing he could find. It was desperately hard work and the two men felt as though they were about to freeze.

It took another half an hour before they were far enough from the harbour and close to where they expected to meet the launch. They could hear the sound of an engine in the distance: for a while it could have been any motor launch or E-boat approaching but, as the vessel approached, they soon recognized it as the familiar sound they had long been waiting for. It was ML 102. Montanaro and Preece had to be helped aboard. They were exhausted, soaked and numb from the extreme cold, and by now their canoe was a wreck.

Later that morning, as sailors and workers at the port of Boulogne went about their business, the outer harbour was suddenly rocked as the charges exploded. They had gone off later than planned but the devastating result was obvious the following day when aerial reconnaissance photographs of the harbour revealed extensive damage to the tanker.

The raid had been a success for several reasons and silenced the critics of such tactics. In June, Montanaro was awarded the DSO for leading the raid, while Fred Preece received the DCM. The troop was later absorbed into Courtney's newly formed 2 SBS. The concept of using canoes to carry out special operations was no longer just an idea but had been well and truly proven.

Chapter Fourteen

Augsburg

17 April 1942

The entry into operational service of the RAF's new four-engine heavy bomber, the Avro Lancaster, had provided Bomber Command's new Commander-in-Chief, Air Marshal Arthur Harris, the opportunity to take his bombing offensive deeper into the heart of Germany. Harris knew the potential of the Lancaster. Its first operational sorties had been carried out in early March 1942 and, within weeks, two squadrons, 44 Squadron based at Waddington and 97 Squadron at Woodhall Spa, were conducting operations. Now Harris wanted to show the Germans that he could attack the Nazi war machine anywhere he liked and at any time, by day or by night.

Rumours of a special operation started spreading around the crew rooms at Waddington and Woodhall Spa. Both squadrons were now training regularly together, particularly at low level, and a special training flight was carried out on 14 April, with 44 Squadron led by a South African, 25-year-old Squadron Leader John Nettleton, still on his first operational tour, and 97 Squadron led by Squadron Leader John Sherwood, two years younger than Nettleton, but already a veteran, having been awarded the DFC and bar. The training flight took each squadron down to the south coast of England where the Lancasters joined up for a long transit north to carry out a simulated attack on Inverness before returning to their bases.

While the crews were of the opinion that one of the big German battleships was their most likely target, Harris had, instead, decided to go for a factory at Augsburg, a thousand miles away and deep into southern Germany. His choice of the Maschinenfabrik Augsburg–Nürnberg Aktiengesellschaft factory was an interesting one as, until that point, it had not been considered one of Bomber Command's primary targets. However, it was believed the factory was responsible for the production of half of the diesel engines required for Germany's U-boats.

At 11.00 am on 17 April the crews of both squadrons were briefed on the target. The gasp of surprise in the audience at Woodhall Spa echoed that at Waddington as the crews now realized it was not to be one of the warships, and when the route was revealed on the big map on the wall, some even thought it was a joke. Who on earth would consider sending them a thousand miles deep into enemy territory in broad daylight to carry out an attack at low level?

As with the training flight just a few days before, the two squadrons were to be led by Nettleton and Sherwood. The plan was a particularly daring one. Six Lancasters from each squadron, flying in two sections of three, were to cross the English Channel from Selsey Bill and coast-in across northern France to the west of Le Havre. The two squadrons were to be just a couple of miles apart and the formations were then to transit south at low level before turning east and passing to the south of Paris. The Lancasters would then set a heading towards Munich, as if the city was the intended target, before finally turning north to Augsburg. The factory was relatively small and so the attack would require pinpoint accuracy from a height below 500 feet if success was to be achieved. It would also need to take place during the last minutes of daylight so that the bombers could return home under the cover of darkness.

Because of the amount of fuel needed to reach the target at low level, each Lancaster would carry just four 1,000lb general-purpose bombs fitted with a delayed fuse of eleven seconds to allow the aircraft to clear the target before the bomb detonated. If, for any reason, the crews could not attack the factory then Munich and Nürnberg were briefed as the alternate targets.

This was to be the first raid of its type and so a number of diversionary raids and fighter sorties over northern France were planned in an attempt to keep the Luftwaffe's fighters away from the attacking force. The weather was forecast to be fine, with good visibility and little or no cloud, all the way to the target. The crews had less than four hours to prepare and to think about what lay ahead. They were used to flying over enemy-occupied territory, but never so deep into Germany, where the chances of surviving if shot down, and then escaping and evading back to England, were slim to say the least.

It was around 3.00 pm when the Lancasters got airborne and set off towards the south coast where the two squadrons were to join up. Flying with Nettleton in B-Baker were Pilot Officer Pat Dorehill as the second pilot, Pilot Officer Desmond Sands, the observer, and the wireless operator, Sergeant Charlie Churchill. Three gunners, Flight Sergeants Len Mutter and Frank Harrison, and Sergeant Buzz Huntly, made up the crew. Because he was the leader of the raid, Nettleton had an eighth crew member on board. Flight Lieutenant Charles McClure, the squadron's bombing leader, was there to help read the maps and to aim the bombs during the final attack while Sands was to concentrate on the navigation.

The two other Lancasters in 44's lead section were flown by Flying Officer Ginger Garwell and Sergeant Dusty Rhodes. Behind them, by about 400 yards, the second formation was led by Flight Lieutenant Nick Sandford, with the two other aircraft flown by Warrant Officers Bert Crum and Joe Beckett, both holders of the DFM and the best of friends.

The diversionary raids had succeeded in luring enemy fighters away from the Lancasters but, as they crossed the enemy coast at little more than 100 feet, the rear section was spotted by Messerschmitt Bf 109Fs returning to their home base. It was a stroke of bad luck for the Lancaster crews. Their route had been planned to avoid all the known enemy fighter airfields in the area, but they were marginally off track and were now simply in the wrong place at the wrong time. Ironically, the enemy fighters were only airborne at the time because of the RAF's diversionary attacks.

Beckett was the first to spot the 109s to his left and well above. Mindful of the order given at the briefing to only break radio silence in an emergency, he rightly considered the threat from the 109s too high to ignore and so called it over the radio. As Nettleton acknowledged the call, the Lancasters closed up within their two formations as the pilots pushed the throttles fully forward and descended to treetop height. The camouflage of the bombers would hopefully enable them to slip through the area unseen from above, but unfortunately for the rear section of 44, one of the 109 pilots had spotted the Lancasters just as he was about to land.

Accelerating fast as the wheels came up, the 109 overshot the airfield before turning towards the bombers to make his attack. Picking on Crum's aircraft first, the lone 109 attacked and, within seconds, more swooped down on their prey. Crum, concentrating on nothing other than following Sandford, while his gunners defended his plane with everything they had, did not see the demise of Joe Beckett's aircraft as it fell astern the formation and plunged into a field. There were no survivors.

Crum was still fighting for survival as his port wing was hit. With his port engines on fire, and with his aircraft now trailing flames and smoke, he instructed the second pilot, Sergeant Alan Dedman, to safely jettison the bombs, before he carried out an almost textbook crash landing into a field. After detonating the secret equipment inside the aircraft, the crew set fire to the Lancaster and set off into the countryside, owing their lives to the immense skill of Crum.

Meanwhile, the lead aircraft of the rear section, flown by Sandford, had become the focus for the marauding fighters. Flying as low as he dared, even under power lines that stretched across the countryside, Sandford pressed on, but the Lancaster's top speed was no match for the three 109s in pursuit. The stricken Lancaster, last seen with all four engines burning, ploughed into the ground, exploding on impact and killing all on board.

In the space of just a minute or so Nettleton had lost half of his force: all three Lancasters had come down within an area covering just a couple of miles. The 109s now turned on the lead section and the aircraft flown by Dusty Rhodes. With his Lancaster's gun turrets soon jammed, it was impossible for the crew to fight back. The port engines were soon on fire, followed by the starboard, and the Lancaster was last seen to pitch up before plunging vertically into the ground.

Four of Nettleton's formation were now gone, with three of the crews killed; there had been no chance at such low level for the twenty-one men. Now it was the turn of the two surviving Lancasters from 44, those of Nettleton and Garwell, to fight for their lives. The Lancasters were hit time and time again but, just as it looked as if they would follow a similar fate, the 109s hauled off, seemingly out of fuel.

Amazingly, the six Lancasters of 97 Squadron, no more than a couple of miles away, had slipped through unnoticed. Their transit from Woodhall Spa had passed without incident but, as they coasted in over northern France, Sherwood had spotted what he assumed to be the six aircraft of 44 Squadron further to the east. Satisfied that his own formation was on track, the fact that he could see the other Lancasters further to the east would account for the reason why the aircraft of 44 strayed too close to the enemy airfield.

The two surviving aircraft of 44 Squadron flew on eastwards, some distance ahead and to the north of the six Lancasters of 97 Squadron, and proceeded to Augsburg without further incident. It was nearly 8.00 pm by the time they approached the town from the south. Nettleton then eased the Lancaster up to get a clear view ahead. He could see that a canal ran north-westwards from the main river and up towards where the factory was located. As he turned towards the area where he knew the factory to be, it did not take him long to spot the chimney stacks ahead and now just a mile or so away.

As they ran towards their target, the two Lancasters were spotted and a wall of light flak and machine-gun fire was thrown into the air in an attempt to stop the attack. Workers at the factory could now hear the noise and looked to the east where they could see the Lancasters flying through the flak and heading straight towards them.

Picking out the buildings of interest, Nettleton and Garwell pressed on, their bomb doors now open. Inside B-Baker, McClure remained as calm as ever, giving minor changes in heading to Nettleton as the Lancaster roared ever closer to their target before shouting 'bombs gone'. Closing the bomb doors as he turned away hard to port to make his escape, Nettleton then took up a heading for home. His aircraft had been hit several times, but not enough to prevent it from getting away. Darkness had yet to fall and they still had a very long way to go.

Meanwhile, in A-Apple it had been much the same, as Flight Sergeant Frank Kirke directed Garwell closer to the target before releasing their bombs. But the crew of A-Apple had not enjoyed any luck. Their aircraft had also been hit repeatedly during the run-in to the factory and was now on fire. Finding it increasingly difficult to control the aircraft, Garwell scanned ahead to see if there was anywhere he could put the aircraft down. But Southern Bavaria is full of dense forests and undulating terrain, and not at all what he wanted to see. Suddenly, though, he saw an area that gave them a chance and he pushed the aircraft downwards towards an open field. As he controlled the Lancaster as best he could, the aircraft slid across the field, breaking in half before it finally came to rest; four of the crew, including Garwell, survived.

Just minutes later, all six of 97's Lancasters were roaring up the valley towards the target. They had all reached Augsburg unscathed, but by the time the first section commenced its run-in towards the factory, every anti-aircraft gun in the area was putting up a barrage of fire. Sherwood did not flinch as he led the charge towards the factory, fast and very low, through what had become a horrendous wall of fire. He could have asked no more of his two wingmen, Flying Officers Darky Hallows and Rod Rodley. Both were relatively inexperienced in terms of operations, with just six and eight ops to their names respectively, but they continued to stick to their leader like glue, just as they had done since leaving Woodhall Spa five hours before.

To anyone observing the scene, it would have seemed all but impossible for anything to get through the defensive barrage that now filled the sky, but the three Lancasters pressed on towards their target. Flying as low as he dared, Sherwood was eventually forced to ease K-King over the chimneys before dropping back down and finally releasing his bombs. Just seconds behind, Hallows and Rodley made their final adjustments before completing their attacks. It was at that point that Rodley saw Sherwood's aircraft emitting smoke as it turned starboard to escape to the north, then K-King burst into flames. As the bombs from 97's lead section exploded on their target, Sherwood's Lancaster smashed into the ground; miraculously, though, Sherwood would survive, although the rest of his crew were killed.

While Hallows and Rodley started their long journey home, the final section of 97 was making its run-in towards the factory. As the last to attack, the rear section was a formation full of experience. It would need to be. The section leader, Flight Lieutenant David Penman, was on his second operational tour and a holder of the DFC. Penman's two wingmen were Flying Officer Ernest Deverill, who had flown more than a hundred operational sorties, mainly with Coastal Command, and had been awarded the DFM two years before, and Warrant Officer Tommy Mycock, another holder of the DFC.

Penman had no desire for his formation to be caught up in the explosions from the previous attacking aircraft and so he decided to hold his formation with a couple of orbits before commencing their attack. The three Lancasters then began their run-in towards the factory, but the formation soon came under intense anti-aircraft fire. By now the defending gunners had established the exact line of attack.

In U-Uncle, Penman held his aircraft as steady as possible, despite being hit several times. He was now just 3 miles from the factory. Alongside him to his right, Mycock's P-Peter suddenly received a devastating burst of gunfire at the front of the aircraft, causing an immediate fire that quickly spread through the aircraft. It was a mortal blow, but Mycroft used all of his experience to hold the Lancaster steady long enough for it to reach the target and for the bombs to be released. Then, P-Peter was seen to pull up and swing to the left before plunging into the ground.

Penman and Deverill succeeded in completing their attacks but, while over the factory, Deverill's Y-Yorker was hit yet again, causing his gun turrets to jam. Somehow, the two Lancasters managed to resume formation and headed for home. It was to be a long return transit for the surviving crews. According to the briefing, it should have been getting dark as soon as the Lancasters were off-target, but it would be another hour before the crews considered it to be dark enough to remain unseen.

The four surviving Lancasters of 97 Squadron landed back at their base at around 11.00 pm, having been airborne for eight hours. No aircraft landed back at Waddington. Nettleton, the only survivor from the six Lancasters of 44 Squadron, was still airborne. His problems were far from over as he suffered navigational problems during the return transit. He eventually landed at Squire's Gate, near Blackpool, just before 1.00 am the following day, nearly ten hours after getting airborne.

Of the eighty-five men who had taken part in the raid, forty-nine were missing, although it would later be discovered that twelve had survived to become prisoners of war. For his outstanding leadership of the raid, John Nettleton was awarded the Victoria Cross. His citation concludes:

Squadron Leader Nettleton displayed unflinching determination as well as leadership and valour of the highest order.

John Sherwood was also recommended for the VC and, as with Nettleton's award, the recommendation was endorsed by Harris. But it appears that someone in the Air Ministry scrawled '*to be recommended for DSO if later found to be alive.*' Miraculously, Sherwood was found alive, although the rest of his crew had not been so lucky, and so he received the DSO instead of the VC. Only the person who wrote on Sherwood's recommendation knows why. Would two awards of the VC for the same raid really have been too much? It had happened before.

In addition to Nettleton and Sherwood, there were a number of other immediate awards for survivors of the raid. From 97 Squadron there was a DSO for David Penman for having demonstrated great skill in the handling of the rear section and for the greatest determination in attacking the target from a very low level in spite of intense and accurate anti-aircraft fire. There was a DFC for Darky Hallows, for taking over the lead section after Sherwood had been shot down, and for displaying great courage and determination throughout the raid. The two other surviving captains, Rod Rodley and Ernest Deverill, both received the DFC, as did Penman's second pilot, Pilot Officer Hooey, and his observer, Pilot Officer Edward Ifould. There were DFMs for Flight Sergeant Brian Louch and Sergeant Tom Goacher (wireless operator and air gunner to Hallows); Sergeants Ron Irons and Ken Mackay (wireless operator and air gunner to Deverill); Sergeant John Ratcliffe (air gunner to Rodley); and Sergeant Doug Overton (air gunner to Penman). Although many felt Tommy Mycock's courage should have been recognized with a VC, he was instead awarded a posthumous Mentioned in Despatches, as were others killed in the raid.

From John Nettleton's crew there was a DFC for each of the officers – Pat Dorehill, Desmond Sands and Charles McClure – and a DFM to each of the rest of his crew – Charlie Churchill, Buzz Huntly, Len Mutter and Frank Harrison. When it was known that Ginger Garwell had survived, he was also awarded a DFC and there were awards for the three other survivors of his crew: a bar to the DFM for his observer, Frank Kirke, and a DFM for his second pilot, Sergeant Laurie Dando, and for the only gunner from his crew to have survived, Sergeant Jim Watson.

Plaudits arrived from all over. At the two squadrons a signal was received from Arthur Harris:

the following message has been received from the Prime Minister – 'We must plainly regard the attack of the Lancasters on the U-boat engine factory at Augsburg as an outstanding achievement of the Royal Air Force. Undeterred by heavy losses at the outset, 44 and 97 Squadrons pierced and struck a vital point with deadly precision in broad daylight. Pray convey the thanks of His Majesty's Government to the officers and men who accomplished this memorial feat of arms in which no life was lost in vain.'

There was also a message from Sir Charles Portal, the Chief of the Air Staff:

I would like 44 and 97 Squadrons to know the great importance I attach to this gallant and successful attack on the diesel engine factory at Augsburg. Please give my warmest congratulations and thanks.

The success of the Augsburg raid has long been debated by post-war historians. The decision to use the Lancaster to carry out a low-level raid by day when its crews had essentially been trained to operate at night has often come under scrutiny, as has the decision to attack a target deep into southern Germany that seemingly did not appear on any of Bomber Command's priority lists. That said, the damage caused by the eight Lancasters that managed to reach the target caused sufficient damage to hold up diesel engine production for several weeks.

Included in the messages of congratulations received at Waddington and Woodhall Spa in the immediate aftermath of the raid, Harris summed up his own thoughts:

The resounding blow which has been struck at the enemy's submarine and tank building programme will echo round the world. The full effects on his submarine campaign cannot be immediately apparent but nevertheless they will be enormous. The gallant adventure penetrating deep into the heart of Germany in daylight and pressed with outstanding determination in the face of bitter and foreseen opposition takes its place amongst the most courageous operations of the war. It is, moreover, yet another fine example of effective co-operation with the other Services by striking at the very sources of enemy effort. The officers and men who took part, those who returned and those who fell, have indeed deserved well of their country.

The Augsburg raid was also a huge propaganda success. The Air Ministry was quick to release a communiqué in time for the national papers, where headlines such as *'War's Most Daring Raid'*, *'Amazing Day Raid by the RAF'* and *'Augsburg Success – Our New Bombers Used – Diesel Works Damaged'* were there for all to see. Nettleton and others who had taken part in the raid suddenly found themselves the subject of newsreels and newspaper reports.

Although the value of the Augsburg raid is likely to remain the subject of debate for many years to come, it must rank amongst the highest achievements in the history of Bomber Command.

Chapter Fifteen

Barricade

14/15 August 1942

The early months of 1942 were difficult for the Allies, and there had been increasing pressure from the Americans and Russians on Britain to carry out some form of positive action in north-west Europe to form an active second front. The British chiefs of staff were right to maintain that it was not the time to try and mount even a limited incursion into north-west Europe, but considered it would be possible to mount a number of small-scale raids across the Channel which, in turn, would divert enemy resources and help relieve the increasing pressure on the Eastern Front.

The man considered best to carry out such raids was Major Gus March-Phillipps, fresh from returning from his successful West African adventure, in particular Operation Postmaster, during which he had led a small group of men in the capture of three vessels off the Spanish island of Fernando Po and then sailed them to Nigeria. March-Phillipps was now asked to form a larger group, of around fifty or sixty men, to carry out more daring amphibious raids, but this time across the Channel.

The elite group he formed was called the Small Scale Raiding Force, but the SSRF operated under the cover title of 62 Commando to avoid attracting too much attention. The unit was to target German strongpoints and signal stations along the northern coastline of France and in the Channel Islands with the aim of gathering vital intelligence. Not only would these raids provide the Allies with vital intelligence, but enemy troops would have to be diverted from other theatres to carry out garrison duties along the coast of northern France and in the Channel Islands to prevent further raids from taking place.

Based at Anderson Manor in Dorset, March-Phillipps began to assemble his team of trained commandos. He had with him members of his *Maid*

Honor crew that had taken part in Postmaster, including Geoffrey Appleyard as his trusted second-in-command, Graham Hayes and Anders Lassen, as well as others from the crew. The rest of the men came from all backgrounds. Half were officers and the other half from the ranks, including some from Allied nations, but all had been specifically hand-picked for the task.

It was soon down to intense training, with the aim of turning the men into masters of their new role. There were new skills to learn, with much time being spent in boats learning how to navigate at sea and how to handle the vessels in all kinds of weather. Time was also spent in the water getting used to swimming in full clothing and keeping equipment and weapons dry. March-Phillipps strongly believed his men should be fully independent and they should not rely on anything or anyone when operating behind enemy lines.

To take a small raiding party across the Channel, March-Phillipps had secured the use of one of the Royal Navy's experimental motor torpedo boats, MTB 344, colloquially known to the men as the *Little Pisser*. With a crew of eight under the command of Lieutenant Freddie Bourne, the *Little Pisser* could carry a raiding party of twelve. She was capable of reaching a speed in excess of 40 knots and was designed to sit low in the water to make visual detection harder. One of her main advantages when operating close to enemy-occupied coasts was that she was able to run relatively silently on an auxiliary engine, thus enabling the raiding party to creep close to the enemy shore without being heard.

The *Little Pisser* had also been adapted to suit the team. The torpedo tubes had been removed to provide room to carry a light landing craft to get the raiding party from the MTB to the shore. The team had acquired a number of small collapsible flat-bottomed assault boats, made with wooden bottoms and canvas sides, known as Goatleys; each Goatley was capable of carrying a dozen or more men and could be quickly assembled in just a few minutes. They also had a Dory, a small, lightweight and shallow-draft boat made of wood with a flat bottom, high sides and a sharp bow. It could also carry a dozen or so men, but was not as flexible as the Goatley once ashore. Two Vickers and two Lewis machine guns had been retained on the MTB to provide some form of defence, but in reality these would prove little match for a more heavily armed German E-boat.

By the middle of June, although training was complete and the SSRF was ready to carry out its first operation, there followed a period of raids being planned and then cancelled for a variety of reasons, such as fog or unusually bad weather in the Channel, or because of problems with the *Little Pisser*'s engine, which continued to ruin many plans. It was also a time when an increasing number of cross-Channel raids were being planned by different units and so clearance to conduct a raid could not always be obtained.

Finally, on the night of 14/15 August 1942, the first raid took place. A German direction-finding station had been located to the north-west of Pointe de Saire on the eastern coast of the Cherbourg Peninsula, and was proving to be a continuous nuisance to Allied shipping in the Channel. The initial plan was to undertake a large-scale assault on the station, including air support, but the headquarters of Combined Operations decided instead to carry out a scaled-down operation using the SSRF.

The operation, called Barricade, was less ambitious but nonetheless daring. The raiding party was tasked with conducting a reconnaissance of the area and with carrying out an attack on an anti-aircraft gun site located near the direction-finding station, killing the enemy or taking prisoners as required. March-Phillipps would lead the raid, with Appleyard as his deputy. Also included in the raiding party of eleven were trusted colleagues Hayes and Lassen, and making up the group were Colin Ogden-Smith, Hamish Torrance, Graham Young, André Desgranges, Alan Williams, Jan Hollings and Tony Hall.

From the briefing given at Anderson Manor it was clear they could expect a difficult landing and approach to the site along what was a rocky part of the French coastline. Speed was always going to be important. German E-boats were freely operating in the Channel and, being fast, well-armed and generally better suited to operating in the open sea, they posed a real threat.

Late in the afternoon of 14 August the raiding party boarded a truck and left the manor for the Royal Naval coastal base of HMS *Hornet* at Gosport where the *Little Pisser* was waiting. Just before 8.30 pm they boarded the MTB and minutes later they set off. Unfortunately, though, the port engine played up once again as it had done during the days leading up to the raid. It was not bad enough to cancel the raid but the crossing had to be made at a reduced speed of 25 knots for the first hour. Then the engine cut out altogether, leaving the MTB proceeding towards France on just its starboard engine at a speed of little more than 15 knots.

The final part of the crossing presented a further risk as the team had to navigate along parts of known shipping lanes to avoid minefields, and so had to take great care to proceed without being spotted or heard. By the time the *Little Pisser* finally arrived off the French coastline it was nearly midnight. The raiding party was now over an hour behind schedule and establishing their exact position off a darkened coastline was not easy. Once satisfied they were approximately in the right place the starboard engine was cut. They then continued slowly and quietly on the auxiliary engine until they were within a mile of the coast, when the Goatley was lowered and the men paddled towards the shore.

The raiders were now getting even further behind schedule. A strong current had meant they landed about 3 miles to the north of St Vaast, nearly a mile from where they should have been, and so by the time they landed on French soil it was nearly 2.00 am. There was now less than an hour to carry out the raid.

It was completely dark and there was no ambient light whatsoever. It felt good to be on French soil but there was no time to hang around. March-Phillipps quickly led his men off, but they soon found they could hardly see further than the man in front, which meant that progress was slower than had been hoped. Furthermore, the fact they had not landed in the right place only added to the confusion, and the darkness made it all but impossible to determine exactly where they were.

Moving as quickly as they could across challenging terrain, the raiding party proceeded towards where the anti-aircraft site was believed to be. It was not long before they could see a building in the distance, and believing it to be part of the site they continued forwards. They then came across a barbed wire fence, but it was easily cut, and March-Phillipps led his men through.

Advancing as quietly as they could, they then came across a second wire fence. Despite their best efforts, the fence proved a difficult obstacle and the men were unable to cut their way through. On the other side of the fence they could see a sentry not too far away. Convinced they had found the right place, March-Phillipps was determined to get through the wire into an attacking position. What they did not know was that they had, in fact, stumbled across an enemy sentry post, complete with heavy machine guns – one of a chain of German defence positions along the northern coastline of France.

With time getting short, the raiders continued to try and cut their way through the wire as quickly and as quietly as possible, but the noise was inevitably heard and the sentry called for help. With four German sentries approaching their position, March-Phillipps decided to make the most of the advantage of surprise and strike first. It was now a matter of dealing with the situation as best they could and causing as much damage as possible before making their escape under the cover of darkness.

The silence was suddenly shattered as the raiders opened fire. As more enemy troops emerged from the building, the commandos continued their attack. Then, just minutes later, and having decided there was nothing more to be gained by hanging around any longer, March-Phillipps ordered his men to make their way back to the beach. Leaving all sorts of commotion behind them, the commandos disappeared into the darkness as quietly as they had arrived.

The Germans had been taken completely by surprise and had no idea of the strength of the attacking force. Furthermore, they did not realize for a long time that the raiders had made a hasty escape, nor did they know in what direction they had fled. A few flares had gone up but to no effect. As the commandos escaped they could hear the firing continuing behind them in the distance as they made their way as quickly as they could back towards the beach, leaving what they believed to be at least three German sentries dead and several more wounded.

The raiding party managed to find their Goatley, and eventually made their way back to the *Little Pisser*, although it took some finding. They again experienced difficulty with the current and by the time they were back on board and heading back across the Channel it was nearly 4.00 am and very nearly daylight. Apart from a brief scare when they thought they had been spotted by an enemy reconnaissance aircraft when it first got light, they arrived safely back in harbour at 7.00 am, more than ten hours after they had first left port.

Operation Barricade had been far from perfect. The raiding party had not found the intended target and so had not achieved their aim, but they had gained valuable experience from landing on the enemy-occupied coastline of northern France and had succeeded in gathering useful intelligence. The operation also proved the concept of small-scale amphibious raids was feasible and signalled the start of a series of daring missions by the Small Scale Raiding Force across the Channel.

Chapter Sixteen

Hess and Goebbels Gun Batteries at Dieppe

19 August 1942

One of the most controversial raids of the Second World War was the raid on Dieppe, which took place on 19 August 1942. By the end of the day, thousands of Allies were dead, wounded or taken as prisoners of war. The Dieppe Raid has since been the subject of much debate, but within the overall operation there were countless acts of great bravery, including those of British commandos at two mighty gun batteries that simply had to be silenced.

The origins of the Dieppe raid were to ease the pressure on the Eastern Front and prevent Germany from committing more resources to the east. The Americans and Russians had both urged Britain to open a second front, but Britain, already heavily engaged in North Africa, the Mediterranean and the Far East, did not have the resources to conduct and sustain a large-scale offensive in north-west Europe. Nonetheless, Winston Churchill had made it clear that he wanted to conduct a major operation during the summer of 1942. Senior military commanders agreed. If the Allies were to eventually carry out a full-scale invasion of mainland Europe, it was essential for a division-size operation to be carried out against a German-held port on the northern coastline of France. To do so would not only help gain a better understanding of large-scale amphibious landings, but would also determine whether the Allies were capable of maintaining forces ashore once a landing had taken place.

A number of ports were considered, but while most were rejected for one reason or another, Dieppe was accepted as a possible target. A coastal town built along a cliff overlooking the English Channel, it was a relatively short distance for raiding forces and so it was possible to make the crossing under the cover of night. Dieppe was also within range of RAF Fighter Command and so raiding forces could be given significant cover from the air.

In April 1942, Mountbatten gave the order for his staff at Combined Operations to commence planning for the raid, which was to be supported by a large array of naval and air assets. One option drawn up was to land a mix of tanks and infantry either side of Dieppe and to then capture the town using a pincer movement over the two headlands flanking the port. Another option was to land tanks and infantry directly onto the beach at Dieppe in a frontal assault, supported by landings on either side of the town. Two heavy artillery gun batteries protecting the approaches to Dieppe – the Hess Battery at Varengeville to the west and the Goebbels Battery at Berneval-le-Grand to the east – would be captured by airborne troops landing ahead of the main attack.

After much discussion it was decided to proceed with the second option, the frontal assault, which would be preceded by a heavy aerial bombardment. Codenamed Operation Rutter, the attack was planned for early July when tidal conditions would be just right for the assault. It would test the feasibility of capturing a port in the face of opposition, understand the problems of operating the invasion fleet, and test the equipment and techniques of the assault.

The scale of the operation meant there were insufficient resources amongst the British Army's commando units to carry out the raid. Therefore, regular army troops would need to be involved, and because there had been increasing pressure from the Canadian government for its troops to take part in operations, the Canadian 2nd Infantry Division was selected as the main attacking force.

Intelligence reports suggested that Dieppe was not heavily defended and the beaches were suitable for the landings. The plan was for two Canadian battalions to assault the main beach, supported by Canadian tanks and engineers, after two other Canadian battalions had landed earlier to attack German gun batteries overlooking the main beach. The British 1st Battalion of the Parachute Brigade were to be dropped to attack the two coastal batteries at Varengeville and Berneval-le-Grand, with a further Canadian battalion acting as a reserve to be committed when and where necessary.

The date for Rutter was narrowed down to the first week of July but, after weeks of training, the combination of unsettled weather and the fact the Germans had spotted and attacked the large gathering of ships required to transport the assault troops across the Channel, resulted in the operation being cancelled.

Although Rutter had been cancelled, its planning was not entirely wasted. The decision to remount the raid, this time called Operation Jubilee, meant plans were resurrected. The main objectives remained largely unchanged, with the only difference being that the large German coastal batteries would be attacked and captured by a seaborne assault, rather than from the air: 4 Commando was tasked to destroy the Hess Battery at Varengeville while 3 Commando was to destroy the Goebbels Battery at Berneval-le-Grand.

Along stretches of the south coast of England the commandos began training for the raid. They would be required to assault the two coastal gun batteries at dawn while the main landings took place on five different beaches along a 10-mile stretch of the coast. A total of 5,000 Canadians and a further 1,000 British troops, including the army commandos and a unit of Royal Marine commandos, and 50 American Rangers were to be supported by more than 230 Royal Navy ships and landing craft and nearly 70 RAF squadrons. It would be the largest amphibious raid of the war.

Tasked with capturing and then destroying the Goebbels Battery, codenamed Operation Flodden, 3 Commando was to be led by Lieutenant Colonel John Durnford-Slater, who had led his men in the raid at Vaagso the year before. His plan was for his force of just over four hundred men to land in two groups on two beaches, codenamed Yellow-One and Yellow-Two, either side of the battery and near the village of Berneval-le-Grand. The Goebbels Battery was known to house three 170mm and four 105mm guns and, situated half a mile inland, it was protected from the sea by steep cliffs. Durnford-Slater would lead the main element ashore on Yellow-One while his second-in-command, Major Peter Young, another veteran of Norway, would land with two troops plus a mortar section on Yellow-Two. The two groups would then carry out a co-ordinated pincer attack against the battery using gullies to conceal their position.

Meanwhile, 4 Commando, led by Lieutenant Colonel Simon Fraser, the fifteenth holder of the title Lord Lovat, who had also served in Norway, would be carrying out an assault on the Hess Battery under Operation Cauldron. The Hess Battery consisted of six 150mm guns in a concrete emplacement just over half a mile inland from the coastal cliffs. Intelligence reports had estimated there were around two hundred men at the battery, with a further two infantry companies in support nearby. The emplacement was surrounded by concrete defences, landmines, concealed defensive machine-gun posts and layers of barbed wire, and was also protected from air attack by an anti-aircraft gun emplacement.

With less than three hundred men, Lovat had a smaller force than Durnford-Slater but he also decided to land his force on two beaches. One group, consisting of C Troop and one section of A Troop, plus a mortar detachment, would be led by his second-in-command, Major Derek Mills-Roberts, and land on the beach at Varengeville. The beach Mills-Roberts had been allocated, codenamed Orange-One, was overlooked by a cliff, but offered two gullies leading to the top, although these were known to be full of barbed wire and other obstructions. The commandos were to scale the cliff in front of the battery and take up a holding position in a wood, half a mile inland, ready to mount a continuous barrage of fire against the front of the battery while the second group, led by Lovat, carried out the assault on the battery. His group, consisting of B and F Troops, was to land on the beach at Quiberville, called Orange-Two. The beach was just over a mile to the west and at the mouth of the small River Saane. It was further away from the battery but the commandos were expected to move quickly inland along the river and then eastwards to the top of the cliffs, where they could attack the battery and its garrison from the rear, although this line of approach was known to be protected by machine-gun posts and barbed wire. The remaining section of A Troop was to be held as a mobile reserve between the two beaches and used as required. Once the battery had been destroyed, the commandos would withdraw using the landing craft at Orange-One.

Having left their temporary bases in Sussex and Dorset, the commandos were transported to their embarkation ports for crossing the Channel; 3 Commando at Newhaven and 4 Commando at Southampton. While 4 Commando's crossing passed uneventfully, the same was not true for the men of 3 Commando. Shortly before 4.00 am, and still about an hour from the coast of France, their landing group was illuminated after being spotted by an armed German convoy in the Channel. The commandos immediately came under intense fire. Their landing craft quickly scattered as they came under attack by fast German S-boats that had been escorting a German tanker. Some of the landing craft were forced to turn back, while others were sunk, effectively halting 3 Commando's main attacking force. They had simply been in the wrong place at the wrong time and had been unfortunate to have been spotted.

Remarkably, though, not all of the landing craft of this group had been sunk or had turned back. Six managed to regroup and continued towards their landing beach. Furthermore, the chance encounter mid-Channel seems to have gone unreported to the coastal defences. To the crews of the German patrol boats, they assumed they had come across a planned raid against their convoy and nothing more. The landing craft of Peter Young had also survived intact and completed the crossing on its own. Determined to press on with the attack, the commandos landed just to the west of Yellow-Two slightly before 6.00 am.

Making their way quickly across the beach, Young then located a gulley leading to the top of the cliffs. Undeterred by the barbed wire and other obstructions that filled the gulley, the commandos reached the top. The Goebbels Battery was already firing on the main landing force, now just a few miles away, but with only eighteen men there was little Young could do. The commandos managed to reach a position within 200 yards of the battery, but a full frontal assault was clearly out of the question; it would have meant certain death.

Young decided the best they could do was to harass the battery as much as possible and to prevent it from inflicting serious damage on the attacking forces. Splitting his men into three small groups, he directed his commandos to cut telephone wires to disrupt communications and continue to fire on the battery for several hours as a constant distraction to the gunners. This seemed to have some effect as no Allied forces were believed to have been lost to the battery. After a couple of hours and hopelessly outnumbered, as well as being all but out of ammunition, Young finally gave the order to withdraw; all his men would make it off the beach and safely back to England.

Meanwhile, the group of six other landing craft that had survived the encounter mid-Channel, a total of around a hundred men, including a handful of US Rangers, had landed on a beach to the east of Yellow-One and opposite Le Petit Berneval. But it was now 5.30 am and they were half an hour behind schedule. The delay of thirty minutes had made all the difference between darkness and first daylight, and the landing craft had been spotted by the German defences. As enemy rounds clattered against the landing craft, causing a number of casualties on board, the commandos were quick to get ashore and reach the safety of a nearby gulley. Having then scrambled to the top, Captain Geoff Osmond had contemplated making a limited assault on the battery as planned, but German reinforcements had already arrived in the area. With such a small force it would have been a suicidal attack but the commandos did manage to take out German defensive positions at Le Petit Berneval. However, as they made their way towards the battery the commandos came under a devastating attack and casualties started to mount.

The survivors of 3 Commando had now been ashore for just over an hour but any hope of continuing the attack was abandoned. The order was given to withdraw to the beach and re-embark. But that was impossible. The commandos were now pinned down. Although the landing craft had managed to return to the beach to pick up the survivors, none of the commandos arrived. Eventually, after waiting as long as they dared, the crews of the landing craft left. Unbeknown to them at the time, the commandos they had come to pick up were still pinned down. Those commandos that were still alive were unaware that there was now no chance of getting away. Although some did make a break across open ground in an attempt to reach the beach, many were cut down. Those that did reach the beach arrived to find their only chance of escape had gone; only burnt-out landing craft were there waiting for them. With no option, Osmond surrendered his men to the surrounding forces.

Although 3 Commando's raid had been disastrous, their colleagues in 4 Commando had been more fortunate. They had set sail from Southampton in the landing ship HMS *Prince Albert* and although they had heard 3's mid-Channel encounter a few miles to the east, their crossing had been uneventful. Having then transferred to their landing craft for the assault as planned, the first group of 4's commandos, led by Mills-Roberts, landed unopposed on Orange-One at around 4.50 am and just before daybreak. They were then able to quickly scale the cliffs and take up their positions, where they were to wait until 6.15 am before commencing their barrage of fire against the battery from the front – the second group were to commence their main assault from the rear fifteen minutes later.

Meanwhile, Lovat's second group had not been quite so lucky. Their landing was met by heavy machine-gun fire from two pillboxes overlooking the beach. Calling for support from the mobile reserve section of A Troop to deal with the enemy positions, Lovat quickly led his two troops off the beach and towards the rear of the battery, where they took up their positions ready for the assault. Behind him, the commandos of A Troop soon dealt with the pillboxes and quickly made their way towards the first group, where they were to join up with the rest of their troop.

For Mills-Roberts and the commandos of the first group, the peace and quiet of the early summer morning was suddenly shattered and the ground shook when the battery unexpectedly opened fire. The convoy carrying the main assaulting troops had been spotted a few miles away and the battery was now engaging the ships. Mills-Roberts decided to wait no longer. Although it was not yet time he decided to engage the battery immediately. Mortars, Brens and rifle fire – everything the commandos had – rained down on the battery; it was the first the Germans knew that the commandos were even there.

A short distance away, Lovat and his group heard the firing. They were making their way towards their assault positions but the going was tough across heavy ground. Leading F Troop was Captain Roger Pettiward. One of 4 Commandos' true characters, Pettiward was a complete gentleman by nature. From a privileged background, and educated at Eton, he had been an adventurous and well-travelled artist before the war, achieving much fame as the cartoonist Paul Crum. Alongside him was his second-in-command, Lieutenant John MacDonald, and 24-year-old Major Pat Porteous, the son of an army brigadier and a former artillery officer, who was acting as the liaison officer between the two assault groups carrying out the attack.

As the commandos of F Troop moved quickly between cottages and an orchard towards their assault position, they were suddenly caught by a heavy burst of enemy machine-gun fire. Pettiward and MacDonald were both killed instantly. As Porteous continued the advance towards the guns he was hit, the bullet passing through his palm and entering his upper arm. Undaunted, he continued until he reached his assailant, disarming him and then killing him with his own bayonet; thereby saving the life of one of the sergeants on whom the German had now turned. With Pettiward and MacDonald dead, and the troop sergeant major wounded, Porteous took command. Without hesitation, and in the face of overwhelming enemy fire, he dashed across the open ground to take command of the remaining commandos of F Troop.

The Fairey Swordfish, known affectionately to its crews as the 'Old Stringbag', achieved some spectacular successes during the early years of the Second World War. One of the most notable was against the Italian fleet at Taranto, on the night of 11/12 November 1940, a raid that would be remembered as one of the most daring in the Fleet Air Arm's history. *(FAA)*

A Bristol Beaufort of 22 Squadron, Coastal Command. From their base at St Eval in Cornwall, the squadron's Beauforts were within striking distance of the Atlantic ports along the Bay of Biscay on the west coast of France, including Brest, where, in April 1941, the mighty German warship *Gneisenau* was located. *(AHB)*

What the outcome of the pursuit of the mighty German battleship *Bismarck* during May 1941 might have been without the heroic intervention of the Swordfish crews will never be known. What is clear, though, is that the damage caused by one or more of the torpedoes launched in their final attack from HMS *Ark Royal* crippled the *Bismarck* to the point that there was to be no escape. *(FAA)*

It was from the Landing Ship HMS *Glengyle* that the men of 11 (Scottish) Commando launched their attack on the Vichy French-held positions at the Litani River. After one unsuccessful attempt to mount the raid, the commandos went ashore on 9 June 1941. *(IWM)*

Led by their squadron commander, Wing Commander Hughie Edwards, the Bristol Blenheim crews of 105 Squadron carried out the daring low-level daylight raid against Germany's second largest port of Bremen on 4 July 1941. *(AHB)*

Flying Officer Kenneth Campbell was posthumously awarded the Victoria Cross for his attack against the *Gneisenau* in the heavily defended port of Brest on 6 April 1941. It was an incredible achievement, given that Campbell had attacked alone and with only one torpedo, to inflict as much damage as he did, and in the face of intense anti-aircraft fire from all around. The result of his attack was that the *Gneisenau* was severely damaged below the waterline and was put out of action for nine months. *(AHB)*

A veteran of the action at the Litani River, Lieutenant Colonel Geoffrey Keyes was killed just five months later while leading the daring raid on what was believed to be Rommel's headquarters at a villa at Beda Littoria in Libya, some 250 miles behind enemy lines. Unfortunately, the German general was not at the villa and the raid was to cost the gallant Keyes his life. Keyes was subsequently awarded a posthumous Victoria Cross, the first of eight VCs won by commandos during the war. *(IWM)*

The small island of Vaagso remains largely unheard of beyond its locality on the western coast of Norway, but the raid that took place there in December 1941 is significant because it was the first time British forces carried out a truly combined amphibious operation involving all three services planning and operating together to achieve a common aim. *(IWM)*

Led by Major Gus March-Phillipps, Operation Postmaster was one of the Special Operations Executive's classic operations of the war. It took place off the west coast of Africa in January 1942, and involved a small group of men tasked with boarding Italian and German ships in the neutral port of Santa Isabel on the Spanish island of Fernando Po and then sailing them to Nigeria. March-Phillipps would then lead the Small Scale Raiding Force during a number of daring raids across the English Channel, but was killed in September 1942 during the disastrous Operation Aquatint. *(IWM)*

Lieutenant Commander Eugene Esmonde, the commanding officer of 825 Squadron, led the heroic attempt by six Swordfish against the three mighty German warships – *Scharnhorst*, *Gneisenau* and *Prinz Eugen* – as they made their daring daylight dash through the English Channel on 12 February 1942. None of the Swordfish returned and amongst those killed was Esmonde, but his gallant leadership earned him a posthumous Victoria Cross. *(FAA)*

An aerial photograph of the villa forming part of the radar site at Bruneval. It was taken by an aircraft of the RAF Photographic Reconnaissance Unit just a couple of months before a force of more than a hundred men of the 2nd Battalion, 1st Parachute Brigade, dropped on the night of 27/28 February 1942 to capture the site, and then dismantle the radar and take parts back to Britain for evaluation. It was the first major British airborne raid of the war. *(AHB)*

The raid on the major port of St Nazaire on the Atlantic coast of France, carried out by army commandos and vessels of the Royal Navy during the early hours of 28 March 1942, has been described as the most daring raid of them all. A former American destroyer, HMS *Campbeltown*, was used to ram the dock gate. She had been extensively modified for the raid to lighten her as much as possible to get over the sandbanks, and, to enable her to approach without being identified, two funnels were removed and the other two modified to give the appearance of a German vessel. The bow was packed with high explosives and timed to explode after the raiders had left the port. *(IWM)*

Five Victoria Crosses were awarded for the St Nazaire raid, the most for a single action of the Second World War. One of those went to Able Seaman William Savage, who continuously manned the gun of his motor gunboat, MGB 314, during the raid, engaging positions ashore with cool and steady accuracy despite being completely exposed and under heavy fire from the port's defences. Eventually, though, the MGB was hit for the last time, killing Savage who was still manning his gun. *(IWM)*

Squadron Leader John Nettleton of 44 Squadron was awarded the Victoria Cross for leading the daring low-level daylight raid by Lancasters against the diesel engine factory at Augsburg on 17 April 1942. *(AHB)*

Commandos returning from the disastrous raid on Dieppe on 19 August 1942. Although they have a German prisoner, captured during the raid, the reality is that this was little consolation for the heavy losses suffered by the Allies that day. *(IWM)*

Colin Ogden-Smith was one of eleven members of the Small Scale Raiding Force to take part in the unit's first raid, Operation Barricade, on the Cherbourg Peninsula on the night of 14/15 August 1942. He would later be killed while serving with the SOE and leading a Jedburgh mission deep behind enemy lines. *(Charmian Musgrove)*

Buried alongside each other in the churchyard at Saint Laurent-sur-Mer, close to where they had fought and died together, are three members of the Small Scale Raiding Force, including its leader, Major Gus March-Phillipps (centre), killed on the night of 12/13 September 1942 during the disastrous Operation Aquatint, the reconnaissance of Saint Honorine-des-Pertes, a small coastal town near Port-en-Bessin in Normandy. The other two buried here are Sergeant Alan Williams (on right of photo) and Private Richard Leonard, whose real name was Richard Lehniger. Lehniger had previously fought against the Allies in 1918, but being half-Jewish and a communist he had later fled Nazi Germany to fight for the Allies during the Second World War. *(Author)*

Major Jake Easonsmith led the raid by the Long Range Desert Group against an Italian-held town and airfield at Barce, deep behind enemy lines, in September 1942. Barce was a main administrative centre for the Italian colonial government of Libya and so was home to a large number of Italian forces; nevertheless, the raid was a resounding success, particularly the attack on the airfield that resulted in thirty-five aircraft destroyed without a single casualty being suffered, and again proved to the Axis that the Allies were capable of carrying out a raid of that type deep in the desert. *(IWM)*

After the death of Gus March-Phillipps, Geoffrey Appleyard took over command of the Small Scale Raiding Force and led the successful raid on Sark on the night of 3/4 October 1942. However, the raid, called Operation Basalt, would have longer-term repercussions stretching far beyond the quiet shores of the Channel Islands as it led to Hitler issuing his Kommandobefehl (Commando Order) just two weeks later, stating that all Allied commandos captured by German forces should be killed immediately, even if in uniform or if attempting to surrender. *(IWM)*

Headquarters section of the Long Range Desert Group. The 30cwt Chevy was the mainstay patrol vehicle of the LRDG at that time. The sturdy design meant that it was extremely reliable: the vehicles were stripped of all but the essentials and a number of modifications for operating in the desert were made, including adding a mix of heavy armament. *(IWM)*

Regarded by many as one of the founders of modern day guerrilla warfare, Orde Wingate was a quite remarkable man. His tactics and, at times, unorthodox leadership of his men, known as the Chindits, during their deep penetration into the jungle of Burma behind enemy lines in early 1943, would influence British military thinking for many years to come. *(IWM)*

Major Blondie Hasler led the daring raid by Royal Marines against enemy shipping in the German-occupied French port of Bordeaux. The raid, later to become better known as the tale of the Cockleshell Heroes, took place in December 1942 and involved a dozen men canoeing 60 miles up a river under the cover of darkness to attack cargo ships in the port with limpet mines before escaping overland to Spain. It was yet another audacious raid carried out during the war but it was to sadly end in tragedy; only Hasler and his canoe colleague, Bill Sparks, survived. *(RM)*

Wing Commander Guy Gibson and his crew about to board their Lancaster for 617 Squadron's legendary attack on the Ruhr dams in Germany during the night of 16/17 May 1943. *(AHB)*

While Gibson looks on, King George VI assesses the damage to the Ruhr dams during his visit to RAF Scampton after the raid. *(AHB)*

Wing Commander Guy Gibson was awarded the Victoria Cross for his outstanding leadership of the raid on the Ruhr dams. Already a holder of the Distinguished Service Order and bar and a Distinguished Flying Cross and bar, he was aged just 24 when he led the raid, but sadly he would not survive the war. He was killed in a Mosquito while acting as master bomber for a raid against Rheydt and Mönchengladbach on 19 September 1944. *(AHB)*

Lieutenant Donald Cameron commanded the midget submarine *X6*, known as *Piker II*, during the attack on the mighty German battleship *Tirpitz*, moored in a Norwegian fjord, on 22 September 1943. Along with the *X7*, *Pdinichthys*, commanded by Lieutenant Godfrey Place, the two X-Craft midgets caused extensive damage to the *Tirpitz*, which resulted in the battleship having to undergo repairs lasting for several months. Cameron and Place were both awarded the Victoria Cross. *(IWM)*

The six surviving crew members of the midget submarines *X6* and *X7* decorated for their daring attack against the mighty *Tirpitz* in northern Norway during September 1943. Left to right: Sub-Lieutenant Dickie Kendall (DSO), ERA Ed Goddard (CGM), Lieutenant John Lorimer (DSO) and Lieutenant Donald Cameron (VC) – all of the *X6*, and Sub-Lieutenant Robert Aitken (DSO) and Lieutenant Godfrey Place (VC) of the *X7*. Sadly, the two other crew members of the *X7* were both killed. *(IWM)*

Mosquito of 464 (RAAF) Sqn at Hunsdon. The squadron took part in the daring low-level daylight raid on Amiens Prison, called Operation Jericho, on 18 February 1944, to free members of the French Resistance awaiting death at the hands of the Gestapo. *(AHB)*

The scene at Pegasus Bridge today. The monument in the foreground on the right marks the spot where the first glider, flown by Staff Sergeant Jim Wallwork, came to rest just yards from the bridge. Next to the monument is a memorial to Major John Howard who led the raid during the early hours of 6 June 1944. *(Author)*

Bruce Ogden-Smith was awarded the Distinguished Conduct Medal and the Military Medal for his daring reconnaissance of several beaches along the Normandy coastline during early 1944 prior to the Allied invasion of Europe. The second mission involved swimming ashore from a midget submarine, night after night, to gather vital intelligence of potential landing beaches for the D-Day landings. *(Angela Weston)*

While the plan for attacking the bridge at Arnhem might have seemed straightforward enough, the task faced by Major General Roy Urquhart's 1st Airborne Division in September 1944 was the most daring part of Operation Market Garden. Urquhart is pictured in front of his headquarters, the Hartenstein Hotel, in the suburb of Oosterbeek. *(IWM)*

Anders Lassen, the fearless Dane who was posthumously awarded the Victoria Cross for his leadership during the raid on Lake Comacchio in April 1945. Considering all that he had been through, and the fact he had taken part in some of the most daring raids of the war, it was tragic that Lassen should be killed just days before the end of the war. *(IWM)*

Leading Seaman James Magennis, the crew's diver on board the midget submarine *XE3*, was awarded the Victoria Cross for his part in the attack against the Japanese cruiser *Takao* anchored in the Johore Straits at Singapore on 31 July 1945. Magennis had risked his own life in extremely hazardous conditions to attach limpet mines to the cruiser, which resulted in the *Takao* being completely immobilized. *(IWM)*

Rallying them, he then led them to their forming-up position where they fixed bayonets ready for the assault.

A pre-planned strike by Allied fighters arrived exactly on time to strafe the battery. It was now 6.30 am and Lovat signalled the assault. The covering fire then ceased and the commandos of the second group attacked. While Captain Gordon Webb led B Troop towards their objective of the battery's buildings, the wounded Porteous led F Troop's charge towards the guns, now less than a hundred yards away. Porteous was immediately wounded for a second time, shot through the thigh, but despite his wounds he continued to lead the men straight to the guns. He was one of the first to reach their final objective, but he was then hit again and finally collapsed from the loss of blood just as the last of the guns was captured. His most gallant conduct, brilliant leadership and tenacious devotion to duty was supplementary to the role he had been given for the assault and was an inspiration to his unit. It was later announced that Pat Porteous was to be awarded the Victoria Cross, one of three VCs to be won during that day.

Demolitions experts then destroyed the six guns with explosive charges while the commandos of B Troop searched the battery buildings and gathered anything of interest for intelligence. The commandos had been ashore for two hours and it was now time to leave. Carrying their wounded, the commandos withdrew to Orange-One where they were evacuated from the beach by landing craft under the cover of a smokescreen. It was still only 8.30 am. Then, having crossed the Channel without incident, apart from some ineffective enemy fire on leaving the beach, the men of 4 Commando arrived at Newhaven shortly before 6.00 pm. It had been a very long day.

As for the main assault on Dieppe by the Canadians, it was a total failure. The naval bombardment had not supressed the enemy defences, the tanks were unable to advance over the shingle beach and the infantry had suffered heavy casualties. Of the main assault force of 6,000 men, over 1,000 were killed and more than 2,000 were captured and taken as prisoners of war (a total casualty figure of some 60 per cent of the attacking force). Naval losses were also severe, with more than 500 casualties, plus the loss of a destroyer and over 30 landing craft. Allied losses in the air were also significant, with around a hundred aircraft lost, more than on any other day of the war. Furthermore, none of the objectives had been met: the assault by

4 Commando on the Hess Battery at Varengeville had been the only success of the whole operation. Even so, 45 commandos had not returned, 17 of whom had been killed, although German casualties were estimated to be around 150.

The assault by 4 Commando was later described as '*a classic example of the use of well-trained troops and a thoroughness in planning, training and execution.*' For his leadership of the raid, Lord Lovat was awarded the DSO and his second-in-command, Major Derek Mills-Roberts, was awarded an MC, as was Captain Gordon Webb.

The men of 3 Commando had also fought with courage, aggression, resilience and dogged determination at Dieppe, but the fight had proved costly, with 140 killed, wounded or taken as prisoners of war; the majority of whom had been killed or captured trying to make it back to the beach. Amongst those killed was 22-year-old Lieutenant Edward Loustalot, a US Ranger attached to 3 Commando. He was the first American to be killed on European soil during the war and one of three rangers killed at Dieppe; Loustalot had been cut down by enemy crossfire while attacking a machine-gun post at the top of the cliff.

For his courage and leadership of the eighteen commandos of 3 Commando, who had landed in the single landing craft to the west of Yellow-Two and had then harassed the battery for some three hours before withdrawing safely back to England, Peter Young was awarded the DSO. His action was later described by Vice Admiral John Hughes-Hallett, the naval commander of Jubilee, as perhaps the most outstanding action of the whole operation.

Although the raid had ended up in a disastrous loss of life, the events at Dieppe would influence Allied planning for later landings in North Africa, Sicily and, ultimately, in Normandy on D-Day. The losses at Dieppe were claimed to be a necessary evil and Mountbatten later justified the raid by arguing that lessons learned were put to good use later in the war: stating that the success at Normandy was won on the beaches of Dieppe, and every life lost at Dieppe in 1942 spared at least ten more in Normandy in 1944. Churchill also claimed that the results of the Dieppe raid fully justified the heavy loss. To others, however, especially the Canadians, it was, and remains, a major disaster.

Chapter Seventeen

Reconnaissance of Saint Honorine-des-Pertes

12/13 September 1942

The summer of 1942 had seen a number of daring and ambitious raids across the Channel but the Small Scale Raiding Force's extraordinary run of apparent immunity, which had characterized their raids so far, came to a tragic end on the night of 12/13 September 1942 when a reconnaissance of Saint Honorine-des-Pertes ended in complete disaster. It proved to be an enormous setback for this small but elite amphibious unit.

Since its close call on the Cherbourg Peninsula during Operation Barricade, and the disastrous Allied raid on Dieppe, the leader of the SSRF, Major Gus March-Phillipps, had decided to leave the northern coastline of France alone; he knew the enemy's defences would have been significantly reinforced with an increased number of patrols all along the coast. For a while March-Phillipps chose to carry out raids on the Channel Islands instead, until such time had passed as he considered it safe to return to France.

With a month having passed since Barricade, and three weeks since Dieppe, March-Phillipps felt that this was the right time to return to the coast of France. The raid he planned, called Operation Aquatint, was to conduct a reconnaissance of Saint Honorine-des-Pertes, a small coastal town near Port-en-Bessin in Normandy, to collect information about the surrounding area and to take at least one guard as a prisoner. Although the area was believed to be free of any major concrete gun emplacements, it was thought there was a network of coastal batteries capable of providing interlocking arcs of gunfire, and German infantry carrying out foot patrols in the area. His plan, therefore, was to land to the east of Saint Honorine and then scale the cliffs to take up a position to the rear of the houses along the seafront, from where his raiding party could carry out a swift attack and take some prisoners before heading back across the Channel.

March-Phillipps decided to lead the raid, taking with him his deputy, Geoffrey Appleyard, although an injury sustained in a raid two weeks before would prevent Appleyard from going ashore. The others selected for the raid were all experienced members of the SSRF. They were: Graham Hayes, André Desgranges, Tom Winter, John Burton, Lord Francis Howard, Tony Hall, Alan Williams, Jan Hollings, Adam Orr and Richard Leonard – the last three all being volunteers from countries in Nazi-occupied Europe and operating with the SSRF under an alias.

The raid was initially planned for the night of 11/12 September, but it had to be cancelled when fog made it impossible for the raiding party to locate its landing site. By the following night the fog had cleared enough to allow the operation to take place. Having left from their home base at Portland, it was just after 10.00 pm when the SSRF's motor torpedo boat, the *Little Pisser*, arrived off the coast of France, close to Barfleur. Having then reduced speed to avoid detection, the MTB manoeuvred around the enemy minefields lying off the shore.

Just after midnight the *Little Pisser* approached the area believed to be the dropping-off point. In the darkness it was difficult to locate the intended landing site. It was so dark that it was almost impossible to clearly make out anything of note, but rather than abort the mission for a second time, the team opted in the end to head for a gulley which they believed to be Saint Honorine. But it was, in fact, Saint Laurent-sur-Mer, about 2 miles further to the west, which, nearly two years later, would become Omaha Beach during the D-Day landings. Although they clearly had no idea at the time, the commandos were about to step into a viper's nest. It was one of the most heavily patrolled areas of that part of the coastline of northern France.

While Appleyard remained on board the MTB, March-Phillipps and the raiding party boarded the Goatley. They had about 400 yards to paddle to the shore and managed to reach it in reasonable time, but having reached the shore they found they were too close to houses to leave the Goatley; it would almost certainly be seen. Having then dragged the Goatley a couple of hundred yards along the water's edge to the base of the cliff to the east, Howard was left to guard it while the main party made their way inland as quickly as they could.

March-Phillipps decided to first reconnoitre the area around the houses along the seafront to find a suitable place to take some prisoners. For the next few minutes everything went more or less as planned. The ten raiders moved silently through the area in an arc that eventually took them back towards the beach. Then, as they approached a track, which crossed in front of them and lay between them and the beach, they heard an enemy patrol approaching. The raiders immediately took cover. Had the enemy patrol not had a dog then the commandos would almost certainly have remained undetected, but the dog picked up their scent. Concerned that they were about to be discovered, and believing they would have the advantage of numbers and the element of surprise, March-Phillipps decided to act first; the intent being for the party to fight its way out of trouble in the same way it had done during Barricade a month before.

The raiders suddenly broke the silence and stormed out of their cover, firing as they raced through the patrol. One grabbed a German in the hope they could still reach the beach and take a prisoner with them as had been the plan. But the noise had alerted a German guard post nearby. Flares suddenly illuminated the beach and a searchlight on top of the cliff now scanned the area as the Germans raked the beach with machine-gun fire and grenades. The commandos were now in a hopeless situation, but fought back as best they could with great courage. All but one, Tony Hall, who had been left for dead on the beach, succeeded in getting back to the Goatley.

Unfortunately, the tide was on its way out and so they now had further to drag the Goatley to reach the water's edge. Using all their strength the commandos got it into the water. Despite the waves crashing ashore, making their task of getting out to sea even more difficult, the raiders somehow managed to get a hundred yards away from the shore before they were illuminated by another flare and a devastating burst of machine-gun fire cut them down.

With the Goatley sinking, the commandos were left to try and swim for the safety of the MTB, but the strong tide made it all but impossible. Reluctantly, they abandoned the idea and made their way back to the shore; there was to be no getting away. Four of the raiding party – Lord Howard, Tom Winter, André Desgranges and Tony Hall – were captured immediately. Hall, in particular, was lucky to be alive. Although he had been left for dead in the desperate dash across the beach, he had in fact been badly wounded and unconscious, and had been quickly picked up by the Germans.

Sadly, though, three of the raiding party were dead. Two of those were Alan Williams and Richard Leonard, a Jewish Sudeten German whose real name was Richard Lehniger, but the biggest loss of all was the gallant Gus March-Phillipps. It appears he had been badly wounded when the Goatley was hit with machine-gun fire and was alive in the water for a while, but his body was later found washed up on the beach.

The flares had also illuminated the *Little Pisser*, waiting 300 yards off the shore, and it, too, now came under attack. Faced with no alternative, Appleyard took the MTB further offshore and cut the engines to make it appear that it had set course for home. He then waited for everything to quieten down while he assessed the damage to the craft. The starboard engine and gearbox had suffered considerable damage, but after a short period of relative calm the boat made its way quietly back towards the shore in the hope that some survivors would be found. Then, having waited for nearly an hour, the silence was suddenly broken again by shells bursting overhead. The MTB had been spotted once more and was now under attack from a seawards direction. Finally, with all hope of picking up the raiding party gone, and with the enemy closing in, Appleyard reluctantly headed back out to sea. The damage to the *Little Pisser* meant the Channel was crossed at a reduced speed, but eventually it arrived back at Portsmouth harbour just before 7.00 am.

While the Germans believed they had accounted for all of the raiders, four of the men had succeeded in getting away. Three of those – John Burton, Jan Hollings and Adam Orr – had managed to swim further down the coastline to make their escape, although they were all subsequently captured. While Burton would survive as a prisoner of war, the two Europeans – Jan Hollings (a Dutchman whose real name was Jan Hellings) and Adam Orr (a Pole whose real name was Abraham Opoczynski) – were less fortunate. Both were handed over to the Gestapo for questioning and their fate remains unknown, although Orr is believed to have escaped with other prisoners in the early weeks of 1945 while being moved from a prisoner camp, in what later became known as the Long March; however, he is believed to have died soon after.

The fourth man to have made his escape was Graham Hayes. Having swum well away from the carnage he went ashore further west along the coast. The exact circumstances of what happened to Hayes over the next six months is not fully clear, but he was smuggled away by the French and apparently made his way to Spain with the intent of returning to England. However, such was the German infiltration of the French Resistance at the time, it appears that Hayes was later betrayed and handed over to the Germans. He was then incarcerated in the notorious prison at Fresnes in Paris, where the Germans held captured members of the SOE and the French Resistance, and it was there, in July 1943, that he was executed.

None of the eleven members of the raiding party that had gone ashore at Saint Honorine-des-Pertes on the night of 12/13 September 1942 had returned to continue the war against the Nazis. It was a tragic loss and Operation Aquatint had been a complete disaster.

Chapter Eighteen

Barce

13/14 September 1942

T he Special Air Service, better known simply as the SAS, needs no
introduction today. Its origins date back to 1940 with the formation
of the Long Range Desert Group, a unit of the British Army made up
of volunteers to carry out deep-penetration raids, and covert reconnaissance
and intelligence missions behind enemy lines. The SAS did not form until
the following year, when it was initially called L Detachment of the Special
Service Brigade, but it soon learned to rely on the assistance of the men of
the LRDG, who had paved the way in the desert war for operations behind
enemy lines. So effective were they that it was later reported that General
Erwin Rommel, Germany's commander of the Afrika Korps, said that the
LRDG caused the Axis forces more damage than any other British unit of
similar strength.

As part of General Archibald Wavell's Middle East Command, the LRDG
operated throughout 1941–42 in the Libyan Desert, deep behind enemy
lines. Their most vital role was known as the 'Road Watch' – clandestinely
monitoring traffic running along the main coastal road from Tripoli to
Benghazi and transmitting the information back to British intelligence –
but probably their most notable action was against Italian forces at Barce in
September 1942.

The deteriorating military situation in the North African campaign
during the autumn of 1942 had prompted four ambitious raids behind
enemy lines. The intent was to disrupt Rommel's ever-lengthening lines
of communication, and these attacks included large-scale raids on the vital
enemy supply ports at Benghazi (called Operation Bigamy) and Tobruk
(Operation Agreement) by commandos and the SAS respectively, and, four
days later, an attack by the Sudan Defence Force on the Jalo Oasis (Operation
Nicety). Although the LRDG was to provide support for all of these raids, it

was also tasked to carry out a subsidiary diversionary raid, called Operation Caravan, on an Italian-held town and airfield at Barce in the Gebel Akhdar in northern Cyrenaica. The key for all four of these operations was surprise, so careful co-ordination and detailed planning would be required if success was to be achieved.

The ancient colony of Barce is about 50 miles north-east of Benghazi and situated on the main coastal road along the northern coast of Libya. It was a main administrative centre for the Italian colonial government of Libya and so was home to a large number of Italian forces. These included a company of military police with armoured cars, a company of carabiniers, a light tank company, an artillery company and a gun battery. There was also an airfield on the north-eastern side of the town.

On 1 September 1942, B Squadron of the LRDG, which consisted of two patrols under the command of Major Jake Easonsmith, left its Egyptian base at Faiyum, some 60 miles to the south-west of Cairo. It was the start of a journey of more than a thousand miles, and the team's task when they arrived at Barce was quite straightforward – to cause as much damage and disruption to the enemy as possible.

A natural leader and with an uncanny ability to out-think the enemy, Easonsmith was described by some as the LRDG's finest patrol commander. He was 33 years old and had been a territorial soldier before being commissioned into the Royal Tank Regiment prior to volunteering for the LRDG. He had been awarded the Military Cross for his first operation in command, when he had recovered the men of L Detachment from a failed raid against Axis airfields at Gazala and Tmimi. Now Easonsmith had a raiding force of forty-seven men to cover the vast distance to Barce in a dozen Chevrolet trucks and five jeeps.

The 30cwt Chevy 1533x2 was the mainstay patrol vehicle of the LRDG at that time. The sturdy design meant that it was extremely reliable. The vehicles were stripped of all but essentials and modified for operating in the desert. The cabs were removed, windscreens were replaced by aero screens, the body was heightened with wooden planks to increase the load and the vehicles fitted with large sand tyres. The trucks were also heavily armed, with a mix of pairs of 0.303-inch calibre Brownings, 0.5-inch Vickers heavy machine guns, 0.303-inch Vickers Ks and Italian-built 20mm Bredas, a particularly popular weapon for such operations because it was lighter than the others, took up less space and had a good rate of fire. The guns were fitted on swivel mountings in the back of the trucks, or on the passenger's doorpost.

The plan was for one of the patrols, called T1, made up of New Zealanders and led by Captain N. P. Wilder, to attack the main target, the airfield situated on the north-eastern side of the town. The other patrol, called G1, made up of British guardsmen and led by Captain Alastair Timpson, would carry out an attack on a barracks at the town.

Because the LRDG was also providing support to the three other raids – Bigamy, Agreement and Nicety – it was important to avoid getting in each other's way when moving across the desert. The route given for Easonsmith's force involved first heading south and then across the great Kalansho Sand Sea, a vast and notoriously difficult part of the Libyan Desert lying below sea level and covered with salt plains, sand dunes and salt marshes, before heading north towards the Gebel Akhdar.

Navigating across the desert was not easy, but the LRDG had become experts. The trucks were equipped with a sun compass and each patrol had a specialist navigator within their team. Easonsmith also had with him Major Vladimir Peniakoff, known as 'Popski', from the Libyan Arab Force. Peniakoff had been born in Belgium to Russian parents and had served in the French Army before transferring to the British Army in 1940. Capable of speaking a number of languages, including Arabic, he was now accompanying the group along with two Libyan tribesmen, who had been given the task of gathering information about the enemy dispositions around Barce and then reporting their findings to Peniakoff immediately prior to the raid.

Because of the long distance to Barce, the group were supported on the journey out by two trucks from the Heavy Section, which would provide fuel for the first 200 miles. They were also accompanied for a while by Captain John Ogilvey's S2 patrol, but they would soon depart on their own mission to Benghazi as part of Operation Bigamy.

The raiders suffered an early setback when Timpson's command jeep overturned on a sand dune, badly injuring both him and his driver. They could not continue and so both had to be evacuated, with command of G1 being passed to Sergeant Jack Dennis. By the end of the first week the raiding force had met up with two more trucks for a further refill of fuel and supplies. A spare truck, loaded with fuel, water and food, was then left

hidden near Bir el-Gerrari as an emergency rendezvous point for the men
on the way home.

By 13 September Easonsmith and his raiding force had reached Benia.
They were now about 15 miles south of Barce and set up camp in preparation
for the raid. It had taken them eleven days to cover a distance of more than a
thousand miles. The camp was set up on a hill where the men could conceal
the trucks amongst a line of olive trees and pines. The day was then spent
preparing equipment and explosives while Easonsmith and Peniakoff,
accompanied by the two local tribesmen as guides, went onwards to the
outskirts of Barce to carry out a brief reconnaissance. Having then returned
to the camp, Easonsmith briefed the men during the afternoon. His plan was
for T1 to attack the airfield, while G1 would carry out a diversionary attack
against the barracks just over a mile to the south-west of the town and then
attack the railway station to the south.

Just after dusk the men moved off northwards in the vehicles towards their
final positions, from which they would mount their raids. Unfortunately,
though, they had been spotted several times, not just on the way across the
desert, but also at their camp immediately prior to setting off. On the way
to the town they were challenged at a police checkpoint, but managed to
capture one sentry immediately, while another was shot and killed as the
raiders attacked nearby buildings with grenades.

The vehicles then continued along the main road towards the town with
headlights on, to give the appearance of an Italian convoy and avoid arousing
any suspicion. The journey to the main town took an hour and at one point
they encountered two small enemy tanks that were guarding the road, but
the Chevy was such a sturdy vehicle that the tanks were brushed aside as
the raiders quickly sped through, although the element of surprise had now
clearly gone.

It was around midnight when the raiders arrived at a fork in the road on the
edge of the town. Easonsmith gave the men two hours to complete the raid
and the convoy then split into their two patrols to carry out their individual
tasks. While GI went off to attack the Campo Maddalena barracks and
railway station, Easonsmith roamed the area in his command jeep, seeking
out any targets of opportunity; he would succeed in finding and destroying a
number of vehicles in the town. Meanwhile, Peniakoff covered the approach
from the south, just in case any enemy vehicles came along, and the medical

officer, Captain Dick 'Doc' Lawson, went with the wireless truck to take up a position to the south-east of the town to set up the rendezvous point once the attacks were complete.

Having split from the others, the men of T1 made their way towards the airfield on the northern side of the town. To get there meant using the main road around the eastern side of Barce. It was now dark and the trucks, led by Wilder in his command jeep, were using their lights. Due to such a bold approach the vehicles continued without raising suspicion. They even passed some Italian vehicles coming the other way.

Although the raiding force had been observed as they made their way towards Barce, it was clear that the Italians were not expecting a raid from the main road leading from the town. But the element of surprise could not last forever and, as the patrol approached the airfield, they were challenged by sentries. As each sentry challenged the approaching vehicles he was individually cut down. The patrol then reached the main airfield gates, but these were closed. They were, however, unlocked, and so the trucks quickly passed through and made their way out onto the airfield.

The airfield was home to an Italian bombing wing equipped with Cant Z.1007 medium bombers and a squadron of Caproni Ca.311 light bomber-reconnaissance aircraft. Before the raiders reached the aircraft they came across a truck and trailer carrying a large amount of aviation fuel. As they opened fire, the night sky was suddenly illuminated by a fireball as the fuel truck and trailer exploded.

The men of T1 had undoubtedly caught the Italians totally by surprise, but there was to be no hiding now. They quickly moved on to one of the airfield buildings, which accommodated the food hall and barracks. While some lobbed grenades inside the building, which quickly caught fire and caught the occupants by surprise, others took out more buildings, a hangar and any vehicles they could find. One group then moved on to a fuel dump, and that, too, was quickly destroyed. They all then moved on to the parked aircraft, shooting at each in turn with incendiary and explosive ammunition.

Using a combination of skilled driving at high speed and the darkness to conceal their position, while also taking advantage of the glow from the burning buildings and aircraft, the raiders worked their way around the airfield. In addition to the machine guns and grenades on board the trucks, some of the men were armed with incendiary devices with a timed fuse. One of those was

Corporal Merlyn Craw. He was in the last truck as it entered the airfield and every time they came to an aircraft he jumped out of the truck and placed a device on top of the wing, usually directly on top of the fuel tank, before making a hasty retreat and then diving to the ground as the device exploded, causing the aircraft to erupt in flames. It was extremely hazardous and a tactic that put the individual at great personal risk, but it worked well.

The raiders of T1 spent an hour at the airfield, at the end of which they had left a scene of utter devastation behind them. The defenders had no answer against the raiders. The airfield defences were there to provide protection from an air attack and were not adequate to provide protection from a raid on the ground. It was estimated that the raiders destroyed more than thirty aircraft and damaged several more, most of which belonged to the bomber wing.

Meanwhile, the raiders of G1, led by Dennis, had reached the barracks after stopping briefly to cut telephone lines. The sound of the attack on the airfield could be heard in the distance and so the occupants of the barracks had already been alerted. The raiders quickly took out a group of the enemy and then pumped machine-gun rounds into the surrounding buildings. As they tried to make their escape, two Italian light tanks intervened, one of which pursued the raiding vehicles all the way to the perimeter fence. But the raiders managed to get away, although one of their trucks became separated from the main group and a jeep was lost in an anti-tank ditch.

Both of the attacks had gone well and much as planned, although two of the local guides and a dozen men of the LRDG were missing; three trucks and a jeep had also been lost, while some other vehicles had been damaged. With both patrols having made it to the rendezvous point, the men gathered as much equipment as they could and set off in the remaining vehicles to make their escape. However, two of the vehicles had suffered significant damage, and by now, every enemy unit in the area was looking for them. Furthermore, it would soon be daylight.

By daybreak the raiders were south of Sidi Salim, but they then suddenly came under attack from an enemy ambush. Although they managed to burst their way through under heavy fire, three men were wounded and another truck damaged. Then, having reached a position of relative safety, they transferred stores to another truck and then destroyed three of the damaged vehicles to prevent them from falling into enemy hands.

The raiders were gradually being hunted down. It was now mid-morning, they had been spotted yet again, and for the rest of the day they came under a number of air attacks. The vehicles were picked off one by one and the men strafed as they took whatever cover they could. Lawson and his medical orderlies continued to tend to the wounded, which now included Wilder, who had been hit in both legs, and Peniakoff, who had been wounded during the escape from Barce. Lawson was even reported to have thrown himself across one of the wounded as protection during one strafing attack. When dusk finally fell, it provided the men with a most welcome rest. At least they were safe from attack from the air, but by then another vehicle had broken down. They were now down to just one truck and two jeeps.

By now the thirty-three remaining men were exhausted. Food and water were in short supply and they still had nearly 800 miles to go before reaching the safety of Kufra. With little option, Easonsmith decided to split the survivors into two groups. Lawson was to go on ahead in one of the jeeps and the truck, with another driver and a navigator, in order to evacuate the six wounded, while the remainder would continue on foot. The walking party was to be split into two smaller groups. Easonsmith would lead a group of fourteen with the remaining jeep laden with stores. The other walking group of ten would only be able to take as much water and food as they could carry, but the plan was for them to pick up the spare vehicle that had been left at Bir el-Gerrari on the journey outbound to Barce.

As darkness fell they headed south. Although they subsequently had to abandon the jeep, Lawson and the wounded reached Bir el-Gerrari the following day. From there they moved on to rendezvous with another LRDG patrol at a remote landing ground near the Kalansho Sand Sea, from where they were eventually evacuated by air.

Meanwhile, the two walking groups plodded on. Easonsmith's group covered 8 miles across the desert before unexpectedly meeting up with another LRDG patrol near Bir el-Gerrari three days later. Easonsmith now organized a search for the remaining ten men, who had yet to arrive at the rendezvous. Three days later they found eight of the men but two had become separated from the group. They had fallen behind and, having decided they would be unable to make it to Bir el-Gerrari, had turned northwards instead. They were extremely fortunate. They eventually came across an Arab camp and were subsequently taken as prisoners of war. By then it was a week after the raid, and it had been six days since they had set off on foot. By the time they were taken into captivity, it was estimated they had covered over 150 miles on foot. As things turned out, there were two further survivors from the raid. They had initially been left behind at Barce, but had walked out on foot and were later picked up by another LRDG patrol.

The raid against Barce was a resounding success, particularly the attack on the airfield, which had resulted in thirty-five aircraft being destroyed without the attackers suffering a single casualty. It proved to the Axis that the Allies were capable of carrying out a raid of that type deep in the desert. Although the raiders were spotted on at least two occasions before they carried out their attack, which meant the Italians should have been expecting a raid at some point, the LRDG had still managed to take the defenders by complete surprise and achieve their objectives. The only other losses, apart from the eight wounded, were eleven men taken as prisoners of war.

Operation Caravan was also a demonstration of great physical and mental courage by those who had taken part. In particular, it had been an extremely long and hard journey home. For his exceptional leadership throughout the raid, Jake Easonsmith was awarded the Distinguished Service Order, as was Wilder for leading the raid on the airfield, and, amongst the other awards, were a Military Cross for 'Doc' Lawson and Vladimir Peniakoff, and a Military Medal for Merlyn Craw.

Chapter Nineteen

Basalt

3/4 October 1942

Following the disaster of Aquatint, it was important for the Small Scale Raiding Force to bounce back as soon as possible and to quickly get back to its winning ways. Yet no one could possibly have imagined that their next raid, to the small island of Sark, would have longer-term repercussions, stretching far beyond the quiet shores of the Channel Islands.

Despite the devastating loss of his closest friend, Gus March-Phillipps, Geoffrey Appleyard remained undaunted when he was given command of the SSRF on promotion to the rank of major. He knew that life had to go on and that the raids should continue; it was what Gus would have expected. Appleyard had understandably decided to leave the northern coastline of France well alone and for the next raid, called Operation Basalt, he decided to conduct an offensive reconnaissance of the small Channel Island of Sark. In addition to the reconnaissance of the island, he wanted to capture some German prisoners and to recover an SOE agent who had been working there.

The German strength on Sark was known to include a heavy machine-gun section, a light mortar group and an anti-tank platoon. Appleyard had recovered from his fractured tibia, suffered during an earlier mission, and was now fit enough to lead the raid. Furthermore, he had better knowledge of the island than anyone as he had been there on family holidays before the war. He decided it would require a raiding party of twelve: seven original members of the SSRF (Appleyard, Anders Lassen, Patrick Dudgeon, Graham Young, Colin Ogden-Smith and his younger brother Bruce, and Corporal Edgar) and five newcomers from 12 Commando, led by Captain Philip Pinckney, who had joined the unit following the losses from Aquatint.

Two attempts to carry out the raid during the third week of September had proved unsuccessful due to poor weather. The second attempt in particular, which had taken place on the night of 19/20 September, had proved most frustrating, as the MTB had reached Sark with insufficient time for the men to go ashore; the memories of Aquatint were still fresh in their minds and so there was no point taking unnecessary risks. The moon conditions then meant that Basalt had to be postponed for nearly two weeks, but finally, on 3 October, approval was given for another attempt to go ahead with the raid.

The same group of twelve boarded the MTB, the *Little Pisser*, at Portland, and soon after 7.00 pm they left the harbour. Making their usual final approach to the island on the auxiliary engine, it was around 11.00 pm when they dropped anchor off Sark and went ashore.

Young was left to guard the Goatley, while another member of the group went off to find the SOE agent. Meanwhile, the main raiding party, with Lassen out in front, clambered up a steep path to the top of the cliff and then along a ridge known as the Hog's Back. It was pitch black, which made progress across the difficult terrain quite slow at times, but the men moved as quickly as they could. After coming across some barbed wire fencing, which was quickly cut, the raiders then heard the sound of a patrol approaching in the distance.

It was not the time to start a battle and so the commandos took cover while the enemy passed nearby. Having successfully avoided the patrol, they next came across a small group of houses about a mile inland. After watching one large house, Appleyard was certain there were no enemy to be found and so he and one of the men went inside. They entered the house to find an elderly lady. Both the occupant and Appleyard were taken by surprise, but somehow the lady remained completely calm, despite having come face to face with two commandos late at night. After Appleyard had explained who they were, she informed him that the Germans were using a local hotel nearby as their headquarters and were also using its annex for accommodation.

By now the raiding party had been on the island for two hours and time was short. They made their way quickly to the hotel and arrived to find just one sentry outside. Lassen was given the task of removing him and, after observing how long it took the sentry to patrol up and down, he crept forward alone to take him out: the silence was broken by a muffled scream. The raiders then entered the annex. Inside they came across a hallway with six rooms where the enemy soldiers were presumably asleep. Appleyard gave each of his men one room to take. They then stormed the rooms at the same time and, one by one, each commando came back out into the corridor with his prisoner.

There were five prisoners altogether and the commandos quickly led them from the annex and took them outside, their hands tied behind their backs. Until that point everything had gone well, but one prisoner then started shouting; the prisoners were not gagged. The others saw this as their opportunity to try and make a break. One prisoner managed to get free, shouting and making as much noise as he could, but he was immediately shot as he made a break back towards the hotel.

By now more Germans were pouring out of the hotel and, when the raiders saw how many there were, they decided to get away. During the rumpus that followed, three other prisoners were shot dead. The only prisoner left alive had seen what had happened to the others and was now stiff with fright. Dragging him with them, the commandos made their way as quickly as they could back towards the Goatley. The whole island now seemed to be awake, but fortunately the raiders found the Goatley without any trouble and quickly got it out to sea, paddling towards the *Little Pisser* as fast as they could. The MTB was ready and waiting for them, the noise coming from the island suggesting to the crew that it was important to get away as quickly as they could. By the time they were heading back across the Channel it was 3.45 am, and three hours later they arrived safely back at Portland.

In the end, the raiders took just the one surviving prisoner with them back to England. Although the raid had been a typical hit-and-run for the SSRF, it would have a much longer and far more significant effect. In the aftermath of Basalt the Germans issued a communiqué stating that German soldiers had been shot while resisting having their hands tied, thereby contravening international law. This then led to Hitler issuing his Kommandobefehl (Commando Order) just two weeks later, stating that all Allied commandos encountered by German forces should be killed immediately, even if in uniform or if attempting to surrender. The communiqué also made it clear that failure to carry out the order would be considered to be an act of negligence, itself punishable under German military law.

In the end, this order would itself be found illegal, and at the Nuremberg trials after the war German officers who had carried out executions under this order were themselves found guilty of war crimes. Nonetheless, from now on the rules by which the Germans would play when it came to the treatment of captured commandos had changed. The British commandos now knew how they could expect to be treated if they were ever captured; not that it seemed to make any difference to the men as they had always known, and accepted, the risks they took.

Chapter Twenty

Cockleshell Heroes

7–12 December 1942

Of all the daring raids of the Second World War, few were more physically demanding than the one carried out by a small unit of Royal Marines on enemy shipping in the German-occupied French port of Bordeaux. The raid, later immortalized on screen in the 1955 film *The Cockleshell Heroes*, took place in December 1942 and involved a dozen men canoeing from the Gironde estuary, in the Bay of Biscay, 60 miles up the river under the cover of darkness and then attacking cargo ships in the port with limpet mines before making their escape overland to Spain. It was yet another audacious raid carried out during the war, but sadly was to end in tragedy.

In 1942 the port of Bordeaux in the south-west of France was a major destination for German blockade-running cargo ships carrying vital goods, such as rubber and raw materials, to help the Nazi war effort. The ships arrived at the port from the Western Approaches via the Bay of Biscay and by sailing up the navigable Gironde estuary, the largest estuary in Western Europe.

Formed from the meeting of the rivers Dordogne and Garonne, just downstream of Bordeaux, the Gironde is approximately 50 miles long and varies in width from about 2 miles at its narrowest, up to 7 miles at its widest point. During the war both the estuary and river were regularly patrolled by up to thirty enemy ships using the port. Furthermore, the river has always had very strong tidal patterns, and even today great care is needed when travelling along it in any kind of vessel.

A daring plan to attack enemy shipping at Bordeaux, by canoeing up the length of the river, was first submitted in September 1942 by the commander of a new and specialist Royal Marine unit, Major Herbert Hasler. Better known as 'Blondie', Hasler was 28 years old and a canoeing specialist. He had been in the Royal Marines for ten years and had earlier served at Scapa Flow and during the campaign in Norway. It was because of his canoeing expertise that he was given command of the new Royal Marines Boom Patrol Detachment (RMBPD) when it had been formed just two months before. His detachment of thirty-four men had been selected because they were all eager to engage the enemy and were indifferent to personal danger, but also because of their intelligence and ability to operate in conditions that others would not even contemplate.

From their base at Lumps Fort on Portsea Island, part of the original eighteenth-century defences for the naval base at Portsmouth, the RMBPD was able to train in the Solent opposite their base and by patrolling Portsmouth's harbour booms at night. Keen to get his unit on operations as soon as possible, Hasler's plan to attack shipping at Bordeaux involved just three canoes. They would be dropped off by a submarine near the Gironde estuary and then paddle the 60 miles up the river at night, avoiding the patrolling vessels as they went and lying up under cover by day, until they reached the port. When they reached the port it was hoped the small team could sink anywhere up to a dozen cargo ships by using limpet mines, before escaping overland to Spain.

Hasler received permission from Combined Operations to carry out the raid on the understanding that the size of the attacking force was doubled and that Hasler would not be allowed to take part: his knowledge and expertise were considered too great for him to be risked in such a raid. While he was pleased to learn that the raid could go ahead, Hasler was not content to remain behind and, having then submitted his reasons for inclusion, he was eventually granted permission to lead the raid.

Much of the training was carried out in the lochs of Scotland and was, unsurprisingly, extremely tough. Not only was there canoe handling to master, there was also training in how to manage limpet mines and how to get off a submarine. Also, because the men's only chance of returning to England was by an overland route to Spain, there was instruction in how to evade enemy forces and, if need be, how to escape once captured.

Brand-new Mark II semi-rigid two-man canoes called 'Cockles' were selected for the raid, with each named after a fish: *Cachalot*, *Catfish*, *Coalfish*, *Conger*, *Crayfish* and *Cuttlefish*. The Cockles were 15 feet (4.6m) in length and had a flat bottom with canvas sides. When collapsed they had to fit through the submarine hatch, which was just 2 feet (0.6m) wide. Each crew was equipped with three sets of paddles and camouflage netting, and to help with navigation they carried a compass and a reel to test the depth of the water. They also carried items such as waterproof watches, a torch, a repair bag should their canoe get damaged, a fishing line and personal rations, including fresh water, for up to six days. Their personal weapons were a Colt .45 pistol and a Fairbairn–Sykes commando fighting knife, and each crew carried eight limpet mines to use against the enemy cargo ships, with a spanner to activate the mines and a magnet to hold the canoe against the side of the ship.

The operation was given the codename 'Frankton', and the twelve men of the RMBPD's 1 Section were selected for the raid, plus one man who would act as a reserve. The twelve men were divided into two divisions, 'A' and 'B', which would work independently to increase the chance of success. 'A' Division was to be led by Hasler in *Catfish*, with 20-year-old Marine Bill Sparks, best described as a wiry young cockney with an infectious laugh. Hasler's two other crews were Lance Corporal Albert Laver with Marine Bill Mills in *Crayfish*, and Lance Corporal George Sheard with Marine David Moffatt in *Conger*. The three Cockles of 'B' Division were to be led by 21-year-old Lieutenant Jack Mackinnon, a Glaswegian, with Marine Jim Conway, just 20 years old, in *Cuttlefish*. The two other crews were Sergeant Sammy Wallace with Marine Bob Ewart in *Coalfish*, and Marine Bill Ellery with Marine Eric Fisher in *Cachalot*.

At this stage only Hasler and his unit's second-in-command, Captain Jock Stewart, knew what the mission was, but the men had understandably started to speculate about what their target would be, with the German mighty warship *Tirpitz*, at that time operating out of northern Norway, considered the most likely.

Hasler was kept informed of the comings and goings of ships at Bordeaux through a number of intelligence briefings. He was confident they could get into the port and was sure the team could do their job, but his concern was more about what would happen after the raid. The escape plan to Spain relied on others, not least the French Resistance, and this would always remain outside of his control. Furthermore, unbeknown to Hasler, or to anyone else at Combined Operations at the time, the SOE was in the process of putting together their own operation inside the port at the same time. As things would turn out, the SOE was in no position to mount a raid at the end of 1942 and so there would be no impact on Frankton, but the fact remains that two separate organizations were planning a similar raid in the same location and at a similar time, which demonstrates a lack of co-ordination between British organizations conducting special operations at the time.

The submarine HMS *Tuna* had been allocated to take Hasler and his team to the Gironde estuary. Finally, it was time to go, and on a cold, damp morning on 30 November, the marines went aboard. Then, with her cargo of six Cockles and all the raiders, the *Tuna* slipped away from her mother ship, HMS *Forth*, and headed down the Holy Loch. It was only now that Hasler briefed his men on what lay ahead.

The mission was scheduled to start on 6 December, but bad weather and the need to navigate through a minefield meant its start was delayed until the following day, by which time the *Tuna* had reached a position about 10 miles from the mouth of the estuary. Using an adapted hoist arrangement slung over the submarine's gun in front of the conning tower, the fully laden Cockles were lowered into the water one by one. But although the crews had practised the disembarkation procedure many times, *Cachalot* got caught as it was passed up through the hatch. With its canvas ripped, and with no time to carry out a repair, the decision was reluctantly made to leave Ellery and Fisher behind.

Hasler was now left with just five canoes to mount the raid. It was early evening as they set off north-east towards the estuary, with *Catfish* in front. Fortunately, the sea was relatively calm, but it was still tough going. The pattern had been set for the men to rest for five minutes every hour, but it still took all their effort to press on. By midnight the men had been paddling for three and a half hours. Hasler had noted the sea becoming rougher as the flood tide pulled the canoes towards the estuary. What was now worrying him, though, was the sound of rough water ahead. This was where the increased volume of water was crashing over the shallows and causing extremely hazardous conditions for all but the most experienced sea campaigners – even by day in an ordinary boat, let alone in a canoe at night.

This had not been expected. Even more worrying for Hasler was the fact that these extreme conditions were not something his relatively inexperienced canoeists had been trained to deal with. He instantly knew they were in trouble, but they simply had to press on. He had briefed his men before they had left the submarine that as long as there remained just one canoe afloat then the mission had to be carried out, and that nothing should stop them. Shouting instructions as best he could, and warning his men to expect waves of up to four feet high and from all directions, he instructed them to try and hit the rough water head-on. It would be the only way of getting through.

Hasler led off in *Catfish* to face the hazardous waters ahead. All the men could do was to try and make their way through and then meet up on the other side. *Catfish* hit the frothing and turbulent waves bow on, the flimsy canoe being tossed around in the water. It was like nothing Hasler and Sparks had ever experienced before, but somehow they hung on. The little Cockle proved remarkably robust and, fortunately, the cockpit cover remained fastened to prevent water from flooding the canoe and causing it to capsize.

An ordeal that must have seemed to take hours was over in a matter of minutes, and *Catfish* was through. All Hasler could do now was to wait for the rest of his crews. One by one the Cockles appeared. Soon there were three other canoes, but there was no sign of the fourth. It was *Coalfish* that had disappeared: the canoe of Wallace and Ewart. There was simply no sign of them. Having considered all possibilities of what might have happened to the crew, Hasler knew there was nothing he could do to help. He knew the rest of them had to press on.

After just four hours Hasler was down to four crews. He had already lost one-third of his raiding force and they had not yet even entered the river. Leaving Wallace and Ewart to their fate, Hasler led the men on, but their troubles were far from over. Soon after passing the island of Cordouan, marking the entrance to the estuary, and just an hour after experiencing the first tidal rush, a second rush of water descended upon them and this time it was even worse than before.

The crews barely had time to brace themselves as waves of up to five feet crashed into them. The Cockles were tossed about once again as the waves caught them, dragging them out of control as the flow of turbulent water took hold. It was all but impossible to resist or counter, no matter what the men tried. One of the canoes, *Conger*, capsized, leaving Sheard and Moffatt clinging desperately to its structure in the maelstrom. The remaining Cockles quickly went to their aid. Then, with the two marines clinging on to the other canoes, Hasler and the others, assisted by the pull of the tide, set about dragging them and the capsized canoe towards the shore and to safety.

For Sheard and Moffatt it was a desperate struggle to hold on in the bitterly cold water, but somehow they did just that. It had been impossible to drain the waterlogged *Conger*, and its weight was now beginning to prove too much to drag any further. They were getting close to the shore around the Pointe de Grave; their main navigation feature, marking the northerly tip of the southern side of the estuary, was just a few hundred yards away. Fortunately, its lighthouse was more of a navigation feature than a searchlight but, nonetheless, the men were clearly exposed. Any sentry looking in their direction would surely have seen them. Furthermore, the tide was dragging them more and more, and, with so much weight in the water, it was making it impossible to reach the shore.

The whole mission was now in danger of being jeopardized. The marines struggled on in the heavy current, attempting to make their way down the southern bank of the river towards the small fishing village of Le Verdon-sur-Mer, but Hasler decided they could no longer continue as they were. Not only did the mission take priority, but he knew it was only a matter of time before hypothermia would put the lives of his men in the water at risk. Faced with no other option, he ordered the sinking of the *Conger* and instructed Sheard and Moffatt to swim the mile and a half ashore and to take their chances on land. Sadly, the two men would not make it. The body of 22-year-old David Moffatt, along with the *Conger*, was found ten days later 60 miles to the north, when it was washed ashore in the Bay of Biscay. George Sheard's body was never found.

It was now the early hours of 8 December. Hasler had already lost half of his force and they had only just entered the Gironde. It had been the force of the sea that had depleted his force, not the enemy. Hasler now faced a further problem. He could see three enemy ships ahead, which looked like small destroyers, lying not far off the jetty at Verdon-sur-Mer. He knew they would have lookouts on board, and no doubt the jetty would be patrolled. He also knew that daylight would be upon them in just a few hours and that he would need to find somewhere safe to go ashore, but first the canoes would have to pass the three destroyers. Hasler told his men they would have to proceed one at a time, keeping as low a profile as possible and separated by some distance to reduce any sound as they paddled. They were to meet up again a hundred yards past the last ship.

Slowly the Cockles made their way past the ships in almost complete silence. Safely past the last vessel, Hasler and Sparks waited for the others to appear. The first Cockle, *Crayfish*, soon appeared, but there was no sign of *Cuttlefish*. Having waited as long as they dared, Hasler decided to continue. He had not heard any gunfire or seen any searchlights from the ships. Furthermore, the water was not rough and so he had no reason to suspect that anything had happened to *Cuttlefish*, but it was nearly dawn and they could not hang around any longer: Mackinnon and Conway would have to continue on their own.

Hasler was now down to just two crews; one-third of his original force. Most significantly though, there were just one-third the number of limpets that had been allocated for the raid; moreover, the first night had not even ended, and there was still a long way to go. The surviving pair of Cockles continued along the river before finally resting at a sandy point along what was mainly a mudbank near Saint-Vivien-de-Médoc. The men managed to drag their canoes ashore and hide them amongst the reeds using their camouflage netting, before settling down to a most welcome meal from their rations. So far they had travelled more than 20 miles but it had been far harder, and more costly, than expected.

Taking it in turns to keep lookout, the men set about getting some well-earned rest. What they had not realized, though, was that the seemingly quiet place they had chosen was a popular spot for the locals in the morning. It soon became obvious they had been spotted and so Hasler took the difficult decision to approach the locals and to speak to them as best he could in the hope they would realize he was British and would not report what they had seen. Using a mix of French and English, the locals suggested it was best if the raiders moved a short distance away, where it was less likely they would be spotted. All Hasler could do now was hope the locals were true to their word and would not report what they had seen.

The four raiders spent the rest of the day anxiously keeping a lookout, almost expecting the Germans to appear at any moment. People came and went close to their hiding place, but the Germans did not come. However, everything else seemed to be going against Hasler and his small team. It had still been less than twenty-four hours since they had left the submarine, but not only were they down to just two canoes, the local French population knew they were there. He had no idea whether he could trust them. Certainly the ones he had met had not tried to raise the alarm, but he knew that locals would talk and that not all of them could be trusted. Furthermore, he was completely unaware of the fate of his other three crews and so had to assume that some of his men may have been picked up by the Germans and their mission may already have been compromised.

That night it was time to move off once more. It was bitterly cold out on the river but, making the best of the high water, the marines managed to cover another 20 miles during the night. They were now about halfway along the river and at the point where it runs due south towards Bordeaux.

Hasler decided to spend the second day hiding up on the eastern bank about 2 miles to the north of the Île de Patiras. Fortunately, the day passed without incident and it was barely dusk when they left their hiding place to set off once again. They knew that the next leg of their journey would be difficult, not least because of the number of small islands in the river, each possibly manned by lookouts. They would have to move as quickly and quietly as possible, taking full advantage of the tidal flow whenever possible.

They should have waited until after dark before making their move because, just as they were reaching the river, they heard a shout. A French farmer nearby had spotted the four marines and so Hasler again found himself having to confront one of the locals. Fortunately, the farmer was friendly, and as the marines moved off once more, they felt confident he could be trusted. He could.

Hasler led the canoes southwards. As they crossed the shipping lanes towards the river's western bank, using the islands as some protection, their journey was interrupted by the occasional sound of boats nearby and the two Cockles had to quickly pull into the reeds and then move off later when they felt it safe to do so.

By the early hours of 10 December the two Cockles were passing through the narrowest stretch of water, alongside the Île Verte, that runs for several miles down towards the Île Cazeau, where the Garonne and Dordogne rivers meet to become the Gironde. The river along this lengthy stretch is just a couple of hundred yards or so wide.

It was a crucial part of their journey where they were at the most vulnerable, but they managed to cover a further 15 miles during the night before Hasler knew they had to find somewhere to hide, otherwise they could be seen by anyone on either bank. They found a place just as day was breaking, but it was far from ideal. There was little cover and so the men spent an anxious day in hiding. Unbeknown to them, Mackinnon and Conway were not far away. They had become separated from the other two Cockles while passing the three enemy destroyers near Verdun-sur-Mer on the opening night. Hasler had been right not to worry that anything had happened to the *Cuttlefish* when it failed to appear after the Cockles had passed the enemy ships: Mackinnon and Conway had simply not been able to spot the other two canoes in the darkness and vast expanse of water. They had, therefore, continued alone, and were now resting on the Île Cazeau, just a few hundred yards from the other two crews.

While the crews of the three remaining Cockles were resting and preparing for moving on that night, albeit in two different locations, two of their colleagues were facing death. Sammy Wallace and Bob Ewart of *Coalfish* had been the first crew to disappear after leaving the submarine. They had capsized during the first raging maelstrom while heading towards the estuary. Although they had managed to swim ashore, finally landing on a beach near Pointe de Grave, they were exhausted and freezing cold, and had lost all of their equipment. With nothing but what they were wearing they decided to seek help from the first house they could find and just hope that the French occupants would be friendly and prepared to help. Having found the buildings on the headland deserted, they eventually found a house with a light on. They took their chance and knocked, but unbeknown to them the house was occupied by German soldiers who were part of the infantry garrison guarding the coastal area. Wallace and Ewart's claim they were sailors washed up ashore was simply not believed. Their camouflaged smocks and commando insignia were all the evidence the Germans needed. Now, after a period of interrogation, the two men faced death in line with Hitler's Kommandobefehl that had stated all captured commandos were to be executed. Sergeant Samuel Wallace and Marine Robert Ewart were executed the following evening. Their bodies were never recovered, but Wallace and Ewart had evidently kept silent during the last hours of their lives. The Germans did not suspect there was still a raiding force on the river and that cargo shipping in the port at Bordeaux was the target.

Hasler now led his two Cockles off once more. It was early evening as they made their way down the Garonne towards Bordeaux. That night they covered just over 10 miles before finding a good hiding place on the western bank of the river opposite the port of Bassens. From their hide they could see two cargo ships at Bassens, which would make suitable targets if need be, and during the day they could monitor shipping going in and out of the main port at Bordeaux.

That night they would carry out their attack. Hasler's plan was for him and Sparks, in *Catfish*, to proceed to the main port at Bordeaux by following the western bank of the river, while Laver and Mills, in *Crayfish*, would cross the river to follow the eastern bank down towards the docks. In the event that Laver and Mills could not find a suitable target in the main port they were to return to attack the two cargo ships at Bassens. After their respective attacks, each crew would then make their own way home.

Soon after 9.00 pm that evening, the two crews wished each other luck and pushed out into the river. They had set their limpets to go off around 7.00 am the following morning and so they now had the night to continue the final part of their long journey and to then locate suitable targets to attack.

Hasler and Sparks arrived at the main port to find the docks at Bordeaux fully illuminated. There was no blackout. Despite all the intelligence they had received before departing for their mission, this had come as a complete surprise. It would make progress difficult, but they simply had to find a way. Clinging to the shadows of the dockside, *Catfish* crawled forward. Ignoring some of the ships deemed unsuitable for attack, Hasler spotted what he was looking for, a cargo vessel of around 7,000 tons called the MS *Tannenfels*.

While Sparks kept the canoe steady against the ship using the magnetic holding device, Hasler placed the first limpet near the bow and below the waterline using his placing rod. The two marines then paddled quietly towards the stern and placed two more limpets as they went. It was now time to find their next target and they soon spotted another cargo vessel moored up against the side of a tanker at the quayside. It would present a good target as they made their escape and so the two men paddled off in search of another target to attack first.

Time would soon be against them and so they did not have long. Struggling to find another cargo vessel, they decided to place two limpets on a German patrol vessel of some 5,000 tons. Then, having successfully laid their charges, they paddled back to the cargo ship moored alongside the tanker. Using whatever shadows they could find they proceeded back towards the ships as quickly as they could. Having reached their targets, they placed two limpets on the cargo vessel, the *Dresden*, and one on the tanker in the area of its engine room. With all their charges placed, Hasler and Sparks paddled silently away.

Meanwhile, Laver and Mills had made their way towards the main port on the eastern bank. Having arrived, they could find no better targets than the two cargo ships back at Bassens and so they returned to place their limpets: five on the large cargo ship SS *Alabama* and three on the smaller SS *Portland*. Fortunately, there was no sign of the enemy and, having placed all their charges, Laver and Mills quickly paddled away.

Hasler and Sparks were making their way back up the river towards the Île Cazeau when, quite remarkably, and totally by chance, they heard what sounded like another canoe. Using a whistle designed to make the mewing sound of a seagull, Sparks called out. The reply he got was quickly followed by the sight of *Crayfish* coming out of the darkness. The marines then paddled the two Cockles back northwards under the cover of darkness, each minute taking them further from where they had laid their charges, before eventually landing past the town of Blaye.

The two crews now bid each other farewell and wished each other good luck. They would have to take their chances in pairs, because staying together as four would rouse far too much suspicion. First, the crew of *Catfish* landed on the eastern bank, followed by the crew of *Crayfish* further to the north. After sinking their canoes, the two crews then set off independently for the Spanish border.

It was around 7.00 am when the first of the limpets exploded. The peace and quiet of dawn was suddenly shattered by the sound of an explosion coming from the quayside at Bassens. Over the next six hours all the limpets exploded, five twisting the hull of the *Alabama* and causing water to pour into the vessel, although the ship managed to stay afloat. Moments later, two limpets that had been attached to the *Portland* became detached and exploded as they hit the bottom. The third limpet had remained attached and exploded nearly three hours later, causing water to burst into the ship.

It was more than two hours later when the first of the limpets exploded in the main port of Bordeaux. Thereafter, there were more explosions as the mines exploded randomly. Two limpets attached to the *Tannenfels* exploded and caused the ship to list by more than 20 degrees. Two more exploded on the stern of the *Dresden* within minutes of each other, which caused serious leaks on board and immediately put the ship out of action. One of the limpets attached to the tanker also exploded, causing damage to its stern and fire damage to the ship. Last of all, and more than two hours after the first explosion at Bordeaux, the limpets attached to the German patrol boat exploded after detaching free from the vessel. For several hours there had been chaos and confusion at the two ports, resulting in the ships requiring repairs that lasted for several days.

Having left the river, Hasler and Sparks made their way inland. They successfully evaded capture and, with help from the French Resistance, they eventually made their way along the celebrated Marie-Claire escape line through Lyon and Marseilles before they crossed the Pyrenees into Spain. Word of their safe arrival in Spain was not confirmed until the end of March 1943, and within two months both men had returned to England.

Their colleagues, however, were not so fortunate. Laver and Mills had initially made good progress, but were caught five days after leaving the river. Mackinnon and Conway had also been captured. After leaving the Île Cazeau on the evening of 10 December they had hit an obstacle in the water near the confluence of the Garonne and Dordogne. The *Cuttlefish* was damaged to the extent that it soon sank, with all its explosives on board, leaving Mackinnon and Conway to swim ashore. Although they managed to evade capture for several days, the two men were eventually caught.

With Sammy Wallace and Bob Ewart having been executed within days of their capture, the outcome for the remaining four marines was bleak. There has been post-war speculation about what happened to them, but it appears they were all eventually taken to the notorious Fresnes Prison in Paris, where they were executed on 23 March 1943. The bodies of Jack Mackinnon, Jim Conway, Albert Laver and Bill Mills were never found.

The story of the Cockleshell Heroes rightly lives on, but it was an extremely costly mission. Of the ten men that left the submarine to carry out the raid, two drowned and six were executed. Only 'Blondie' Hasler and Bill Sparks survived. Both were deservedly recognized for their part in the raid. Hasler received the Distinguished Service Order and Sparks the Distinguished Service Medal. And rightly so. Few DSOs or DSMs can have been harder earned. Admiral Louis Mountbatten, the commander of Combined Operations, later described the raid as '*the most courageous and imaginative of all the raids ever carried out by men of Combined Operations.*'

Chapter Twenty-One

Chindits

February–April 1943

Regarded by many as one of the founders of modern-day guerrilla warfare, Orde Wingate was a quite remarkable man. Having developed his ideas of using unconventional and irregular forces to carry out raids behind enemy lines during his time in East Africa in 1941 – ideas that would soon be adopted by Special Forces operating in the North African campaign – Wingate's deep penetrations into Burma during 1943 would influence British military thinking for many years to come.

When the Japanese invaded Burma in January 1942, Wingate was offered to the Commander-in-Chief India, General Sir Archibald Wavell, as it was thought there might be a role for his irregular style of warfare in the jungle. When Wingate arrived in the Far East he was tasked with organizing guerrilla warfare in Burma by carrying out long-range penetrations behind enemy lines. Wingate believed that troops supplied from the air could operate for long periods in the jungle and could disrupt the enemy's lines of communication while also causing great havoc by operating behind enemy lines.

While not everyone agreed with Wingate's ideas or tactics, Wavell was intrigued and so he gave Wingate a new brigade of troops to create a long-range penetration unit. Wingate's new brigade, the 77th Indian Infantry Brigade, formed in the area around Jhansi in northern India during the summer of 1942 and soon became known as the Chindits: the word being a somewhat corrupted version of the name of a mythical Burmese lion, the *chinthe*.

Half of the Chindits were British and made up of men from the 13th Battalion the King's Liverpool Regiment and men from the former Bush Warfare School in Burma, which were formed into 142 Commando Company. The other half of the brigade consisted of the 3rd Battalion of the 2nd King Edward VII's Own Gurkha Rifles, a rifle regiment of the British Indian Army, and the 2nd Battalion the Burma Rifles, a composite unit formed from depleted battalions of Burmese troops that had retreated to India.

The standard British Army brigade and battalion structures were considered unsuitable for what Wingate had in mind and so he initially reorganized his force into eight columns, although this would later be revised to seven when carrying out operations. Each column was large enough to be capable of inflicting a heavy blow on the enemy while being small enough to disperse into the jungle and evade capture if outnumbered. Each column, therefore, consisted of an infantry rifle company armed with three 2-inch mortars and nine Bren light machine guns, a support group armed with heavier weapons, including two Vickers machine guns and two light anti-aircraft guns, and a reconnaissance platoon from the Burma Rifles, plus a sabotage group from the Commando Company.

Wingate also recognized the importance of air support, communications and medical support, and so small detachments of each were attached to the column's headquarters. The heavy equipment, such as heavy weapons, radios, ammunition and food, were carried on mules, and so more than fifty mule handlers were attached to each column. Each British column numbered just over 300 men, while the Gurkha columns had about 70 more. Two or more columns were commanded by a group headquarters, with the whole force commanded by Wingate's brigade headquarters.

Wingate took charge of the brigade's training in the jungles of central India. His men were to become experts in long-range penetration missions deep behind enemy lines. He not only had to prepare his men for guerrilla warfare against the Japanese, but teach them how to survive in the jungle. A training centre was set up at Saugor in the state of Madhya Pradesh, with much of the training carried out during the rainy season when conditions were at their toughest. The men got used to penetrating the jungle on foot with their main tactic being that of surprise. Even though there were mules to carry the heavier equipment, each man was required to carry more than 70lb of personal equipment. This was made up of his weapon (a rifle or Sten gun), ammunition, grenades, a machete or Gurkha kukri knife, a groundsheet and other personal items, plus enough rations for seven days. The men were also taught how to be resupplied from the air, with stores being dropped by transport aircraft, and how to make use of close air support instead of artillery.

Early training methods were unconventional and not always popular amongst the officers. They also proved too hard for many of the men, who were simply not used to operating under such conditions. A very high sick rate amongst the men, sometimes as high as 70 per cent, led to many having to be replaced by new drafts from elsewhere in the army. But Wingate had the support of Wavell and so his training methods and style of leadership never came under any close scrutiny.

By the end of 1942 the Chindits were ready to commence their first penetration into Burma. The plan was for Wingate's brigade to be part of a co-ordinated operation, with the army, into northern Burma, but when the planned offensive was cancelled, Wingate persuaded Wavell to allow him to proceed into Burma anyway. Wingate successfully argued that the Japanese needed to be disrupted and that deep penetrating raids behind enemy lines could only be perfected over time by actually carrying them out, rather than conducting yet more training.

Under the name of Operation Longcloth, Wingate and his 3,000 Chindits set out from Imphal on 8 February 1943. Five days later they crossed the Chindwin River, the largest tributary of Burma's main river, the Irrawaddy, where the brigade divided into two main groups.

1 Group, led by Lieutenant Colonel Leigh Alexander, the commander of the 3rd Battalion 2nd Gurkha Rifles, and totalling about 1,000 men supported by 250 mules, went south. Alexander had two Gurkha columns: 1 Column led by Major George Dunlop, formerly of the Royal Scots, and 2 Column led by Major Arthur Emmett of the Gurkha Rifles. Once the group had proceeded far enough to the south, the plan was for the two columns to swing eastwards, with the task of deceiving the enemy into believing that their group was the main British attack. They openly followed local trails and paths, and even received a large air drop as a way of alerting the Japanese to their position.

On 3 March they arrived at their main target, the railway at Kyaikthin. Dunlop's column was tasked with destroying a railway bridge while Emmett's, accompanied by Alexander's headquarters, would continue on to the railway station under the cover of darkness. However, the jungle made radio communications difficult and the two groups soon lost contact with each other. Unbeknown to Alexander and Emmett there was a Japanese ambush lying in wait on both sides of the railway embankment and 2 Column was about to stumble across it. The guides out in front of the column could do nothing as a large explosion signalled the start of the battle. Japanese machine guns then rained bullets down on the Chindits while grenades were lobbed into the fray. The battle then descended into hand-to-hand fighting, with bayonets and kukris flashing in the moonlight. It was carnage.

Alexander managed to extract his headquarters from the battle and now decided to head eastwards to the planned rendezvous with Dunlop's column. Four days later they met up and Alexander was able press on towards the Irrawaddy River. For Emmett, however, it was a different story. His column had been badly mauled. Those who had survived the encounter at Kyaikthin made their way back west towards the Chindwin and eventually back to India.

Meanwhile, the second group, 2 Group, had crossed the Chindwin and proceeded eastwards. It was a much larger force of around 2,000 men supported by 850 mules. Commanded by Lieutenant Colonel S. A. Cooke, formerly of the Lincolnshire Regiment and now attached to the King's, it had five columns: 3 Column led by Major Michael Calvert of the Royal Engineers; 4 Column led by Major Philip Conron of the Gurkha Rifles; 5 Column by Major Bernie Ferguson of the Black Watch; 7 Column was led by Major K. D. Gilkes of the King's; and 8 Column was led by Major Walter Scott, also of the King's. The columns were reinforced by 6 Column, which had been broken up to bring the others back to full combat strength, and the 2nd Burma Rifles, commanded by Lieutenant Colonel Lyndon Wheeler, was also attached to the group.

Having crossed the Chindwin, each column moved independently. This gave the columns flexibility, mobility, independence and security, and meant that they did not have to rely on each other. They could go anywhere they wanted and would be difficult to hunt down. Each column had its own task and was to be resupplied from the air by a detachment of DC-3 Dakotas of 31 Squadron.

Two of the columns, those led by Calvert and Ferguson, proceeded towards the main railway in Burma that ran north–south through the country. Calvert, known to his men as 'Mad Mike', had initially been commissioned into the Royal Engineers, but more recently had commanded the Bush Warfare School in Burma, where he trained officers and men to lead Chinese guerrillas in their war against Japan. On 4 March, Calvert's column reached the valley containing the railway linking Mandalay and Indaw. His men successfully demolished the track in seventy places, as well as destroying key railway bridges. Two days later Ferguson's column arrived and did more of the same.

Although the railway was only temporarily disabled, the attacks by the two columns had proved a valuable point to the enemy. Until now the Japanese had been led to believe that the Chindits they had earlier encountered in the jungle were nothing more than small groups gathering intelligence. It was only after the attacks on the railway that they realized the size of the British force now operating behind their lines and the fact that these forces were capable of carrying out many forms of guerrilla warfare.

The Japanese had been caught by surprise and this now meant that valuable resources would have to be diverted away from major units for the protection of vital assets. They had also failed to realize that this northern group was being resupplied from the air, so much of the Japanese effort had gone into cutting their land supply chain from the west.

Although two of his columns were forced to withdraw to India because of casualties suffered during attacks by the Japanese (4 Column had now withdrawn from the northern group in addition to 2 Column from the southern group), Wingate decided to take the rest of his force deeper into Burma. Spurred on by the success against the Burmese railway, he decided to cross the main Irrawaddy River.

The Chindits crossed the Irrawaddy using whatever means they could. The river was a mile wide in places and so it meant commandeering local boats so that the men could cross in small groups. Conditions on the other side of the river were extremely hard. There were large areas where there were no established roads or paths and the men were left to hack their way through dense jungle with their machetes or kukris. There were even occasions when elephants were used. Not only were large expanses very dry and inhospitable, they found the areas where it was possible to operate full of Japanese. Unsurprisingly, the roads were regularly used by enemy vehicles and British supplies dropped from the air were often intercepted by the Japanese as they became more familiar with how the Chindits were operating.

Wingate knew the return journey to India would be more hazardous, as the two major rivers would be patrolled by enemy forces, but still he pressed on. His rules of the jungle were also hard. He had always directed that wounded or sick men would have to be left behind, although such rules were not always adhered to by those officers expected to carry them out: wounded or sick men tended to be carried on mules, or left behind in villages under the care of the locals – anything but leave them to the Japanese.

With no major British land offensive underway, the Japanese were able to focus their effort on hunting down and then destroying the Chindit force operating in Burma. Three Japanese infantry divisions were involved in the hunt and regularly patrolled the major rivers. The Chindits had now been behind enemy lines for six weeks and had advanced so deep that they were in danger of exceeding the maximum range for air resupply. With food and water increasingly hard to come by, the men were exhausted. Furthermore, the Japanese had increased the number of patrols as they continued to hunt down the Chindits; finally they managed to trap Wingate's men in an ever-shrinking box between the Irrawaddy and Shweli rivers.

At the end of March Wingate was ordered to withdraw his men to India, although breaking out of Burma would be extremely hard. Having met with his senior commanders to decide the best way to return, Wingate split his force so that his men could make their way home using a number of routes. The majority would try to go back the same way they had come. This would mean crossing the Irrawaddy again, which would undoubtedly be guarded, but it was also thought that the Japanese would consider this the least likely route back because of the river. Once across, these Chindits would be able to disperse into smaller groups to make evading the enemy easier as they went back towards the Chindwin. While this would be the main return route, one column would continue eastwards to China while other men would return via northern Burma.

With the decisions made, all non-essential equipment was abandoned and the mules turned loose. An airstrip was built in a jungle clearing to evacuate the wounded. Air supply drops even included rubber dinghies and lifebelts to assist with the river crossings.

The return to India was every bit as hard as expected, and sadly many did not make it back. Some did not even make it to the main rivers as they were captured by the waiting enemy. Among them was Leigh Alexander, the commander of the southern group. After joining up with George Dunlop's column he had led the men across the Irrawaddy and, at the time the order had been given to withdraw to India, his men had been the furthest east of all the Chindits. Alexander had decided to head towards the Kachin Hills on the Chinese Yunnan Province border, believing it to be safer than returning by the same route. By 10 April his group had reached the banks of the Shweli, but they lacked equipment to cross the fast-flowing river. Two aborted attempts to reach the northern bank had resulted in the loss of many men. Now, with fewer than 500 men, Alexander decided to head west to the Irrawaddy. It was hard going. Exhausted, hungry and lacking water, the men reached the river. Those that were able managed to cross the river using whatever local boats they could find. Numbers were reducing all the time and there were now just 350 of the group still together. Then, on the morning of 28 April, while resting on a hill overlooking the Mu River, they came under attack. Amongst those killed was Alexander, he was caught full in the blast of an exploding mortar bomb and later died of his wounds.

Others to die during the expedition included Lyndon Wheeler, who had commanded the 2nd Burma Rifles attached to the northern group, and Philip Conron who had led 4 Column of the same group. Conron died on 3 April and Wheeler died the day after. Neither of their bodies were ever recovered.

Continuously harassed by the Japanese, the survivors of Wingate's force finally returned to India by several different routes and in varying numbers throughout the spring of 1943. They returned in groups ranging from a complete column to just a couple of individuals. In the end, casualties turned out to be high. Of the 3,000 men who had gone into Burma, around one-third were lost. Those that had survived had been away for three months and had covered a thousand miles behind enemy lines, having crossed two major rivers and fought off jungle diseases and the Japanese. However, of those that did return, about one-third were in a poor condition and suffering from tropical diseases, such as malaria and dysentery, and malnutrition, and not considered fit enough for further operational duty.

Although no major battles had been fought, or any ground won, the expedition was deemed to be a success. The Chindits had shown what a well-trained and determined force could achieve deep behind enemy lines. They had shown that it was possible to infiltrate the enemy and then cause disruption and havoc in difficult jungle terrain.

Many lessons had been learned from Longcloth, not least the importance of good communications and the valuable role of air support when conducting operations deep behind enemy lines. This had not been done before. Furthermore, the problem of how to deal with the wounded and those suffering from tropical diseases, who, therefore, needed to be removed from the battle, had to be addressed. Simply abandoning their men to the awful fate meted out by the Japanese was not considered a viable option by the leaders.

Although this first Chindit expedition had been hard and costly, there were many positives to take from it. This was the first time the British had fought back against the Japanese. Up until that point the Japanese soldier had been considered invincible in the jungle. The Chindits had proved this was not the case and this had done much to raise the morale of the British and Indian troops in the region. For the Japanese, the Chindits had proved to be a thorn in their side. They had been forced to divert significant resources to counter them and now had to allocate more resources to protect their vital lines of communication.

News of the success of the Chindit expedition reverberated back to London. Wingate received a second bar to the DSO he had won previously and was then promoted to the rank of major general and appointed as Commander of Special Forces India Command. In early March 1944, a second and much larger expedition, involving six brigades, was mounted into Burma. Sadly, however, on 24 March, the eccentric, but quite brilliant, Orde Wingate was killed in the early stages of the operation, while visiting Chindit-held camps in Burma, when the aircraft in which he was travelling crashed into hills near Bishenpur; he was 41 years old.

Chapter Twenty-Two

Vemork Heavy Water Plant, Telemark

27/28 February 1943

Few, if any, raids could have had a greater impact on the outcome of the Second World War than the one carried out in 1943 by a small group of saboteurs from the SOE against the Vemork Norsk hydro-electric plant in Norway. The raid, later immortalized on screen in the 1965 film *Heroes of Telemark*, was to sabotage the plant and so prevent the Nazis from acquiring deuterium oxide, otherwise known as heavy water, which could have been used in the production of nuclear weapons. It has since been described as the SOE's greatest raid of the war, but, had the raid not have been successful, the outcome of the Second World War might have been quite different.

Today, the original power plant at Vemork is an industrial museum located near the town of Rjukan in the county of Telemark, but its importance dates back to before the Second World War when Norsk Hydro built the first commercial plant to produce fertilizer. A by-product of the process was the production of deuterium oxide, one of two substances necessary for moderating neutron energy emissions in a nuclear chain reaction (graphite being the other). Prior to Germany's invasion of Norway in 1940 the extant supply of heavy water was removed by the French and, in turn, found its way to Britain after the Nazi invasion of France. But the plant in Norway was still capable of production. Understandably concerned that the Nazis would use the facility to produce heavy water for their own weapons programme, the Allies commenced a series of attempts to destroy the plant, or at least, stop its production.

The SOE had a trusted agent, Einar Skinnarland, working within the plant, and he was able to pass detailed information to the British. Skinnarland was 24 years old and a graduate of the engineering college in Porsgrunn. He had made his way to Britain on board a coastal steamer and, coming from

Telemark and having lived near the plant all his life, he had been a natural recruit for the Norwegian Independent Company 1, which had been set up in 1941 to carry out operations on behalf of the SOE.

With members of his family already working within Vemork, it was relatively easy to insert Skinnarland back into the country and to find him work within the plant. At great personal risk to himself, he used his radio to pass valuable information to Britain, such as a detailed layout of the plant and working schedules within it, which could then be used for detailed planning by a demolition party.

The first major attempt to destroy production took place in October 1942 when British Combined Operations mounted a raid to destroy the plant. Under Operation Grouse, a four-man team of Norwegian commandos were trained by the SOE and parachuted into Norway. Grouse was led by 23-year-old Second Lieutenant Jens-Anton Poulsson, and he and his three team members – Arne Kjelstrup, Knut Haugland and Claus Helberg – were all locally born and knew the area well. They were dropped onto the vast and mountainous Hardangervidda plateau in the central part of southern Norway as an advanced party for Operation Freshman, due to be mounted the following month by thirty British Royal Engineers of the 9th Field Company, 1st Airborne Division. The engineers were due to land in two Horsa gliders on a frozen lake near the plant, but although Grouse had gone much as planned, Operation Freshman proved to be a disaster. One of the gliders crashed after its Halifax tug flew into a mountain, killing all on board the Halifax and causing severe casualties on board the glider, while the second Halifax could not locate the landing site. It was decided to abort the operation and return to base, but the glider then broke free in bad weather and crashed, causing yet more casualties amongst those on board. Although there were some survivors from both of the gliders, they soon fell into German hands and were subsequently tortured by the Gestapo before being executed under Hitler's Kommandobefehl.

Not only was Freshman a failure, but it was now quite clear to the Germans that the Allies were determined to destroy the hydro-electric plant. The Allies knew this, but it was essential that another attempt be made. The Grouse team had survived and so it was now important for the men to remain undetected until a further attempt could be undertaken. For the four Norwegians high up on the plateau overlooking the plant it was a long winter, but they remained undetected until a fresh attempt could be made; they were now to operate under the changed codename of Swallow.

On the night of 16 February 1943, under the codename of Operation Gunnerside, six Norwegian commandos, led by Joachim Rønneberg, boarded a converted Halifax bomber of 138 Squadron at RAF Tempsford. Rønneberg was another young Norwegian who had fled to Britain after the German occupation to join the Norwegian Independent Company. He was now 24 years old and a lieutenant, and was selected to lead the raid because of his steadiness and inspirational leadership qualities. He had been trained well and so had his team – Knut Haukelid, Fredrik Kayser, Kasper Idland, Hans Storhaug and Birger Strømsheim – all of whom had also fled their country after occupation, and were now equally determined to return home and hit back at their occupiers. They were all excellent skiers and fully at home in the mountains, and so were perfect for such a raid.

Just hours later the Gunnerside team parachuted into Norway. They quickly gathered their supplies and set off to find the men of Swallow, but gale force winds and severe blizzards meant the conditions were harsh. Much of their time was spent sheltering in a remote hunting cabin and it took the team five days to travel the 30 miles to meet up with Swallow.

Once together, the combined team began to make preparations for the raid, which was due to take place on the night of 27/28 February. The Germans had clearly expected the British to mount a further raid in the immediate aftermath of their failed attempt and so the defences at the hydro–electric plant had been significantly reinforced. The number of guards patrolling the facility and its surrounds had been increased, mines had been laid outside the plant and the whole area was covered by floodlights. Furthermore, the single bridge spanning the deep ravine above the main river providing water to the plant, which was the main route in and out of the facility, was heavily guarded.

None of this was unexpected to the SOE and this was one of the main reasons behind the decision to leave the plant alone in the immediate aftermath of Op Freshman. Now, though, after more than three months, it was hoped that the German defenders had become more relaxed, complacent even, during what had been a long and extremely hard winter, even for the Norwegians. It was hoped that the bitterly cold weather would mean there would be a reduced number of guards outside the main plant, and even the guards who were outside would hopefully be more focused on trying to keep warm rather than maintaining a sharp lookout for intruders.

To cross the river by using the main bridge was clearly out of the question and so the raiders decided to descend into the deep ravine. It was over 600 feet deep and the sides were steep. It was such a difficult route that the Germans had considered it impassable, but it was to prove the weak point of their defences. When the raiders reached the bottom they had to ford the icy river before climbing up the far side. Fortunately, the river level was low and they had been able to make good time. Having climbed back up the far side, the raiders then followed a railway track into the plant. The railway was rarely used, but even so, it came as a welcome surprise to find it unguarded; they were able to make their way into the plant without encountering any problems.

From information provided by Skinnarland the raiders had been able to plan their attack in detail. The idea was to split into two teams, one to sabotage the plant while the other kept a lookout.

It was around midnight when Rønneberg and Kayser crawled inside the building through a cable shaft. They found the room containing the heavy water cylinders guarded by just one person, a Norwegian. Apart from being caught by surprise, the guard turned out to be friendly and provided no opposition. Two more members of the team, including Strømsheim, soon joined them, having entered the building through a window.

Remarkably, the team had been able to enter the plant without being spotted or encountering any opposition. They quickly set about placing their explosive charges on the heavy water electrolysis chambers and then attached a short delayed fuse to give them just enough time to make their escape. Before leaving, they placed a British Sten sub-machine gun next to the chambers to make it clear to the Germans that it was the work of the British and not the Norwegian Resistance, in the hope that this would prevent any reprisals against the local population.

With the men having made their escape, the explosive charges detonated as planned, destroying the main electrolysis chambers. Although the noise was deafening inside the plant, outside the sound of the muffled explosion largely went unheard; although some guards seemed to hear the noise, they associated it with the sound of machinery in the plant rather than any act of sabotage.

The heavy water had been destroyed, as had the equipment critical to the operation. The Germans dispatched a huge force to try and find the commandos but none were caught. Five of the team, led by Rønneberg, skied 250 miles to make their escape to Sweden; it took them two weeks. The rest stayed behind in Norway and simply disappeared back into the population without ever being found. The raid was, without doubt, a success. Eighteen heavy water cells and more than 1,000lb of heavy water had been destroyed, with the production of heavy water stopped for several weeks.

However, the Germans fully intended to continue using the plant to restore production and, by the summer of 1943, the damage had been repaired and production fully restored. With German defences at the plant substantially increased, the Allies realized that mounting a further raid on the ground would most likely end up failing and prove too costly, and so a series of air raids were carried out instead. One daylight raid in particular, carried out by more than a hundred American B-17 bombers during November, caused extensive damage.

The Germans were convinced that more air raids would hamper production and so decided to abandon the plant and transfer its heavy water production to Germany. This would involve moving the extant stock of heavy water and the critical components required for production.

With five of the Gunnerside team having escaped to Sweden, the only trained commando still in the area was Knut Haukelid, who had remained behind in Norway. Haukelid was informed of the German plan to remove the stock of heavy water and its equipment across Lake Tinnsjø, one of the biggest lakes in Norway and one of the deepest in Europe, using the railway ferry operating on the lake. The ferry, called the *Hydro*, connected the railway on either side of the lake and carried raw materials and fertilizer from the hydro–electric plant to the port at Skien. While destroying the heavy water and equipment on the train was considered, there were too many uncertainties. Complete destruction could not be guaranteed and so the ferry presented the most obvious way of destroying the heavy water and its equipment. The *Hydro* simply had to be sunk.

With the support of a small team, Haukelid put together a plan to sink the ferry as it crossed the deepest part of the lake, where it was nearly 1,500 feet deep. Unfortunately, the ferry also carried passengers and so, to minimize the number of civilian casualties, Haukelid was able to get someone on the inside of the plant to make sure the crossing of the lake took place on a Sunday when the ferry was known to carry fewest passengers.

On Saturday, 19 February 1944, Haukelid received notice that the heavy water and equipment was due to be transported the following day, with the heavy water drums carried in railway cars. That evening, he and three saboteurs boarded the ferry. While one of the saboteurs, Knut Lier-Hansen, distracted a crew member, Haukelid and Rolf Sorlie went below deck to set the charge. It took them nearly two hours to set the 20lb of plastic explosive where it would do the most damage. The explosive was set in a circular pattern to blow out part of the hull and cause the ferry to sink quickly, but not so quickly as to prevent passengers and crew from escaping overboard. While the ferry needed to be sunk at the deepest part of the lake, Haukelid was also keen to ensure that the sinking took place close enough to the shore to give everyone the best possible chance of reaching safety.

Having placed the charge, the saboteurs left the ship and Haukelid immediately set off for Sweden. The *Hydro* sailed as planned the following morning. It was a cold but calm day, but the peace and quiet of another Sunday morning on the lake was suddenly shattered as the explosive blew. The ferry immediately turned towards the shore, but the *Hydro* sank soon after with the loss of eighteen on board, including the crew of seven and eight German soldiers. The *Hydro* went straight to the bottom with the heavy water and vital equipment still on board. It would not reach Nazi Germany.

There were many decorations awarded for the raid against the plant and the follow-on attack on the ferry. Amongst their own Norwegian decorations for bravery, both Joachim Rønneberg and Knut Haukelid were awarded the DSO by the British for their courage and leadership; Rønneberg for the Gunnerside team and Haukelid for the sinking of the *Hydro*. Other members of the team were awarded the MM and there was a DCM for Einar Skinnarland, who had provided such vital information from inside the plant. The heroism of those involved meant the top secret war against heavy water production became internationally known and the saboteurs rightly became national heroes.

Chapter Twenty-Three

Dam Busters

16/17 May 1943

The men of 617 Squadron, the legendary Dam Busters, probably require no introduction, as the heroic raid they carried out against the dams in the heart of Germany's Ruhr valley must rank as the most famous of all the raids carried out by the RAF during the Second World War.

From early plans drawn up before the war, it was considered essential to hit the German war machine in the heart of its industrial areas, and so the dams in the Ruhr valley had been studied in great detail long before hostilities had even commenced. Although the Ruhr did not rely totally on water from the dams for the generation of electricity, it was estimated that it consumed around 25 per cent of Germany's water. The two most important reservoirs, one on the Möhne and the other on the Sorpe, held about three-quarters of the total water available in the Ruhr valley, and so any breach of their dams would impact on hydro-electricity generation, as well as causing mass destruction in the area through severe flooding.

At that early stage, there was neither the weapon nor the aircraft to deliver an attack on the dams but, as the war progressed, Barnes Wallis, the assistant chief designer at the Vickers-Armstrong Aviation Section at Weybridge in Surrey, worked on ideas to breach the dams. His initial ideas were along the lines of designing a massive bomb to be dropped from high altitude that would create shock waves underground, which would cause large-scale destruction of any targets in the area. The Air Ministry refused to sanction any such design and so Wallis turned his thoughts to other ideas.

After countless experiments, Wallis concluded that exploding a weapon against the surface of a dam would cause a shock wave capable of weakening the structure, and that successive detonations would eventually result in the destruction of the dam. According to his estimates, he concluded that just 6,000lb of explosives would be required. Trials began in 1942 as Wallis worked on a method to deliver such a weapon accurately onto its target, while further tests were carried out to determine the exact amount of explosives required. The result was the construction of prototype bombs, initially spherical in shape, to be dropped from a very low altitude and designed to bounce across the water to the target. Five drops were made using a modified Wellington bomber before the decision was made to install the new weapon, codenamed Upkeep, into a Lancaster.

The bouncing bomb, as it was later to become better known, weighed 9,250lb, of which 6,600lb was the main explosive charge. It was designed to be carried beneath the Lancaster by two v-shaped arms. Rotating the weapon backwards meant that, on impact with the water, it would start decelerating as it bounced towards the target. Having calculated the rate of deceleration, Wallis was then able to determine its release point, a distance that was eventually calculated to be between 400–450 yards from the target, with the weapon being dropped from a height of just 60 feet, while the aircraft maintained a speed of 220mph.

To carry out such a vital raid it was decided to form a new squadron. Time to form and train it was limited and so it would need to include some of Bomber Command's finest Lancaster pilots and crews. Chosen to lead the squadron was Wing Commander Guy Gibson. Although he was still just 24 years old, Gibson was a Bomber Command veteran with more than 170 operations under his belt, for which he had twice been awarded the DSO and twice the DFC.

Gibson was instructed to form a new squadron at RAF Scampton in Lincolnshire. All he knew at the outset was that his squadron would be required to carry out a special mission. At that stage he had no idea of where or when, although he would later be told that the mission required flying at low level and at night. Even before this, Gibson had started assembling his crews, picking some of the best pilots he knew, with 617 Squadron officially forming on 21 March 1943.

The squadron was made up of twenty-one crews, plus engineers and support staff, and as the crews started to arrive at Scampton, rumours started to spread. Never before had so many highly decorated people been gathered together in one place and on one squadron. Amongst them were the two flight commanders, Squadron Leader Melvin Young, better known as 'Dinghy' after twice coming down in the sea and surviving in inflatable dinghies, and with a DFC and bar for his two operational tours, and Squadron Leader Henry Maudslay, just 21 years old but already a holder of the DFC. The rest of the squadron included seventeen other holders of the DFC and eleven of the DFM. While not all of his squadron members would be highly experienced, particularly some of the air gunners, Gibson had, nonetheless, been allowed to put together a most formidable line-up. He was then given ten Lancasters to start the team's training.

One of the squadron's first tasks was to photograph several lakes around the country, with the crews being told this was for the benefit of the operational training units rather than having any relevance to their future task. Gibson was now getting more information regarding the type of mission the squadron would be carrying out. He had also been given a general briefing by Wallis and shown films of a new weapon being trialled, but he still did not know the target. Meanwhile, work was being done to modify the Lancaster to carry the new Upkeep weapon. Twenty-three aircraft were required, with the modifications including the removal of the bomb doors to mount the gear for rotating the weapon and the removal of the dorsal gun turret to reduce the weight. There was also a hydraulic motor to drive the rotating gear installed in the cabin.

The crews were now aware that they would be required to fly at very low level and deliver a weapon from a height of just 60 feet. How to achieve this had become a challenge. The aircraft's normal pressure altimeter was not accurate enough and even the more sensitive radio altimeter was not considered reliable, particularly when the aircraft was turning. The method adopted was to fit two Aldis lamps to the aircraft – one in the nose and the other at the rear of the bomb compartment – angled so that the beams converged on the surface when the aircraft was at a height of exactly 60 feet. It had also been necessary to improvise when it came to determining the exact range for the release of the weapon by using a piece of wood with a sighting point and two nails. The idea was for the bomb aimer to look through the sight and, when the two nails were lined up with objects at a specific distance, the aircraft was at the correct range to release the weapon.

By the end of April training was progressing well and many modified aircraft had been delivered to Scampton. The first successful release of Upkeep had also taken place and trials using the Aldis lamps at night soon followed. Any problems that were encountered were simply overcome by the crews and ground personnel.

From studies of German records it was apparent that the water level in the reservoirs would be at their highest in mid-May, and when also taking into account the moon conditions, it was decided to carry out the raid on the night of 16/17 May.

The plan for the attack, codenamed Operation Chastise, was for nineteen aircraft to attack in three sections. The first section of nine aircraft, led by Gibson, was to attack the Möhne dam and, if successful, fly on to attack the Eder. The second section of five aircraft would attack the Sorpe dam. The third section, also of five aircraft, would act as a mobile reserve and were briefed to attack any of the primary targets should the dams not be breached.

It was just after 9.30 pm on 16 May when the first wave took off in three sections of three, with Gibson leading in 'AJ-G George'. All had gone well until crossing the Rhine, when one of the aircraft in the second section, 'B-Baker', flown by 23-year-old Flight Lieutenant Bill Astell, was hit by flak. His aircraft was seen to fly on for a while before becoming engulfed in flames. It crashed to the north-west of Dorsten; there were no survivors.

Pressing on towards their target, the Lancasters continued at low level, with Gibson's lead section arriving unscathed over the Möhne soon after midnight. Gibson was the first to attack. By now the Lancasters had been spotted and his aircraft was immediately subjected to intense anti-aircraft fire from defensive positions on the ground. Gibson pushed on and released his weapon at exactly the right point. Moments later his Upkeep hit the dam, and, looking back to their target, the crew saw a huge column of water rise above the dam. They had hit the target, but excitement turned to disappointment after the water had settled and the crew could see the dam was still intact.

Next to attack was Flight Lieutenant 'Hoppy' Hopgood in 'M-Mother'. During the run-in his aircraft was repeatedly hit by ground fire, causing the Upkeep to be released late. Hopgood's Lancaster was seen staggering away from the dam when it blew up. Although it looked to the others circling above as if the crew had all been killed, it was later discovered that two had miraculously survived.

Gibson knew the Lancasters were going to be continuously vulnerable to ground fire and so he decided to escort the third aircraft, 'P-Popsie' flown by

Flight Lieutenant Micky Martin, during its attack. Martin successfully ran the gauntlet of ground fire, but his Upkeep was released early and exploded short of the dam.

Martin now joined Gibson to escort the fourth Lancaster, 'A-Apple', flown by Dinghy Young. The three Lancasters thundered in towards the dam as the German defenders continued to throw everything they could at the attackers. Despite the intense anti-aircraft fire, Young held his aircraft steady for long enough to complete the attack. His Upkeep was seen to strike the dam with devastating accuracy, causing cascades of water to flow over the parapet, but there was still no breach.

The fifth aircraft, 'J-Johnny' of Flight Lieutenant Dave Maltby's crew, now took up its position to attack. Running the gauntlet like the others had done before, Maltby pressed on with precise accuracy. Just as he was releasing his Upkeep the dam was suddenly seen to begin to collapse; the previous attack by Young had delivered the vital blow needed to breach the dam.

The crews of the seven surviving aircraft of the first wave spent the next few moments circling above the reservoir to watch the spectacular sight, as thousands of tons of water burst into the valley below. Realizing there was still more to be done, Gibson instructed Maltby and Martin to head for home while he took the others on to the Eder. It took a while for Gibson to locate the Eder, but when they arrived the crews were relieved to find the dam was undefended. However, the location of the dam meant it was clearly going to require great flying skill to approach the target and then to recover safely once the attack had been made.

With Gibson watching over, the first Lancaster to attack the Eder dam was 'L-Leather', with the Australian, Flight Lieutenant Dave Shannon, at the controls. His Upkeep was seen to hit the target and seemed to cause a slight breach. Next to attack was Maudslay in 'Z-Zebra'. His Upkeep was seen to be released late and it hit the dam without bouncing, exploding on impact and catching the Lancaster full in the blast. While others watched, some believed they heard a faint transmission from the stricken aircraft, but nothing was heard from the crew again. From evidence collated later, Maudslay's aircraft had apparently survived the explosion, but is believed to have been shot down by flak near the Dutch–German border on its way home; there were no survivors.

The last aircraft to attack the Eder dam was Pilot Officer Les Knight's 'N-Nut'. His Upkeep was delivered with great accuracy and hit the dam. As the remaining crews watched, the breach gradually widened before a great tidal wave swept down the valley. With the Möhne and Eder dams breached, the four remaining Lancasters turned for home.

Of the second wave tasked with attacking the Sorpe dam, two aircraft were forced to return early; Flight Lieutenant Les Munro's 'W-Willie' was hit by flak and Pilot Officer Geoff Rice's 'H-Harry' lost its Upkeep after clipping the waves en route to the target. What happened to two of the others is unclear, as nothing further was heard of them after leaving Scampton. One aircraft, 'E-Easy', flown by Flight Lieutenant Robert Barlow, crashed close to the Dutch–German border and the other, 'K-King' of Pilot Officer Vernon Byers, was shot down by flak off the island of Texel near the Dutch coast. This left the crew of the lead aircraft, 'T-Tommy', flown by Flight Lieutenant Joe McCarthy, to attack the Sorpe dam on their own. Although they hit the target there was no breach.

The third wave, led by Pilot Officer Bill Ottley in 'C-Charlie', had also suffered badly en route to the dams. Ottley's aircraft appears to have blown up, having been hit by flak soon after crossing the Rhine; amazingly, the rear gunner, Sergeant Frank Tees, was thrown clear and survived to become a prisoner of war. The second aircraft, 'S-Sugar', flown by Pilot Officer Lewis Burpee, was shot down by flak over the airfield at Gilze-Rijen with no survivors. The last of all nineteen aircraft to get airborne, 'Y-York' flown by Flight Sergeant Cyril Anderson, was forced to return to base with its Upkeep still intact. His rear gun turret was unserviceable and, although Anderson had pressed on, he was forced to alter his route to avoid known enemy defences. The large detours, combined with misty conditions, had made low-level navigation all but impossible and he fell behind schedule. With the hours of darkness rapidly slipping away, he reluctantly returned to Scampton.

This left just two aircraft of the third wave to attack the dams. One, 'F-Freddie', flown by Flight Sergeant Ken Brown, attacked the Sorpe dam. The Upkeep was seen to hit the dam but there was no breach. The other aircraft, 'O-Orange', flown by Flight Sergeant Bill Townsend, attacked the Ennepe dam, but without success.

Back at Scampton the ground crews and support staff waited for the Lancasters to return. The first two to arrive back were those of Maltby and

Martin; they had both been ordered back after the successful breach of the Möhne dam. Some forty-five minutes passed before the next aircraft, Shannon's, landed, and soon after came Gibson and then Knight.

By 4.30 am these were the only five aircraft from the first wave to have made it back. There was no sign of Young's aircraft. It would later be discovered that his Lancaster had been shot down by a German coastal flak battery with the loss of the entire crew. From the second wave, Joe McCarthy's aircraft returned from his attack on the Sorpe dam and, with daylight now getting close, Brown's aircraft returned from the third wave. The last to land was Townsend, by which time it was 6.15 am.

With two of the primary dams breached, resulting in widespread devastation caused by the flooding, Chastise was understandably considered a success, but the raid had proved costly for the squadron. Eight of the nineteen Lancasters had failed to return, with the loss of fifty-three aircrew.

A total of thirty-four gallantry awards were made to the survivors of the raid, the most notable being the award of the Victoria Cross to Guy Gibson for leading the raid. His citation included:

> *Under his inspiring leadership, this squadron has now executed one of the most devastating attacks of the war – the breaching of the Möhne and Eder dams. The task was fraught with danger and difficulty. Wing Commander Gibson personally made the initial attack on the Möhne dam. Descending to within a few feet of the water and taking the full brunt of the anti-aircraft defences, he delivered his attack with great accuracy. Afterwards he circled very low for thirty minutes, drawing the enemy fire on himself in order to leave as free a run as possible to the following aircraft which were attacking the dam in turn. Wing Commander Gibson then led the remainder of his force to the Eder dam where, with complete disregard for his own safety, he repeated his tactics and once more drew on himself the enemy fire so that the attack could be successfully developed. Wing Commander Gibson has completed over 170 sorties, involving more than 600 hours operational flying. Throughout his operational career, prolonged exceptionally at his own request, he has shown leadership, determination and valour of the highest order.*

The surviving officer pilots who had carried out their attacks – Les Knight, Joe McCarthy, Dave Maltby, Micky Martin and Dave Shannon – were all awarded the DSO, while the two non-commissioned pilots who attacked the dams, Ken Brown and Bill Townsend, were both awarded the CGM. In addition to the pilots, fourteen DFCs and twelve DFMs were awarded to other surviving members of the crews. The daring attack by the legendary Dam Busters has rightly taken its own special place in the history of air warfare.

Chapter Twenty-Four

Midgets Against the *Tirpitz*

22 September 1943

The heroic attack by the crews of three Royal Navy midget submarines, known as X-Craft, against the mighty German warship *Tirpitz*, carried out in a remote fjord in northern Norway in September 1943, was a remarkable act of seamanship and personal bravery. It was surely one of the most courageous British raids of the Second World War.

The *Tirpitz* was the second of two *Bismarck*-class battleships built for the Germany Navy. Work was completed on her during early 1941 and she was commissioned into the German fleet. At 43,000 tons, the *Tirpitz* was heavier than her sister ship, making her the heaviest ship built by any European navy at that time, and, like the *Bismarck*, she was armed with a main battery of eight 15-inch (38cm) guns in four twin turrets.

After successful completion of her sea trials, *Tirpitz* was held at Kiel as part of a temporary Baltic Fleet, which also included the heavy cruiser *Admiral Scheer*, to prevent the possibility of a break-out by the Soviet Baltic Fleet at Leningrad. It was while she was at Kiel that the first attempts were made by RAF bombers to destroy the *Tirpitz*, but without success. Then, in early 1942, and under the cover of poor weather, the *Tirpitz* sailed to Norway to deter an Allied invasion and to tie down much needed Royal Navy assets. While there she also presented a significant threat to Allied convoys heading for the Soviet Union.

The *Tirpitz* moored in the Fættenfjord just to the north of Trondheim. To protect her from air attack the mooring was next to a cliff and anti-aircraft batteries were set up around the fjord. Torpedo nets and heavy booms at the entrance to the fjord protected her from an underwater attack, while the ship was heavily camouflaged to make visual detection more difficult. But although she was well defended, her movements were severely restricted, not helped by a shortage of fuel, and she rarely ventured out.

Many air attacks were made in an attempt to destroy the *Tirpitz*, but all without success. A daring attempt was even made during October 1942 by two Chariot human torpedoes, but, again, without success; rough seas caused the Chariots to break away from the fishing vessel towing them before either could be launched.

After the Allied convoys to the Soviet Union ceased temporarily during 1943, the *Tirpitz* and the German battleship *Scharnhorst*, also now operating out of Norway, were free to roam together. By early September, RAF reconnaissance flights and intelligence reports from Norway confirmed that the two great warships were moored in the Kåfjord in northern Norway.

Determined to take out both *Tirpitz* and *Scharnhorst* once and for all, the British decided to mount a raid, but with air attacks having proved unsuccessful, as well as being heavy on resources, a new idea was put forward instead – to use the new X-Class midget submarine. This would be the first time the new midget submarines would be used operationally and, under Operation Source, a series of underwater attacks were planned to neutralize Germany's two great warships, as well as the pocket battleship *Lützow*, which happened to be in nearby Langfjord at the time.

The concept for the X-Craft was for it to be towed to the area in which it was to operate: about 50 feet underwater and 200 yards behind its mother submarine on the surface. It was tricky business. The two vessels rarely seemed in harmony with each other, particularly with a rough sea, and the only break from the harsh conditions on board the midget was when it surfaced every six or so hours to recharge the batteries, and to open its hatches to get some much needed fresh air through the vessel. Tows could take several days and because conditions on board were tough, two crews were used: the passage crew of three being replaced by the fresh operational crew for the mission, with the transfer of crews carried out using a rubber dinghy between the two vessels. The operational capability of the X-Craft was largely down to the endurance of its four-man mission crew (commander, pilot, engineer artificer and a specialist diver), but could last, in theory, for several days and cover anything up to 500 nautical miles when on the surface, or up to 80 miles when submerged. Then, once the mission was over, the X-Craft would rendezvous with the towing submarine for the passage home.

Described as something looking rather like a cigar tube and tapered at both ends, the X-Craft was just over 50 feet in length and about 5 feet in diameter, and weighed 35 tons. There was a narrow deck running along the top of the hull but, unlike a conventional submarine, the X-Craft had no conning tower and there were no torpedoes or guns on board. On the surface it was powered by a 4-cylinder 42hp diesel engine, which gave the X-Craft a maximum speed of 6–7 knots and also recharged the batteries. When submerged it was powered by a 30hp electric engine, giving the X-Craft a speed of up to 5 knots when under the water. Its weapons were two concrete detachable side charges, clamped snugly around the port and starboard sides of the hull, with two tons of amatol in each and detonated by delayed fuses; the idea was to drop the charges on the seabed underneath the target and then escape. The craft was also fitted with electro-magnets to avoid detection by anti-submarine detectors on the seabed. Surfacing and diving was achieved by means of three ballast tanks along its length, which gave the vessel an operating depth down to around three hundred feet. Aquaplanes were used to manoeuvre the X-Craft up and down when beneath the surface, with small trimming tanks used to keep the vessel level. The only way the commander could view what was going on around the vessel was through a slim periscope.

For the attack on the three German warships in northern Norway it was decided to use six X-Craft. Three – HMS *X5*, *X6* and *X7* – were tasked with attacking the *Tirpitz*, while two more – *X9* and *X10* – would attack the *Scharnhorst* and *X8* would attack the *Lützow*. They would slip under the protective torpedo nets and each drop their two powerful mines on the seabed under their target.

The attacks were planned to take place sometime during 20–25 September, with the exact date of attack depending on how long the passage of 1,000 miles across the North Sea would take and how long it would then take for the X-Craft to make their way up the fjord to carry out their attack.

Leaving their depot ship, HMS *Bonaventure*, in Scotland on 11 September, the six X-Craft were towed out to sea by four S-Class and two T-Class conventional submarines. The six submarine pairs transited across the North Sea in parallel and approximately 10 miles apart, their route taking them through the Faroe and Shetland Islands and then north-eastwards towards northern Norway.

The transit across the North Sea was not without incident. One of the X-Craft destined for the *Scharnhorst*, the *X9*, was lost after it became separated during the tow. It is believed the vessel was trimmed bow-down due to the rough sea conditions, which probably resulted in the midget submarine plunging to the bottom with the loss of all three men on board. A second vessel, the *X8*, also failed to make it to northern Norway after it developed serious leaks in the side-mounted demolition charges. These had to be jettisoned, but they exploded near the craft, causing significant damage and resulting in her having to be scuttled.

Only four X-Craft were left to carry out the attack and so the plan was revised. Three were to attack the main target, the *Tirpitz*, as had been originally planned, leaving the fourth to attack the *Scharnhorst* alone; the *Lützow* was the lowest priority target and would be left alone.

Just over a week after leaving Scotland the submarines were in position to release the four remaining X-Craft. The operational crews now replaced the passage crews and began preparations to commence their attack. It was just before dusk on 20 September when the midgets slipped away from their mother submarines to start the journey of around 100 miles to their targets. For those left on board the mother subs, it was now a matter of waiting for the midgets to return.

As things turned out, the single midget heading for the *Scharnhorst*, the *X10*, suffered technical problems almost immediately after setting off; it had also been discovered that the *Scharnhorst* was not at her normal mooring. The attack, therefore, had to be abandoned. What had started as a planned attack by six X-Craft against three German warships was now down to just three midgets against the *Tirpitz*.

The first of the three, the *X5*, affectionately known to its crew as *Platypus*, was commanded by a young Australian serving with the Royal Navy, 21-year-old Lieutenant Henry Henty-Creer. On board were his three crew members: 22-year-old Sub-Lieutenant Tom Nelson, Acting Sub-Lieutenant Alastair Malcolm and 22-year-old Engine Room Artificer 4th Class Ralph Mortiboys.

The second craft, *Piker II*, was commanded by 27-year-old Lieutenant Donald Cameron of the Royal Naval Reserve. When he had volunteered for the midget subs a year earlier he was officially too old, but this fact was overlooked because of his vast maritime experience and because he was just the kind of man needed for such a job. Having first commanded one of the development craft, the *X3*, he was now in command of the *X6* with his crew of 21-year-old Lieutenant John Lorimer, Sub-Lieutenant Dickie Kendall and Engine Room Artificer Eddie Goddard.

The third vessel, *Pdinichthys*, was commanded by 22-year-old Lieutenant Godfrey Place, the only regular Royal Navy officer amongst the early X-Craft volunteers. Place had transferred to the submarine service in 1941 and was awarded the DSC while serving as first lieutenant in HMS *Unbeaten* in the Mediterranean. He was already an experienced midget sub operator, having commanded the second experimental craft, the *X4*, before he was given command of the *X7*. With him on board were his crew of Sub-Lieutenant Robert Aitken, Lieutenant Bill Whittam, also just 22 years old, and Engine Room Artificer 4th Class Willie Whitley.

The three X-Craft headed off towards the fjord, but it is not known for certain what happened to *X5* and its crew. It appears they were later spotted in the fjord near the *Tirpitz* and it is believed the craft sank having been hit by enemy fire, although it is not known whether any charges were ever laid. Unfortunately, no wreckage was ever found (although parts have recently been recovered that may have belonged to the *X5*) and none of the crew's bodies were ever recovered. Whatever happened to *X5*, the crew did not survive to tell their tale.

Meanwhile, *X6* and *X7* penetrated through an enemy minefield and entered the fjord the following day, surfacing alongside a small island under the cover of darkness to recharge their batteries. They now had a passage of a further 50 miles up the fjord to reach their target.

The fjord was known to be vigilantly patrolled by the enemy and had numerous defences, including anti-submarine and torpedo nets, gun defences and listening posts. Life on board the midgets was cramped and great self-control was required by the crews to fight any fears of claustrophobia. It was not easy to move around inside, particularly around the centre of the vessel where the four men had to live and work. The commander spent most of his time at a small chart table where he took care of navigation, using the periscope as and when required. Just a couple of feet away was the first lieutenant, who would be on the hydroplanes ensuring the craft maintained the correct depth while monitoring the gauges and levers that controlled the craft. The engine room artificer was at the helm steering while maintaining the engines. There was much that could go wrong and to maintain the diesel engine meant crawling through a small hatch and then lying on the fuel tank to work in an extremely cramped space. Unless the fourth member of the crew, the diver, was required for diving duties, he helped in any way he could; particularly with the catering on board. When he was needed for diving, the task of getting into a diving suit inside a midget submarine was far from easy. When he was required to leave the vessel he did so through a small wet and dry compartment in the forward section, flooding it first to equalize the pressures inside and outside the vessel so that the hatch could be opened. As for rest and sleep, while two crew members remained on watch there was just about enough space for the other two to lie on boards on top of the batteries in the bow to get whatever rest they could. Condensation was always a problem and had to be dealt with as best as possible to avoid electrical failures on board.

In the early hours of 22 September the two X-Craft dived once more. The first obstacle was the outer perimeter anti-submarine net. If the crews could not find a way of getting through it then the divers would have to cut a way through. Cameron on board the *X6* and Place on the *X7* watched through their periscopes. The gate through the outer net had been opened to allow a trawler through and so both midgets quickly dived beneath its wake and got through the outer defence without having to cut the net.

Having passed through the outer defences the X-Craft proceeded slowly along the fjord. Then, in an attempt to avoid another vessel crossing their path, the *X7* ran into a torpedo net at a depth of 30 feet. The bow had caught in something that Place could not see. There was no chance of cutting their way out – the diver's equipment was simply not strong enough – so their only hope was to try and wrestle the *X7* free; first by going full astern and then fully forward, and by flooding and blowing the ballast tanks. Finally, after more than half an hour of trying, the craft broke through the net.

Meanwhile, on board the *X6* the starboard charge had flooded soon after setting off, causing the vessel to list by some 10 degrees, though Cameron was satisfied that the vessel was handling well enough to continue. But now the list had got worse, making the periscope almost useless and so Cameron decided to continue on the surface under the cover of darkness, using the rough water of a nearby trawler to help conceal the sub's position. The two X-Craft worked their way up the fjord and through the enemy defences. There were several vessels in the fjord, but finally, just before 7.00 am, they sighted the *Tirpitz* little more than a mile away.

The depth of the fjord where she was moored was estimated to be about 30 fathoms (180 feet). Given the shallow running of torpedoes, the anti-torpedo nets only went down to about 50 feet and so there was plenty of room for the midgets to pass beneath.

By now the *X6* was just beneath periscope depth. Cameron decided to surface once more to get a good look. He could see what looked like a gap in the torpedo net ahead, through which a small boat had just passed. He found the gate and in no time the *X6* was through. Cameron could now see the bow of the *Tirpitz* on his port side and less than 200 yards away. He then manoeuvred the craft under the surface to take it towards the battleship's stern, but then there was a huge bump. They had run into a rock.

The impact had momentarily pushed the bow of the *X6* above the surface. Cameron was quick to react and took the midget back down to 70 feet but, unbeknown to the crew on board, the midget had been spotted by one of the battleship's many lookouts. The alarm was immediately raised and the crew on board the *Tirpitz* set about closing watertight bulkheads as gunfire rained down into the water, more in hope than anything else.

Fortunately for the crew on board the *X6*, they were too close for the *Tirpitz* to bring any heavy guns to bear. Cameron now had to decide where the *Tirpitz* was using his last known information. Having set course, the *X6* soon bumped into its hull. Whichever part of the mighty battleship it was, this was their only chance to lay their charges and in no time at all they had dropped both charges, which, as it happens, settled on the bottom beneath the port bow.

The *X7*, meanwhile, had reached the protective anti-torpedo net about the same time as the *X6* had first been spotted. Place took the craft down to a depth of 70 feet to slip beneath the nets. At first they could not get under and so they tried going down further. Eventually the midget got through and when they surfaced for a few brief moments, Place could see the *Tirpitz* just 30 yards away. Then, at a depth of just 20 feet, he headed straight towards the battleship.

The *X7* ran into her side and then slid under the keel. The crew then manoeuvred the craft fore and aft in line with the *Tirpitz* to position underneath the aft turret before jettisoning the starboard charge. Place then manoeuvred his craft slowly forward alongside the hull for about 70 yards to the forward turret where they dropped the port charge. The crew could now hear the sound of explosions as those on board the *Tirpitz* lobbed grenades into the water around the ship where the *X6* was believed to be and fired at anything and everything they saw.

On board the *X6* the crew knew there was no chance of escape. They could not see where they were going and the vessel was leaking badly. The torpedo net would be closed and every ship in the fjord would be looking for them. Depth charges would soon be raining down on them and Cameron knew that it would only end in a grim death if they continued any longer. He then took the *X6* to the surface. They surfaced to find they were just 50 yards from the *Tirpitz*. The crew quickly set about destroying everything and, before opening the hatch to surrender, the sea cocks were opened to scuttle the midget. Their job was done. Having then boarded an enemy launch they were taken on board the *Tirpitz*.

The delayed charges were timed to go off about an hour after being set, but the timing could not be relied upon. Meanwhile, on board the *X7* the crew had set off back down the fjord, but again became tangled in a torpedo net. Now they were stuck, only this time they could not break free.

It was at 8.12 am that the charges blew. The blast somehow threw the *X7* clear of the net, but she had suffered severe damage and was now increasingly difficult to control. Although the crew tried to stay hidden beneath the water, the craft broke the surface several times. They had now been spotted and were coming under continuous fire from the *Tirpitz*. The *X7* was hit several times, causing damage to her hull and periscope, and they dived again, but there was clearly no chance of escape. There was no option other than to abandon the *X7* and to surrender. Somehow the crew managed to surface the stricken vessel. Place then climbed out and waved his white jumper at the *Tirpitz*, but in her low state of buoyancy, more water started spilling into the midget submarine and she started to sink once more. Place managed to escape just before the *X7* sank to the bottom. He was then captured and taken on board the *Tirpitz*. Godfrey Place was now a prisoner of war.

Still on board the *X7* were the three other crew members. Now stuck on the bottom of the fjord, the crew discussed what to do. They knew the vessel was damaged and there was also the risk of being destroyed by enemy fire and depth charges, and so they decided to abandon the craft using the emergency breathing apparatus, rather than to try and get the *X7* back to the surface.

The procedure for abandoning the X-Craft involved flooding the vessel to equalize the pressure inside and out so that the hatch could be opened. With their breathing apparatus on, the crew opened the valves and started to flood the craft. Some of the valves could not be fully opened and so the flooding procedure was taking far longer than it should have. As the water level rose the batteries fused, giving off fumes and forcing the men to start breathing on their oxygen supply. There was nothing the crew could do but wait. There was no light and they could not talk to each other. They just had to sit there and wait, each man with his own private thoughts.

There were two hatches by which the crew could escape, but during the escape attempt only Robert Aitken survived. Having reached the surface he was captured and taken on board the *Tirpitz* as a prisoner of war. The body of Bill Whittam was later discovered, but that of Willie Whitley was never recovered. It appears he ran out of oxygen before attempting to leave the vessel.

It appears that the mines of both X-Craft went off almost simultaneously, causing extensive damage to the *Tirpitz*. Although she was not in danger of sinking, there was a large indentation in the bottom of the ship, and bulkheads in the double-bottom had buckled. More than a thousand tons of water had flooded the ship's fuel tanks and the void spaces on the port side, making the ship list and causing serious damage to generators. There was also mechanical damage to parts of the ship. One of the turrets was damaged, and significant heavy-lift equipment would be required to repair it – equipment that was not available in Norway at the time – and the ship's two float planes were destroyed.

The extensive damage caused by the two X-Craft put the *Tirpitz* out of action, and it would be another six months before repairs were complete.

For their leadership and courage during the raid, Donald Cameron and Godfrey Place were both awarded the Victoria Cross. The bravery of the four other survivors of the midgets was also recognized: the three officers – Robert Aitken, Dickie Kendall and John Lorimer – were all awarded the DSO, while Eddie Goddard received the CGM.

The crippling of the *Tirpitz* had come at a vital time and offered some respite for the Royal Navy's Arctic convoys. Numerous operations followed as the British again attempted to blow up the mighty warship before eventually, on 12 November 1944, Lancasters of RAF Bomber Command succeeded in destroying the *Tirpitz* once and for all.

Chapter Twenty-Five

Reconnaissance of the Normandy Beaches

January 1944

As the men of the British XXX Corps went ashore on Gold Beach during the morning of 6 June 1944, D-Day, few, if any, would have spared a thought for those brave young men that had earlier risked their lives to identify the beach as a suitable landing site for the operation.

One of those brave young men was 25-year-old Sergeant Bruce Ogden-Smith, one of the most colourful and courageous characters of the Second World War. Talked into taking part in special operations by his older brother Colin, himself a commando, Bruce Ogden-Smith's first experience of carrying out daring raids occurred with the Small Scale Raiding Force during the summer of 1942. After the disbandment of the SSRF he had joined the fledgling Special Boat Section and operated in the Middle East. By the end of 1943 he was back in England and serving with a clandestine naval unit called the Combined Operations Assault Pilotage Parties, based at Hayling Island near Portsmouth. Its members, known as COPPists, risked their lives to gather information on proposed landing beaches and inshore waters, often under the noses of the enemy land and sea patrols.

If the D-Day landings were to be a success then it was vital for the Allied planners to understand many things, such as the construct of the enemy defences located in the coastal towns of Normandy, but other things that needed to be understood were, perhaps, less obvious. Amongst these latter considerations was an appreciation of the natural hazards that the landing force faced, such as the tides and currents, and what was beneath the surface. For example, planners needed to know if there were any hidden underwater banks, rocks, or any man-made hazards placed under the surface that would act as defensive obstacles, and, of course, they needed to understand the gradient and composition of the proposed landing beaches. This required gathering lots of samples for analysis back in England prior to a landing taking place. It was hazardous but vital work.

On New Year's Eve 1943/44, Ogden-Smith, with a young officer of the Royal Engineers, 23-year-old Major Logan Scott-Bowden, both part of a group of specialists called COPP 1, left the south coast of England in a motor gunboat to take part in Operation KJH. Their task was to survey the area around Ver-sur-Mer on the Normandy coast, which had been identified as a potential landing beach and would later become Gold Beach during the D-Day landings. Aerial photographs and local knowledge had suggested that just below the sandy top layer of the beach there were extensive levels of soft peat, which, if true, could cause major problems for tanks and other heavy armoured vehicles as they went ashore. It was, therefore, necessary to find out whether the beach could withstand the weight of large numbers of heavy armoured vehicles.

As they crossed the Channel the two men changed into their loose-fitting but rather bulky rubber swimsuits and strapped on their backpacks. There was much to carry and so their packs were far from light. They contained everything the men would need once ashore – wire cutters, a wrist compass, a waterproof torch, a waterproof writing tablet, emergency rations, sampling equipment and a sand-coloured fishing line marked with beads every ten yards for measuring. The packs also contained their personal weapons, a Colt .45 and a commando knife, although they had no intention of getting involved in a fight; Scott-Bowden and Ogden-Smith worked on the assumption that they would only ever be spotted if they were unfortunate enough to come across an over-eager sentry.

The two men were then transferred to a smaller craft, which took them to within a short distance of the shore. Then, when about 400 yards from the beach, Scott-Bowden and Ogden-Smith climbed overboard and swam towards the shore. The sea was bitterly cold, quite rough and the current strong. They were dragged further to the east from the point where they had hoped to land, but they were both strong swimmers and managed to reach the shore near enough where planned.

Once ashore they initially lay low at the water's edge to survey the scene. The beam from a nearby lighthouse meant that the men had to keep lying flat on the beach, but other than that, as had been hoped, the fact that it was New Year's Eve meant there was little enemy activity around.

While continuously probing for mines, they worked their way slowly along the beach, taking various measurements as they went and stopping occasionally to take out the metal augers from their backpacks. Taking a number of core samples from different parts of the beach, they then stored them in special containers ready for analysis back home.

It took Scott-Bowden and Ogden-Smith several hours to complete their task. They also had to remove all signs of them having been on the beach at all. Had they not have done so, the Germans would have known that the beach had been surveyed. Then, having completed their task, the two men then crawled back to the water's edge. By now they were heavily laden with samples and the waves kept throwing them back to the beach, but eventually they managed to struggle through the surf and back out to sea where their craft was waiting. They then rendezvoused with the MGB and made it back to Newhaven before dawn.

The reconnaissance carried out that night was to be the first of several extraordinary beach reconnaissance missions. Once the Americans heard about what the British had successfully achieved, the two men were asked to carry out similar surveys of more potential landing beaches along the Normandy coast to the west of Port-en-Bessin and at Vierville-sur-Mer. This would require a longer mission of a few days to cover all the beaches. Because they could not afford to waste valuable time at night travelling backwards and forwards across the Channel, it was decided that the next mission would use an X-Craft midget submarine. This would allow the men to spend more time each night surveying the beaches and then remain off the coast of Normandy during the day.

Reconnaissance missions such as this could only be carried out in dark periods when there was little or no moon and so it was more than two weeks later, on 16 January 1944, before Scott-Bowden and Ogden-Smith boarded the midget submarine at HMS *Dolphin* in Gosport. Their mission was given the codename Operation Postage Able and they would be in good hands. The midget sub, HMS *X20*, was one of the Royal Navy's latest X-Craft and commanded by Lieutenant Ken Hudspeth, an experienced midget submariner who had already been awarded the first of his three DSCs for commanding the *X10* during the attack on the *Tirpitz*; Hudspeth would go on to become one of Australia's most highly decorated naval officers of the war. Also on board were the other two members of the crew – Sub-Lieutenant

Bruce Enzer and Lieutenant Commander Nigel Willmott, the founder of the COPP, who would command the overall mission.

With five men on board, conditions were cramped. The *X20* was then towed across the Channel by a navy trawler to within a few miles of the French coast before the midget sub made its way to a position off the Normandy coast, where it would spend the next four days.

At dawn on 18 January the *X20* submerged. A fishing fleet with enemy armed guards provided an unwelcome complication to their plan, not only because of the lookouts on board, but also because of the fishing nets beneath the surface, but, threading their way through the nets, they then took up a position just off the shore. Having then raised the periscope to observe the scene ashore, they were surprised to see hundreds of soldiers preparing enemy defences along the seafront. With no option but to turn away, the *X20* withdrew back out to sea.

For that night's reconnaissance the decision was made to return eastwards along the coast and to survey the beaches there. Scott-Bowden and Ogden-Smith then swam ashore, taking with them the necessary equipment to complete their task. Once ashore they proceeded in the same manner that they had done before, taking measurements and samples along the beach before returning to the *X20* before dawn. Only once was there a possible problem, when an enemy patrol passed close by.

The next day followed a similar pattern as the men first surveyed the scene from the midget sub at periscope level before Scott-Bowden and Ogden-Smith went ashore once more to work their way along the next beach. On this occasion they had a close call when the flashlight from a sentry shone straight in their direction, but the two men kept face down in the sand and, after a few nervy minutes, the sentry moved away. Somehow they had remained unseen. They then went about their task in their normal cool manner. This time they took back samples from a shingle bank, which could prove a problem for vehicles going ashore.

By the end of the second night they had surveyed the beaches at Vierville-sur-Mer, Colleville-sur-Mer and Saint Laurent-sur-Mer, the same beach that had witnessed the disaster of the Small Scale Raiding Force's Operation Aquatint sixteen months before. All these beaches would later make up the area of Omaha Beach on D-Day for landings by the American V Corps.

On the third night the two men were due to go ashore yet again, only this time further to the east off the Orne estuary, an area that would later become Sword Beach, but by this stage the weather was worsening. With such vital information about several beaches already gathered, and with so many samples already on board, they could not risk their mission now because of bad weather. Nor, perhaps, could they push their luck any further; they had been incredibly lucky so far. Besides, Scott-Bowden and Ogden-Smith, as well as the rest of the crew, were exhausted. And so the decision was made to return to Gosport. The *X20* arrived back at *Dolphin* on 21 January.

As a result of the work by Scott-Bowden and Ogden-Smith, the Allies were able to make detailed models of the landing beaches in preparation for the landings on D-Day. This allowed planners to assess the effectiveness of the landing techniques being developed and the movement of vehicles and men over the beaches.

These had been extremely tiring and hazardous missions. Altogether, Scott-Bowden and Ogden-Smith had sampled thirty potential landing beaches. Parts of the coastline were mined, and even the beaches that were not mined were regularly patrolled by sentries. Furthermore, the missions had been physically demanding. The two men had spent long periods in extremely cold water, bringing on cramp and severe exhaustion.

For these first beach reconnaissance missions from an X-Craft, Bruce Ogden-Smith was awarded the Military Medal for Operation KJH and the Distinguished Conduct Medal for Postage Able, while Logan Scott-Bowden was awarded the officer equivalent of the Military Cross and the Distinguished Service Order. Both men would later get to see the fruits of their labour when they were assigned to American forces as guides at the head of the D-Day landings on Omaha Beach.

Chapter Twenty-Six

Amiens Prison

18 February 1944

It was just before midday on 18 February 1944 when the local inhabitants of Amiens heard the thunderous sound of aircraft approaching at low level. Looking up from the Albert to Amiens road, they could see Mosquitos at treetop height and heading at high speed towards the prison, where it was reported that some 700 members of the French Resistance were awaiting certain death at the hands of the Gestapo. They were witnessing the opening moments of Operation Jericho, and the aircraft they could see were Mosquitos of 140 Wing, led by a man who was, to many, the archetypal English hero, Group Captain 'Pick' Pickard.

The formation of the RAF's 2nd Tactical Air Force at the end of 1943 had given the airfield of Hunsdon in Hertfordshire a new lease of life. Three Mosquito squadrons – 21, 464 (RAAF) and 487 (RNZAF) Squadrons – moved in from Sculthorpe in Norfolk to operate as 140 Wing, part of 2 Group, as a specialist wing tasked with carrying out low-level precision raids against the enemy.

Leading the wing was Group Captain Charles Pickard. With a DFC and a DSO with two bars, Pickard was 28 years old and had already experienced a varied and exciting operational career. He had flown Wellington bombers and Whitleys, during which time he had led the air component of the successful airborne raid against the German radar installation at Bruneval, and had flown Lysanders when he clandestinely transported agents of the SOE to and from France. He was also well known to the British public, after appearing as the skipper of a Wellington bomber 'F for Freddie' in the 1941 propaganda film *Target for Tonight*, and was considered by many to be the archetypal English hero.

The Hunsdon Wing was equipped with the Mosquito Mk VI fighter-bomber. It was capable of a top speed in excess of 350mph at low level and was an aircraft that could hold its own with the best of the Luftwaffe's single-engine fighters around at the time. As a fighter-bomber, its wing structure had been reinforced to enable it to carry either a 250lb or 500lb bomb on racks housed in streamlined fairings under each wing, or up to eight 60lb rockets, in addition to its internal bomb load of two 250lb bombs, or a 500lb bomb, while four 0.303-inch Browning machine guns were mounted in the nose.

The mix of Brits, Aussies and Kiwis at Hunsdon seemed to work very well and the wing soon became experienced in low-level precision attacks. Raids included attacks against German V-1 sites across the Channel, but it was to be a daring low-level raid against a prison in the French city of Amiens that was to propel the wing into the limelight.

The city of Amiens lies in the Picardy region of France, about 70 miles to the north of Paris, and had been under German occupation since May 1940. By early 1944, many members of the French Resistance had been captured and imprisoned at Amiens. Some had been betrayed by collaborators and it was believed that the entire Resistance movement in the region was at risk. Some of the Resistance leaders had already been executed and it was believed that many more, maybe up to a hundred patriots, were to be executed on 19 February.

Details of the prison were sent to London by members of the Resistance still operating in the area, and when two Allied intelligence officers were captured and imprisoned at Amiens, a request was made for a precision air attack against the establishment so that prisoners could make their escape. Even if an air attack was to prove unsuccessful, many believed it better to be killed in an Allied air attack than to be executed by the Nazis.

The prison was located alongside a long straight road and surrounded by high walls. From information obtained from inside the prison, it was known that the guards took their meals in a block adjacent to the main building, and that the changeover of guards took place at lunchtime. Therefore, it was decided that an attack carried out during the lunch period would stand the best chance of success as it was the only time when most of the prison guards would be in the same place at the same time. As well as destroying the mess hall, the prison outer walls would have to be breached and the buildings where the prisoners were housed would need to be sufficiently damaged to allow them to escape. However, with an estimated 700 inmates at the prison, some loss of life amongst the prisoners was considered inevitable and so the raid had to be personally approved by Winston Churchill.

The task for carrying out the raid was given to the 2nd Tactical Air Force and, when it found its way on to the desk of the Air Officer Commanding 2 Group, Air Vice-Marshal Basil Embry, he was keen to lead the raid himself. Embry chose his trusted 140 Wing at Hunsdon for the mission. However, because of his close involvement with the planning of the Allied invasion of Europe, due sometime within the next few months, Embry was denied his wish to lead the raid. He simply knew too much, in the event he was shot down and taken as a prisoner of war. With Embry not allowed to lead the raid, responsibility was passed to Pickard.

The raid was scheduled to take place on any suitable day after 10 February, but was continuously delayed due to poor weather over Europe, which worsened considerably throughout the month with low cloud, poor visibility and snow. With the deadline of 19 February looming, the raid was eventually planned for 18 February, just twenty-four hours before the executions were due to take place.

At 8.00 am on the morning of the raid the crews gathered at Hunsdon for their briefing. The attack was planned to take place just after midday, with eighteen aircraft taking part, six from each squadron, accompanied by a photo-reconnaissance Mosquito from the Photographic Reconnaissance Unit (PRU). The Mosquitos of 487 (RNZAF) Squadron were given the task of attacking the prison's outer walls, which were 20 feet high and 3 feet thick, and to bomb the mess hall where the guards would be having lunch. The Kiwis, led by Wing Commander Irving Smith, were to cause a breach in two places to allow both areas to be used for escape, while the Aussies of 464 (RAAF) Squadron, led by Wing Commander Bob Iredale, were to bomb the main prison walls. Pickard would remain at the rear of the second formation. He and his long-term and highly decorated navigator, 23-year-old Flight Lieutenant Alan Broadley, a holder of the DSO, DFC and DFM, would assess the damage once the first two waves had completed their attacks. If no prisoners were seen to be escaping then he would call in the third wave of 21 Squadron, led by Wing Commander Danny Dale, to carry out the unpleasant task of bombing the prison. In the event of anything happening to Pickard's aircraft, the crew of the PR Mosquito would carry out the visual assessment instead.

The Mosquito crews were briefed to expect eight Typhoons from Westhampnett and Manston to escort them to Amiens, and so the route from Hunsdon would initially take them down to Littlehampton to join up with their escort. The large formation was then to cross the Channel to northern France, coasting in at Tocqueville, before proceeding to Senarpont and then north-eastwards to Bourdon. Keeping the formation some 20 miles to the north of Amiens, the route then took the attackers east to a point just to the south of Doullens and then south-east to Bouzincourt before turning right, passing to the west of the town of Albert, to commence the target run south-westwards to Amiens; the attack on the prison was to be made from the north-east. Off-target, the attackers were to head to Saint-Sauveur, 5 miles to the north-west of Amiens, before heading for Senarpont and returning across the Channel using the same route as inbound to the target. Zero hour, the time for the first attack, was to be at midday, but the weather clearly remained a problem. However, there was no chance of delaying anymore and, with just two hours until the raid was due to take place, the decision was made to go.

Just before 11.00 am the Mosquitos took off from Hunsdon and climbed into the gloom. The weather over southern England was far worse than many of the crews had ever flown in before. Four aircraft ended up losing sight of the formation and returned to base, while a fifth aircraft suffered an engine problem and also had to return.

Just thirteen aircraft were now left to carry on to Amiens: nine to carry out the raid and four in reserve. Things then got worse. The weather at Manston was appalling, with very low cloud and heavy snow showers, which prevented many of the Typhoons from getting airborne; those that did manage arrived overhead Littlehampton too late.

At Westhampnett, however, the weather was slightly better, but there appears to have been a misunderstanding with the timings for the rendezvous and the plan for the attack, resulting in the Typhoons getting airborne hastily and without being fitted with long-range fuel tanks. There was also a problem with bad weather over the Littlehampton area where they were due to join up with the Mosquitos. Four Typhoons did manage to find the Mosquitos of the second wave and joined up, and they were soon followed by four more, and then a further three Typhoons managed to join up with the three Mosquitos of the third wave.

After coasting in over northern France, the formations flew at low level across Tocqueville, Bourdon, Doullens and Albert before picking up the old Roman road leading direct to the prison. By the time the clock in the mess hall struck midday, the Mosquitos of the lead wave were just a couple of miles away to the north-east.

The anti-aircraft guns had now spotted the attackers and a wall of flak filled the sky. A minute later the first Mosquitos struck. Because of the poor visibility, Smith had reduced speed to less than 200mph to ensure the attack was carried out with pinpoint accuracy. Reducing the speed increased the vulnerability of the Mosquitos to ground fire, but it was the only way they would have any chance of success. Smith led the first three aircraft into attack against the eastern outer wall, while the other two aircraft of his formation carried out a diversionary attack against a nearby railway station before running in from the north-west to attack the prison's northern wall.

The attack by Smith's lead section resulted in success. Attacking from a height of just 50 feet, their 500lb bombs breached the northern wall as planned, although the eastern wall seemed to have remained intact. It was now the turn of the Aussie crews of 464. They were now a further aircraft down as one Mosquito had been hit by flak as the formation approached Amiens, and having jettisoned their bombs the crew had headed back home. The four surviving Mosquitos had to initially hold off because of the eleven-second delayed fusing from the bombs of the Kiwis ahead, and by the time the Aussies attacked a couple of minutes had passed since the first attack.

Given that the eastern wall still appeared intact, two Mosquitos ran in towards the prison to bomb the wall, one from the north-west and the other from the north-east, although, from the air, it was not clear whether the eight 500lb bombs dropped had managed to breach the wall. Meanwhile, two other Mosquitos ran in towards the main building at a height of 100 feet. Again, one aircraft ran in from the north-west while the other attacked from the north-east to give the defending gunners as much of a problem as possible. Having successfully run the gauntlet of anti-aircraft fire, the two Mosquitos released their eight 500lb bombs with devastating accuracy. A direct hit was observed on the guardhouse, killing many of the guards inside and allowing the prisoners to start making their escape.

Pickard was circling ahead and had seen the attacks. He could now see a large number of prisoners running towards the breached wall and could see the damaged building and demolished guard towers. Assessing the damage caused, he could see that any further attack would put the escaping prisoners at more risk and so he called off the final wave, instructing Dale to take the four remaining Mosquitos of 21 Squadron back home. Above Pickard at around 400 feet was the Mosquito of the PRU, which had been circling overhead to film the attack.

As the remaining Mosquitos made their escape, one of 464's aircraft, flown by Squadron Leader Ian McRitchie, was hit while escaping to the north-east of Amiens and had to crash-land near the town of Albert. McRitchie was fortunate to escape with his life and was taken as a prisoner of war, but his navigator, Flight Lieutenant Richard Sampson, was killed.

By now, the raid had attracted a number of enemy fighters in the local area. Focke-Wulf FW 190s at the nearby airfield of Glisy, on the eastern side of Amiens, had received warning of the raid; some of the Mosquito crews had even seen the 190s preparing for take-off as they ran in towards their target. As soon as they were airborne the 190s headed for the Mosquitos but they were too late to prevent the attack. They were, however, in time to catch the stragglers as they made their escape from Amiens, but the escorting Typhoons were quick to step in and managed to force most of the 190s away.

Pickard had been the last to leave the target area. He then circled the wreckage of McRitchie's aircraft to ascertain if there were any survivors, but, as he did so, he was spotted by two of the 190s. The burst of cannon fire that followed blew the Mosquito's tail section away, causing it to flip over and dive into the ground. It then blew up. The Mosquito had come down at St Gratien, some 8 miles to the north of the prison. Pickard and Broadley were both killed.

For the other Mosquitos the return transit went much as planned, although the weather remained bad. One of 487's aircraft, that flown by Pilot Officer Max Sparks, had earlier been hit by flak but managed to make it back to base, although his wheel collapsed on landing; Sparks and his navigator were unhurt. Two Typhoons, both from 174 Squadron, were lost. One was shot down by an FW 190 about 4 miles to the north of the prison and crash-landed near Poulainville, with the pilot surviving to become a prisoner of war, while the other, flown by Flight Sergeant Henry Brown, failed to return to Westhampnett; it is not known what happened.

The RAF later announced that Operation Jericho was a success but, like many raids analysed in the post-wear era, it has since been the subject of much controversy. Nearly 260 prisoners managed to escape, including many important members of the Resistance, but about 180 of these were later recaptured, while around 100 prisoners were killed during the raid, and a further 70 wounded. It appears that many prisoners had refused to try and escape for fear of reprisals against their families.

In the aftermath of the raid some historians considered it to have been an unnecessary raid that served little or no purpose. There has also been doubt raised as to whether the French Resistance had ever requested the raid in the first place, as no executions appear to have been scheduled or expected to take place on that day. But whatever the truth, there can be no doubting the courage of the Mosquito crews who took part in Jericho. They had been left in no doubt as to the urgency of the raid and had pressed on through awful weather conditions to deliver their attack. Furthermore, the loss of the outstanding Pickard and Broadley had been a devastating blow, not only to 2 Group, but to the nation. Their bodies were recovered from the wreckage of their Mosquito and given heroes' graves; they remain buried at St Pierre Cemetery on the north-eastern outskirts of Amiens.

Basil Embry, the AOC of 2 Group, was to later write of Pickard:

It is impossible to measure Charles Pickard's loss to the RAF and Britain, but in courage, devotion to duty, fighting spirit and powers of real leadership, he stood out as one of the great airmen of the war, and a shining example of British manhood.

Chapter Twenty-Seven

Pegasus Bridge

6 June 1944

The Allied invasion of north-west Europe, called Operation Overlord, commenced on 6 June 1944. Better known as D-Day, it was one of the most famous days in recent history and images of thousands of men landing on five beaches stretching along the Normandy coastline – Gold, Juno, Omaha, Sword and Utah – will remain forever. The day witnessed many heroic actions, but the first took place several hours before the initial landing craft had even gone ashore. The glider-borne assault, carried out by a small force of men from the Oxfordshire and Buckinghamshire Light Infantry and the Glider Pilot Regiment, was to capture, and then hold, two bridges crossing the River Orne and Caen Canal. The bridges have since become better known as Pegasus and Horsa, and Major John Howard's coup de main has become legendary in the annals of airborne operations.

Sword Beach, the easternmost of the five landing beaches, stretched 5 miles from Ouistreham to Saint Aubin-sur-Mer and was where the British 3rd Infantry Division was due to go ashore. It was also the closest beach to Caen, one of the major objectives, which was just 10 miles away. Being on the extreme eastern flank of the Allied landings meant that British units going ashore on Sword would be vulnerable to German counter-attacks. It was vital, therefore, that the main approaches to the beach were denied to the enemy, and this meant capturing and holding two key bridges: one crossing the Caen Canal at Bénouville and the other spanning the River Orne at Ranville, just a few hundred yards further to the east.

A daring plan was put in place for a small force of 180 men to land next to the bridges in gliders. The assault was planned to take place several hours before the first Allied landings and so surprise was the key to success. If all went according to plan, the assault force would be able to quickly capture the two bridges. Meanwhile, paratroopers of the British 6th Airborne Division were to be dropped to the east of the River Orne to establish an airborne bridgehead and to reinforce the small force holding the two bridges as quickly as possible. This would allow units coming ashore on Sword to move rapidly across the bridges – the only exits eastwards – to consolidate the airborne bridgehead. Capturing the bridges would also deny their use to the enemy, in particular German armoured units, to counter-attack the beach landings.

Chosen to lead the raid was Major John Howard of D Company, 2nd Battalion Oxfordshire and Buckinghamshire Light Infantry. Following a period of intense training leading up to the invasion, most of which was done at night, the men of D Company were put to the test during a number of rehearsal exercises involving the capture of bridges. For the assault Howard was given extra men, with D Company increased in size from its normal four platoons to six. The extra men were to be taken from B Company and so Howard chose the two platoons commanded by the subalterns Sandy Smith and Dennis Fox to join his own platoon commanders: Lieutenants Den Brotheridge, David Wood, Tony Hooper and Tod Sweeney. Planning continued with information about the bridges coming from several sources: aerial reconnaissance photographs, detailed intelligence from members of the French Resistance on the ground, and a scale model for Howard to study. With his fellow officers, Howard was able to form a plan.

Howard had available to him a total force of 181 men, which were to be carried in six Horsa gliders. He would be on board the lead glider with the men of 1 Platoon and would land at the bridge over the Caen Canal. Led by Brotheridge, the platoon would be the first men on the ground and so they had the vital task of destroying an enemy pillbox and seizing the bridge. The platoon would then cross the bridge to seize and hold the western end while 2 Platoon, the next to land, and led by Wood, would remove any opposition on the eastern bank of the canal. The last glider to land at the bridge would be carrying the men of 3 Platoon, led by Smith, who would go straight to the western side to reinforce 1 Platoon. The plan for capturing the bridge over the Orne at Ranville was essentially the same. Howard's second-in-command, Captain Brian Priday, would land in the first glider and oversee the attack with the men of 4, 5 and 6 Platoons, led by Hooper, Fox and Sweeney, carrying out the assault.

The six platoons were to be accompanied by twenty sappers of the airborne specialists, 249 Field Company of the Royal Engineers. Once the bridges had been captured, the sappers' task would be to crawl all over the structure and remove any explosives or wires that might be found.

The six Horsa gliders that would be used to carry Howard's men to Normandy would be flown by men of the Glider Pilot Regiment. Part of the British airborne forces since early 1942, the glider pilots were volunteers from the British Army but trained by the RAF. They had the immensely challenging task of getting the gliders down on the ground as close to the bridges as they possibly could, and, once on the ground, augmenting the assaulting force.

Poor weather meant that D-Day was delayed by twenty-four hours from its planned date of 5 June. The news came as a disappointment to Howard and his men. They were ready to go. Then, during the late evening of 5 June, the men boarded their gliders at Tarrant Rushton in Dorset.

It was just before 11.00 pm when the lead glider was towed down the runway by its Halifax tug and limped into the air. Within five minutes all six gliders and tugs were heading for Normandy in two formations of three. The Horsa was considered to be very manoeuvrable for a glider but conditions were not going to be ideal. A strong breeze and patchy cloud between the launch point and landing zone had been forecast, which would provide a challenge for any glider pilot in daylight during peacetime, let alone at night and at war.

At the controls of the lead glider was 24-year-old Staff Sergeant Jim Wallwork, an experienced pilot who had taken part in the Sicily landings the year before. Sat alongside him was his co-pilot, Staff Sergeant John Ainsworth. Behind the two pilots was Howard. The dozen or so training flights beforehand had done little to help the men get used to the extremely cramped conditions on board and the nauseous feeling of being towed, but at least that would soon be over. When it was time to be released it came as something of a relief.

It was seven minutes after midnight when the glider jerked for the last time as it was released from the tug. There was then silence: the drone of the tug's engines had disappeared. The Halifax tugs now reverted to their role as bombers and continued on to Caen where they were to carry out a light diversionary attack as a way of distracting the enemy defences.

For those on board the gliders there was no turning back. Sat next to Howard was Brotheridge, who was to lead the main assault on the bridge.

Howard knew that the capture of the bridges would depend largely on surprise and speed. If the gliders could get down safely, and if the opposition was to be as expected, then he was confident they could capture the bridge intact, but holding it until relieved would be a different matter. As they continued the descent, the door was then removed, but all they could see was cloud. The twenty-eight men of 1 Platoon now prepared themselves for action.

As Wallwork swooped down towards his designated landing zone it was very dark. A layer of cloud prevented the moon from providing any light. Meanwhile, on the ground the German defenders did not suspect a thing. The recent poor weather had convinced many commanders that an attack was far from imminent and the German soldiers at the two bridges had settled in to what appeared to be another routine night of duty.

The route took the glider over the French coast at Cabourg, about 5 miles to the east of the mouth of the River Orne and some 10 miles from their bridge. Behind them, at one-minute intervals, were the two other gliders destined for the same small area next to the bridge over the canal. The second glider, flown by 23-year-old Staff Sergeant Oliver Boland, had the men of Wood's 2 Platoon on board. The gliders were separated to minimize the risk of collision, which was just as well because the darkness meant the pilots could hardly see a thing, let alone each other. All three were heading for the same landing zone and were effectively on their own.

In the lead glider Wallwork still could not see the landing zone. Fortunately, he had spotted Cabourg as he coasted in, and from there he and Ainsworth had used dead reckoning to find the bridge. It was a procedure they had used many times in training and involved flying on a known heading for a certain length of time, but for navigation to be accurate they had to assess their speed across the ground and make the right allowance for the wind that was pushing the slow wooden glider in one direction. It was then time to turn hard right for a few moments before making another hard right turn onto a northerly heading towards the bridge. They were now descending rapidly to a height of 500 feet and reducing airspeed down to around 100mph, a manoeuvre quite unpleasant for those inside; however, Wallwork and Ainsworth could still not see anything to confirm they were in the right place.

Meanwhile, minutes behind and some way further to the west, approaching the mouth of the River Orne, the second formation of gliders were manoeuvring towards their landing zone on the western side of the river and to the north of the bridge. The pilots were encountering the same difficult weather conditions as the first formation and navigation was equally as difficult. Unfortunately, the pilot of the lead glider, with Priday and Hooper's 4 Platoon on board, had mistaken the mouth of the River Dives for the mouth of the Orne. The confusion was complete when the pilots spotted a bridge across the Dives that they assumed to be their bridge over the Orne and landed. They were, in fact, more than 12 miles away from where they should have been and the men were now left to make their way through the enemy lines towards Ranville. Fortunately, the other two Horsas had passed over the right estuary and were now running on the correct southerly heading along the Orne. They had a straightforward descent and run-in to their bridge.

Back in the lead glider of the first formation, Wallwork was on his final run-in towards the bridge despite the fact he could still not see anything of note. He was now just 200 feet above the ground and at his final landing speed of just below 100mph, with the door open ready for impact. He was committed to land, but at that stage he still did not know where. Suddenly, the cloud broke enough to allow some lunar light to reflect off the river and the canal. Through their remarkable skill, he and Ainsworth had got the glider to the right place. They could now make out the bridge just over a mile away.

Aware that there were two gliders behind him and heading for the same area, Wallwork decided to bring his glider to rest as close to the bridge as he could. This would take him into the barbed wire defences at the far end of the landing zone and next to the bridge. He had to keep his speed up because of the weight on board and so in order to stop quickly it would mean the use of the Horsa's chute: a technique untried and not favoured. Nonetheless, it would be the only chance they would have of stopping in such a short distance, although it would inevitably bring the glider to a sudden stop and undoubtedly cause injuries to some of those inside.

The men behind him were braced ready for impact. As the wheels touched down the chute was deployed, which lifted the tail and caused the

Horsa to lunge momentarily back into the air. Then, with the chute having been discarded, the glider crashed back down to the ground with the wheels ripped off. Wallwork had managed to put the glider down in the perfect position between the canal on his left and a large marsh pond on his right. As the Horsa finally crashed through the barbed wire, bringing the glider to an abrupt halt, the two pilots were both catapulted through the cockpit and out into the open – still strapped to their seats, which had broken free. Inside the glider the men were stunned and most had been temporarily knocked unconscious by the impact. It would take a few seconds for them all to come round.

According to the records it was sixteen minutes after midnight when Wallwork landed his glider in exactly the right spot. It was an achievement later described by Air Chief Marshal Sir Trafford Leigh-Mallory, the commander of the Allied air forces on D-Day, as '*the greatest feat of flying of the Second World War.*' Anyone who has visited the site will appreciate just how difficult a task it was and just how skilful Wallwork and the other glider pilots had proved to be.

Just yards away at the bridge, the German sentries were still unaware of what was happening. They had heard a sound but they had seemingly dismissed it as soon as they had heard it. It was very dark and so nothing could be seen in the direction of the sound. Whatever they thought it might have been, they would not have expected it to have been from an enemy glider landing in such a small space. Had the German sentries seen the glider then the outcome of the assault might well have been different: the men of 1 Platoon would have been trapped inside, making it almost impossible to escape. Fortunately for the raiders, and for the invasion forces soon to land on Sword, that was not to be the case.

The raiders had taken the defenders completely by surprise, and with the Germans failing to recognize what had happened, the men of 1 Platoon immediately took the initiative. Led by Brotheridge, they stormed off the glider and went straight into action. Now the German sentries realized the gravity of the situation they were in but it was too late.

It was at that moment that the second Horsa landed exactly as planned, but to avoid running into the back of the first glider, Boland released his chute and turned hard starboard towards the pond. In doing so the glider broke into two, with the front section finally coming to rest just short of the boggy marsh.

By now Brotheridge was leading 1 Platoon across the bridge and dealing with the enemy as they appeared. With his men alongside him, he then charged towards a machine-gun post entrenched on the far bank of the canal and quickly took it out with a grenade. At that moment he fell. He had been shot through the neck and was now lying mortally wounded at the western end of the bridge, with no cover from the enemy fire. Den Brotheridge would later die from his wound, making him the first British officer to die on D-Day.

Wood's platoon had now rallied outside their broken glider and moved forward to Howard's position, where he had set up a temporary command post with his radio operator. With 1 Platoon seemingly taking care of the bridge, Howard sent Wood and his men to clear the north-eastern side of the bank. At that point, the third glider landed.

The sound of German Spandau machine guns and British Bren and Sten guns could be heard all around as more men of 1 Platoon charged across the bridge. For the next few minutes the battle raged as they disposed of a second machine-gun position on the far bank. The first two groups of raiders were now being supported by Smith's 3 Platoon, whose men had recovered from their impact on landing and had now joined the fray. As Smith led his men across the bridge, a grenade went off next to him, catching him in the blast – quite incredibly, he escaped with relatively minor wounds.

Howard now awaited word from the bridge at Ranville. With Priday's lead glider having landed miles away, Fox's Horsa landed 300 yards to the north of the correct bridge on the western side of the river. It was just four minutes after Howard's glider had landed and everything had gone according to plan. Fox now rallied his men and led them off towards the bridge. They were greeted by a burst of machine-gun fire, but the enemy position was soon taken out and Fox's platoon reached the bridge and quickly crossed to the eastern bank.

A minute behind them, Sweeney's glider landed even shorter and nearly half a mile from the bridge. Sweeney quickly gathered his platoon and they soon arrived at the bridge without encountering any opposition. The bridge at Ranville was already secure but, soon after, a section of Sweeney's platoon challenged a group of four approaching the bridge. It happened to be a German patrol, and in a devastating burst of fire all four of the enemy were killed.

Back at the canal bridge at Bénouville the battle was still raging and word of what was going on at the river bridge had yet to reach Howard. On the eastern side of the canal 2 Platoon had been weeding the enemy out of their positions, but in doing so Wood had been hit in the leg. Howard now faced the fact that all three of his platoon commanders at the canal bridge had become casualties, but moments later the night fell silent. The bridge had finally been captured intact.

A search by the sappers on the canal bridge revealed the enemy had wired the bridge for demolition but no explosive charges had been placed. The attack had clearly come as a complete surprise but it had cost the deaths of two of the raiders. Apart from Brotheridge, a lance corporal had died in one of the gliders on landing.

Howard now received word that the river bridge was also in their hands and had been taken without suffering any casualties. Both bridges had been captured intact in just fifteen minutes since the gliders had landed. While his radio operator continuously transmitted the code words 'Ham and Jam', signifying the capture of both bridges, Howard knew that his men would have to hold both bridges until reinforcements arrived. There was still another six hours until the first Allied troops were due to come ashore and so Howard had to hope that 6th Airborne's drop to the east of the Orne had gone according to plan so that reinforcements could arrive as soon as possible.

The main threat to Howard's forces would come from the west rather than the east. He knew there were enemy tanks out there that would have little trouble taking back the bridges if the enemy fully realized what had gone on.

Howard decided to reinforce his defence of the canal bridge by pulling one platoon away from the river bridge so that he could get men, armed with an anti-tank weapon, dug-in along the road approaching the canal bridge from the west. Sure enough, two tanks soon approached. Sergeant Wagger Thornton, armed with a PIAT, a portable anti-tank weapon, was perfectly concealed in his hiding position. He now waited patiently for the right moment to fire. His patience paid off. Whereas others might have fired too early, thereby reducing the chances of securing a hit, Thornton waited until the tank was just 50 yards away. He then fired, his round striking the centre of the tank and triggering a chain of explosions inside it that could be seen and heard for miles around. The commander of the second tank had seen the devastation in front of him and, believing the strength of the enemy forces to be far greater than it actually was, quickly withdrew. The Germans would wait until dawn before commencing a further attack; one accurate round from the PIAT had prevented further attacks during the night and had gained Howard some valuable time.

Meanwhile, the 6th Airborne's drop to the east had become scattered, but Howard and his men did not have to wait too long for reinforcements to arrive. Just over two hours after the bridges had been secured the first men of the 7th Parachute Battalion arrived from the east. Once the paras had relieved his men to the west of the canal, Howard relocated to a position between the two bridges where his men would be held in reserve.

The paras took up their positions as they waited for the inevitable counter-attack. By the time the German commanders in the area had realized what had happened, it was too late. As Allied forces started to land on the beaches, the Germans realized they had been deprived of this vital artery and would not be able to counter the landings without first having to overcome stiff opposition at the bridges. There was still sporadic enemy fire coming in from the surrounding area and an attack on the canal bridge during the morning by two enemy motor gunboats, trying to withdraw from the harbour at Ouistreham back to Caen, was repelled by one of Howard's men using a PIAT. The round exploded inside one of the wheelhouses, causing that gunboat to jam against the bank of the canal; the crew were taken prisoner.

With the exception of one further attack by a gunboat from the south during the afternoon, which was again quickly and easily repelled, the situation at the bridges finally stabilized. The western side of the canal was secured and Allied forces were pushing out to the east to consolidate the earlier landing by 6th Airborne. Then finally, at around midnight, and twenty-four hours after his men had first landed, Howard was able to hand over his responsibilities.

Howard had been given 181 men to take and hold the bridges but he had ended up with far fewer. The platoon that had landed more than 12 miles away still remained unaccounted for, and the glider pilots and sappers had left the bridges as soon as it had become safe to do so; they had done their job. Furthermore, the two platoons that had reinforced his own company, those of Smith and Fox, were now handed back to B Company, leaving Howard with less than eighty men and just one other officer fit for battle.

For his outstanding leadership of the raid, John Howard was awarded the DSO. The combination of daring fighting prowess and endurance throughout such a difficult mission had resulted in success. Only two men had been killed and fourteen wounded, far fewer than had been expected.

Chapter Twenty-Eight

The Bridge Too Far

17–26 September 1944

The town of Arnhem has become immortalized in books as well as the epic 1977 film *A Bridge Too Far*. Its main bridge crossing the Nederrijn, the Dutch Lower Rhine, from which the film took its name, was the northernmost objective for the Allies during Operation Market Garden, one of the most famous military actions of the Second World War. After nine days of intense fighting, the shattered remnants of the British 1st Airborne Division were withdrawn. They left behind them some three-quarters of the original force, who had been killed, wounded or taken as prisoners of war. Although the bridge was, indeed, 'a bridge too far', the courage of those who fought at Arnhem will never be forgotten.

By September 1944 the Allies had broken out of the Normandy beachhead and had quickly swept their way through France and Belgium. Now well poised to enter Holland, there were differences of opinion amongst senior commanders as to what to do next. While most favoured continuing into Germany across a broad front, Field Marshal Bernard Montgomery, commander of 21st Army Group, proposed a bold plan – a single thrust northwards through Holland, to bypass the German Siegfried Line, and to open the door into Germany's industrial heartland of the Ruhr.

The plan, called Market Garden, was for the American 101st and 82nd Airborne Divisions to capture and secure key bridges at Eindhoven and Nijmegen while the northernmost bridges at Arnhem – a road bridge, a rail bridge and a pontoon bridge – would be captured and held by the British 1st Airborne Division, which was to include the attached Polish 1st Independent Parachute Brigade. With the bridges in Allied hands, the British Second Army, led by XXX Corps, would then punch its way up the airborne corridor and cross the Rhine within two days.

While the plan might have seemed straightforward enough, the task faced by Major General Roy Urquhart's 1st Airborne Division was the most daring. There were two significant problems. The first and biggest problem of all was the fact that not enough aircraft were allocated to Urquhart to enable him to conduct a single lift, and so three lifts would be required. The second problem, which may have been less of an issue had a single lift been an option, was where to land. Much of the ground in that part of Holland was considered too soft and damp for glider landings. There was, however, a large area about 4 miles to the north of Arnhem where paratroopers could be dropped, but the ground was not considered suitable for gliders. The only place in the surrounding area considered suitable was to the west of Arnhem, where the ground was higher and, therefore, firm enough, but this area was 8 miles from the three bridges.

There was a further problem, too, and that was the accuracy, or lack of it, of the intelligence received prior to the raid taking place. The Allies believed there were no significant enemy forces in the region, no more than brigade-size at worse, but information received from the Dutch Resistance suggested that the 2nd Panzer Corps, which had been withdrawn from Normandy, was now reorganizing in the Arnhem area. But it seems that any concerns raised simply fell on deaf ears.

Urquhart's division consisted of the 1st and 4th Parachute Brigades, under the command of Brigadiers Gerald Lathbury and Shan Hackett respectively, with each brigade consisting of three para battalions. There was also the 1st Airlanding Brigade led by Brigadier Pip Hicks; this was the division's only glider-borne infantry unit and consisted of the 1st Borders, 7th King's Own Scottish Borderers and 2nd South Staffords. The division also consisted of elements of the artillery, engineers, ordnance, medical, signals, reconnaissance and security, as well as two wings of the Glider Pilot Regiment.

The main task, the capture of the road bridge at Arnhem, was given to 1st Parachute Brigade, and so the first lift would carry Lathbury's men and those of the 1st Airlanding Brigade tasked with securing and holding the landing zones. To carry three para battalions to their drop zone, just to the north of Heelsum, required more than 160 American Dakotas, while nearly 300 aircraft of the RAF would tow the gliders carrying the 1st Airlanding Brigade and the 1st Airlanding Light Regiment of the Royal Artillery to their landing zones to the north and west of Wolfheze.

Lathbury gave the task of capturing the main bridge to Major Freddie Gough's 1st Airborne Reconnaissance Squadron. Having landed in gliders, his men were to advance quickly through the town from the west and secure the bridge. They would be supported by the 2nd Parachute Battalion, commanded by Lieutenant Colonel John Frost, who had led the raid on Bruneval more than two years earlier. Frost would lead his men south from their drop zone and follow the northern bank of the Lower Rhine to the bridge. Meanwhile, John Fitch's 3rd Parachute Battalion was to move from its drop zone and approach the bridge from the north, where the men would help form the main defence, while the 1st Battalion, led by David Dobie, would secure a perimeter to the north of Arnhem.

The second lift was to take place the following day and would include Hackett's 4th Parachute Brigade. They were to be dropped to the north-west of Wolfheze on the furthest drop zone from Arnhem. The total lift required more than 120 Dakotas, with 300 tugs towing the gliders carrying the rest of the Airlanding Brigade. Once on the ground the paras were to secure an even larger perimeter around the town. A further thirty-five transport aircraft of the RAF would drop much needed supplies to those already on the ground. Then, on the third day, more than a hundred Dakotas would drop the Polish Parachute Brigade on the southern side of the river while nearly fifty gliders would deliver the rest of the brigade to the north-east of Oosterbeek at the closest landing zone to Arnhem.

Operation Market Garden began on Sunday, 17 September. The vast air armada carrying the 1st Parachute Brigade and 1st Airlanding Brigade crossed the Dutch coast and the first airborne units landed on Dutch soil soon after midday. The landings were mainly unopposed, and within a couple of hours the para battalions had formed up and set off towards their objectives, as had the 1st Airborne Reconnaissance Squadron tasked with taking the bridge. Meanwhile, the men of the Airlanding Brigade took up defensive positions around the landing zones ready for the 4th Parachute Brigade's arrival the following morning.

The landings had taken the Germans totally by surprise. They were unprepared and now confused and so could initially offer only a token resistance. However, as the paras made their way into Arnhem, the Germans were quick to blow the railway bridge. Furthermore, the pontoon bridge was missing its central section and so this left the steel road bridge as the only way of crossing the river.

By the early evening of the first day, only lead elements of Frost's 2nd Battalion had managed to reach the undefended northern end of the road bridge. Their advance had been slowed by the strength of welcome from many of the local Dutch population. Having finally arrived at the bridge, Frost immediately began securing buildings around its ramp and organizing his defences, but he was now out of radio contact with two of his companies.

Although elements of Frost's battalion had reached the bridge in relatively quick time, the rest of the main body of the first lift had been halted on the outskirts of the town. The Allied advance had also been hampered by poor communications. The wooded terrain around the town caused problems with the radio sets, making it at times impossible to maintain communications between the advancing paras and their headquarters back at the landing zones. The problem was so bad that Urquhart decided to follow the 1st Parachute Brigade into Arnhem so that he could maintain contact with his senior commanders, most notably Lathbury; however, this would end up with him becoming cut off from his own divisional headquarters for the next two days.

As dusk fell, the men of A Company of Frost's 2nd Battalion were dug-in on the northern side of the bridge. Major Digby Tatham-Warter now observed the German forces across the bridge and decided to try and seize the southern side of the bridge before nightfall. He gave the task to one of the platoon commanders, Lieutenant Jack Grayburn.

As darkness fell, Grayburn led his men along the ramp and onto the bridge. His platoon had split and were progressing forward on either side of the girders along the edges of the road, but they were soon spotted and immediately came under heavy fire from two 20mm guns and from machine guns from an armoured car. Grayburn was hit almost immediately, the rounds hitting him fully in his shoulder. There was no cover on the bridge but in spite of his wound he pressed on. However, the enemy fire soon became too intense and casualties were starting to mount, and so he was faced with no option but to order his men to withdraw. He then personally directed the withdrawal until all his men were back on the northern side of the bridge. Grayburn was the last to leave.

Away from the bridge, the reconnaissance squadron and paras had run into unexpected resistance on the outskirts of Oosterbeek in the western suburbs of Arnhem. The advanced unit of the reconnaissance squadron had been ambushed and so was forced to withdraw while the paras decided to split up. The 3rd Battalion remained dug-in at Oosterbeek while Dobie took the 1st Battalion northwards, but they soon encountered more defenders on the edge of the town. Unable to form a defensive perimeter to the north of Arnhem, and unable to contact Lathbury, Dobie decided to support Frost's battalion at the bridge.

By the early hours of 18 September, German reinforcements had started to arrive at Arnhem and Frost's men at the bridge were surrounded. Frost had a fighting force of between 300–400 men, but attempts by the 1st and 3rd Battalions to reach them during the night had proved unsuccessful. His men of A Company were now occupying buildings on either side of the ramp nearest the river, with Grayburn's platoon occupying a house in a vital position overlooking the bridge.

Throughout the morning a battle raged and the paras of A Company came under continuous attack from tanks, mortars, machine guns and infantry as German armoured units crossed the bridge from the south. While the first vehicles attempting to cross had been halted by the paras, more armoured vehicles arrived, simply knocking the wreckage to one side and pressing on into the town. The house where Grayburn and his men were dug-in was very exposed and difficult to defend, but the platoon held out.

While Frost's men remained dug-in at the bridge, the rest of the division had been making several attempts to reach them, but were unable to break through the German defences now surrounding the bridge. In Urquhart's absence, Hicks had taken temporary command of the division and established its headquarters at the Hartenstein Hotel in Oosterbeek. Realizing Frost's perilous situation, he sent the main element of the 2nd South Staffs into Arnhem to link up with the 1st Parachute Battalion and to reinforce attempts to reach the bridge.

Back in southern England, the second lift had been delayed due to fog, but poor communications meant that much of the essential information did not get through to the landing and drop zones. Equally, those already on the ground to the west of Arnhem had been unable to warn those back in England that the landing and drop zones had now increasingly come under attack; the Germans had received sufficient reinforcements to hassle the Airlanding Brigade defending the zones and there were an increasing number of strafing attacks by the Luftwaffe, as enemy planes were now appearing in larger numbers over Arnhem.

The arrival of the 4th Parachute Brigade was now several hours overdue, and when they did arrive during mid-afternoon they jumped into heavy fire from the ground which killed or wounded several of them. But as soon as the men were ready to move off, Hicks sent the newly arrived 11th Parachute Battalion and the rest of the 2nd South Staffs into the town and the two other battalions of the 4th Parachute Brigade, the 10th and 156th Battalions, to take up positions to the north-west of the town.

Meanwhile, the situation inside the town had become more confused as the battle resorted to street-to-street and house-to-house fighting. Soon after first light on 19 September, Dobie's 1st Parachute Battalion, supported by remnants of the 3rd Battalion, led an advance along a narrow front. Almost immediately the lead battalion was spotted and came under heavy fire, bringing the advance to a halt. The men of the 1st Battalion were caught out in the open and came under heavy fire from three sides as enemy forces, with heavier cannon mounted on half-tracks and armoured vehicles, had positioned themselves along the southern bank of the river. Behind them the 3rd Battalion had been forced to withdraw immediately.

As the 11th Parachute Battalion and the 2nd South Staffs joined up with the 1st and 3rd Battalions of the 1st Parachute Brigade in the western suburbs of Arnhem, it was hoped there were now sufficient numbers to break through to Frost at the bridge. The 2nd South Staffs had been following the main road on the left flank while the 11th Parachute Battalion took up the rear, but the South Staffs were quickly cut off and most of the battalion was overcome during the morning. The 11th Battalion were also exposed and had soon become overwhelmed while trying to take the high ground to the north. With no chance of breaking through, the remaining 500 or so men of the four battalions retreated westwards back to Oosterbeek, although many had become casualties or had been captured.

The four battalions had fallen back in some disarray and all four commanding officers had become casualties; John Fitch (3rd Parachute Battalion) had been killed, while David Dobie (1st Parachute Battalion),

George Lea (11th Parachute Battalion) and Derek McCardie (2nd South Staffs) had been wounded and taken prisoner.

The remnants of the battalions were now organized into defensive positions by Lieutenant Colonel 'Sheriff' Thompson, the commanding officer of 1st Airlanding Light Regiment. Now known as Thompson Force, defensive positions were set up at Oosterbeek Church and its surrounding area, with the outlying forces led by Major Dickie Lonsdale, the second-in-command of the 11th Parachute Battalion.

North of the main railway line that ran into Arnhem, the paras of the 10th and 156th Battalions had encountered the enemy while trying to occupy the high ground in dense woodland to the north of the town. They would eventually be forced to withdraw to a landing zone near Wolfheze where men of the King's Own Scottish Borderers were defending the area in preparation for the arrival of the glider-borne elements of the Polish Parachute Brigade. The two para battalions combined had withdrawn with little more than 500 men and had lost almost all of their transport.

The raging battle that had unfolded in the suburbs of Arnhem during the morning had kept the Germans fully occupied. Fortuitously for Urquhart it gave him the opportunity to escape out of the town and back to his divisional headquarters. Appalled by the situation he now found his men to be in, he sent Colonel Hilaro Barlow, the deputy commander of the 1st Airlanding Brigade, into Arnhem to co-ordinate the battalions. But Barlow never reached Arnhem and was never seen again.

Back in England, more ground fog had hampered the third lift. When the Poles did arrive, the gliders came down in the middle of a raging battle and many Poles became casualties. It was during the afternoon that the RAF flew its first major resupply mission, with more than 160 aircraft involved. By now, the Germans had established where the drop zones were located and had moved a number of anti-aircraft flak units into the area.

The unwavering efforts of the RAF to resupply the 1st Airborne Division, and the courage of the air transport crews, did not go unnoticed by those on the ground, who were now being pressed into a small area. To ensure the drops were as accurate as possible, the aircrews had to fly at less than 1,000 feet over the drop zones.

Despite the intense anti-aircraft fire in the vicinity of the drop zones, the transport crews still pressed on. One of those aircraft was a Dakota of 271

Squadron, flown by Flight Lieutenant David Lord. While approaching the drop zone at 1,500 feet his aircraft was hit in the starboard wing and the engine caught fire. Lord would have been fully justified in abandoning his run-in, but having been told that his crew were uninjured he decided to press on to complete the drop, fully appreciating that the troops on the ground were in desperate need of supplies. With his starboard engine burning furiously, Lord took the Dakota down to its drop height but his stricken aircraft had now been singled out by the anti-aircraft gunners. Keeping his aircraft as steady as possible Lord pressed on while the supplies were dropped. At the end of the run he learned that two containers had still to be dropped. The wing of the aircraft was now in danger of falling off, but instead of heading for safety he elected to go round again for a second run to drop the remaining supplies. The Dakota was still under intense anti-aircraft fire and it took several minutes to complete the second drop. Only when his task had been completed did he order his crew to abandon the aircraft.

The Dakota was now down to 500 feet but, as the crew were preparing to jump, the starboard wing broke off and the aircraft fell in flames. There was only one survivor, Pilot Officer Harry King, who had been flung out of the aircraft as it fell. King was captured and taken as a prisoner of war, but after his release at the end of the war he was able to tell the full story of Lord's heroic act and extraordinary sacrifice. David Lord was posthumously awarded the Victoria Cross, the only member of Transport Command to have been so recognized.

Meanwhile, reinforcements were still trying to reach the besieged paras at the bridge. During the afternoon 24-year-old Captain Lionel Queripel, of the 10th Parachute Battalion, was leading a small composite company of paras, consisting of men from the three battalions of the 4th Parachute Brigade that had been cut off from their main force. They had been following the main road running along the embankment towards the town when he and his men came under continuous and heavy enemy fire. During one heavy attack from a machine-gun position, which had been extremely accurate and had resulted in considerable casualties, Queripel reorganized his men and led them on towards the enemy strongpoint, first down one side of the road and then the other, while all the time coming under increased fire. One of his sergeants had been hit and badly wounded, but Queripel picked him up and carried him back to the regimental aid post, all the time under continuous fire, and himself suffering wounds to his face. In spite of his own injuries, Queripel continued to lead the attack, finally killing the machine-gun crews and capturing an anti-tank gun.

Unable to press on, the men were forced to withdraw with the rest of their battalion. Later in the day Queripel again found himself cut off with a small group of men and suffering from further wounds in both his arms. In spite of his own wounds, as well as being under further heavy fire from machine guns and mortars, he continued to rally and inspire his men. However, the situation had now become desperate and he ordered his men to withdraw while he insisted on remaining behind to cover their escape. Armed with only an automatic pistol and a few remaining hand grenades, Lionel Queripel was last seen covering the withdrawal of his men – he was killed while doing so. It was an act that would later see the gallant young officer posthumously awarded the Victoria Cross.

At the bridge, the paras continued to hold out, but, without any resupply or reinforcements, their position was becoming weaker by the hour. The Germans were now using mortars, artillery and tanks against the buildings and houses to blast the defenders out of their hiding places. The heavy bombardment was typically followed by infantry assaults, but the paras held on. Renewed enemy attacks against the house in which Grayburn and his platoon were holed up increased in intensity but, as the young platoon commander organized and rallied his men, they continued to repulse the attacks. Eventually, however, the house was ablaze and Grayburn finally gave the order to evacuate. He now led his men, as well as other survivors from the company, to new defensive positions covering the approaches to the bridge, where he re-formed them into a fighting force.

As the battle of Arnhem entered its fourth day, the 1st Airborne Division had been weakened so much that, of the nine battalions that had been landed, only one, the Border Regiment of the Airlanding Brigade, still existed as a unit. Urquhart decided that the only way to hold out until the arrival of XXX Corps was to withdraw his remaining forces and consolidate them inside a defensive box.

At the bridge, Frost's defensive perimeter was shrinking hour by hour as casualties mounted and ammunition ran low. He had finally managed to make contact with divisional headquarters, only to hear that reinforcements were increasingly unlikely. In the afternoon Frost was wounded in the leg by fragments of a mortar bomb. Command of the battalion was passed to Tatham-Warter, with Grayburn, in turn, taking over command of A Company, while Freddie Gough assumed overall command of all forces at the bridge.

Grayburn had extended the defences by organizing a series of fighting patrols to prevent the enemy from gaining access to key buildings in the immediate vicinity of the bridge, which would have prevented its defence. The enemy responded by bringing up more tanks, which resulted in Grayburn's positions coming under more intense fire and gave him no option but to take his men to an area north of the bridge.

As the Germans squeezed the defences of the paras, they laid demolition charges under a section of the bridge next to the southern river bank in case the advancing Allies were to reach the bridge and capture it from the south. Immediately recognizing what was happening, Grayburn organized and led a fighting patrol to temporarily drive the enemy back off the bridge while members of his patrol removed the fuses. In doing so, Grayburn was wounded once again, this time in the back, but he still refused to be evacuated. Finally, an enemy tank approached. It was so close to him he could do nothing to stop it. In full view of the tank, Grayburn succeeded in directing the withdrawal of his men back to the main defensive perimeter, but he was then caught by a burst of machine-gun fire from the tank. The gallant Jack Grayburn was killed instantly, his body falling into the river.

British casualties were continuing to mount. The building housing the headquarters of the 1st Parachute Brigade, with some 200 wounded men crammed into its cellars, had been under continuous attack throughout the day. There was no option other than to ask for a brief ceasefire to allow the evacuation of the wounded, rather than to leave them to suffer an awful end in the burning rubble. Remarkably, just after nightfall, the Germans agreed, and during a truce that lasted for two hours, the British wounded, including Frost, were taken into captivity.

At Oosterbeek, the Germans had launched a series of heavy attacks against Lonsdale's men. Determined to overrun the defenders, one major attack involved infantry, tanks and self-propelled guns. In charge of one British 6-pounder anti-tank gun defending the main road into Oosterbeek was 22-year-old Lance Sergeant Jack Baskeyfield of the South Staffs. His gun crew had already destroyed two enemy tanks and at least one self-propelled gun at a range of less than 100 yards, but Baskeyfield was now wounded in the leg and the rest of his crew had been killed or badly wounded.

Baskeyfield refused to be taken to the regimental aid post and continued to man his gun alone. The next attack soon came but he continued to fire at the enemy, keeping the tanks at bay, until his gun was out of action. He then crawled, under intense enemy fire, to another 6-pounder gun nearby, the crew of which had been killed, and continued to man the gun single-handedly. He managed to engage another enemy self-propelled gun and scored another direct hit. However, whilst preparing to fire another round he was killed by an exploding shell from an enemy tank. The superb gallantry of Jack Baskeyfield was an inspiration to those around him and his actions were later recognized by the award of a posthumous Victoria Cross, although his body was never recovered.

By the afternoon the mixed force had become so weak that it was forced to withdraw back towards the church. With Thompson maintaining command of the artillery, the South Staffs and the glider pilots, Lonsdale took command of the remaining paras; their defensive positions now formed a finger-shaped perimeter extending from the Lower Rhine at its base out about a mile into Oosterbeek and no more than half a mile wide.

Back at the bridge, only 150 or so paras remained and, by the early hours of 21 September, it had become impossible for them to hold out any longer. They were crammed together in wrecked buildings and cellars amongst the dead and wounded, and attempts to break out to reach the defensive perimeter at Oosterbeek had proved unsuccessful. With no chance of reinforcement, resistance from the last group of paras at the bridge ceased. They had been asked to hold out for two days but they had been there for nearly four.

Major Digby Tatham-Warter was one of those taken prisoner. He later escaped captivity, and on his return to England, wrote a report on the events at the bridge, which led to the posthumous award of the Victoria Cross to Jack Grayburn for his supreme courage, leadership and devotion to duty from the time he arrived at the bridge during the evening of 17 September, until his death on 20 September. Although he had been wounded and was clearly in much pain, and even though he was tired and short of food, Grayburn's courage never flagged. His body was eventually recovered in 1948 and buried in the Arnhem Cemetery at Oosterbeek.

The besieged British forces at Arnhem had now been boosted after making contact with advanced artillery units of XXX Corps, although the latter's advance northwards along what had become known as 'Hell's Highway' had not been anywhere near as quick as anticipated. The plan now was for the survivors of the airborne division to establish themselves in and around Oosterbeek, with the intention of holding a bridgehead on the north side of the river until the arrival of the rest of XXX Corps.

In the south-east of the perimeter, Thompson Force had become Lonsdale Force, after 'Sheriff' Thompson was wounded. One officer responsible for the defence of this part of the perimeter was Major Robert Cain of the South Staffs. The Germans made repeated attempts to break through his position, a vital part of the perimeter, but Cain had already destroyed an enemy tank after going out alone to a house, armed with a PIAT. Cain engaged the tank from just 20 yards, so its gunner then turned its machine guns on the house where he was lying. As the building was repeatedly hit, Cain was wounded and hampered by falling masonry, but continued firing until he scored several hits and immobilized the tank. He now managed to drive away more tanks and a self-propelled gun by his fearless use of his PIAT; each time, he left the relative safety of his cover to go out into the open to engage the enemy.

Cain was everywhere, rallying and inspiring his men and he would not give up during the hard days ahead as he continuously refused rest or medical attention in spite of the fact that he had suffered multiple wounds. Robert Cain would later be awarded the Victoria Cross and, of the five recipients of the VC for Arnhem, he was the only one to have survived the action. His award was the second to the 2nd South Staffs for Arnhem, making it the only battalion to have received two VCs for the same action during the Second World War.

The arrival of the Polish Parachute Brigade late in the afternoon, albeit two days later than planned, briefly took the heat off the British at Oosterbeek. The Poles had dropped south of the river under intense fire and, fearing an attack against the southern end of the bridge, the Germans sent forces south of the river. Unfortunately, though, the Poles were needed north of the river. The British at Oosterbeek had seen the Poles drop, but there was no way of contacting them. In any case, the Poles had no way of crossing the river and so they were eventually forced to take up defensive positions at Driel.

Urquhart was convinced that senior British commanders had not grasped the true gravity of the situation at Arnhem, and so, on 22 September, he sent two of his officers across the river in small dinghies to report to the headquarters of the Poles and to send a signal to Lieutenant General Brian Horrocks, the commander of XXX Corps, asking for reinforcements and supplies.

An improvement in the weather did allow some close air support by Allied aircraft to take place, but without communication with the aircraft, and without any form of forward air control, it was impossible to ensure the attacks were delivered in the right place and at the right time. Later that day, leading elements of the 43rd Wessex Division linked up with the Poles at Driel but an attempt to get elements of the Polish Brigade across the river that night was unsuccessful, due to enemy fire, as well as the exceptionally strong current of the Lower Rhine.

By 23 September the situation inside the thinly held perimeter was desperate, with little or no food, little water and with ammunition becoming dangerously low. The Germans had already worked out that the Allies were trying to reinforce the Oosterbeek perimeter from the south and continued to concentrate on cutting off the northern bridgehead, while also carrying out attacks against the Poles on the south side of the river. These attacks were soon beaten off as more of XXX Corps arrived in the south. The Poles had also managed to get a small number of troops across the river to join the 1st Airborne's defensive perimeter, but, in reality, these did not arrive in sufficient numbers to have any impact on the battle taking place on the river's northern side.

During the afternoon of Sunday, 24 September, there was a further temporary ceasefire at Arnhem, again lasting for two hours, but this time allowing 450 British wounded to be evacuated from the Oosterbeek perimeter. An attempt to reinforce the besieged airborne division by putting two companies of the 4th Battalion Dorset Regiment across the river during the night proved fruitless. The position of the crossing point was poorly advised, and of more than 300 men of the Dorsets who crossed the river in driving rain, all but 75 landed amongst the German positions and were immediately captured.

The senior Allied commanders now decided to abandon the idea of crossing the Lower Rhine and decided instead to establish its new front line at Nijmegen. It was also decided to withdraw the surviving elements of the airborne division from its bridgehead on the northern side of the Lower Rhine back across the river.

At dawn on 25 September the survivors of the 1st Airborne Division received the order to withdraw, although the withdrawal could not take place until nightfall. In the meantime, those stranded inside the perimeter would somehow have to survive another day. The Germans made a significant thrust along a narrow front and aimed at the eastern part of the perimeter, achieving some success and finally breaking through part of the British lines, but the attack was met with determined resistance as the British defenders somehow found the strength to beat off the attackers.

As the British prepared to withdraw, every effort was made to stop the Germans knowing that they were about to do so. Then, during the night, engineer units began to ferry the men of the 1st Airborne out of Oosterbeek and across the river. By the early hours of the following morning, some 2,400 men had been evacuated, leaving 300 men still on the north bank to surrender at first light. It was not until later in the morning that the Germans realized most of the defenders had got away.

Of more than 10,000 men that had gone into Arnhem with the 1st Airborne Division, nearly 1,500 had been killed and another 6,500 were wounded, missing or captured. The Germans had suffered heavily, too, with similar numbers killed and a further 2,000 wounded.

With no secure bridges over the Lower Rhine, the Allies were unable to advance further northwards and, during the next few weeks, consolidated their line at Nijmegen. The position remained largely unchanged until February 1945, when the Allies advanced east on the Rhineland instead of north towards Arnhem as originally planned. For the Allies the battle for Arnhem had proved extremely costly. The 1st Airborne Division had lost nearly three-quarters of its strength and did not see action again. The bridge at Arnhem had, indeed, proved to be a bridge too far.

Chapter Twenty-Nine

Lake Comacchio

1–8 April 1945

The story of daring raids would not be complete without mention of the operation that witnessed the last moments of the life of one of the bravest men to have served with British Special Forces during the Second World War. That man was Anders Lassen, a fearless Dane and a quite extraordinary soldier, who was posthumously awarded the Victoria Cross for his actions at Lake Comacchio on 8 April 1945. At the time of his death Lassen was still only 24 years old and he remains the only member of the Special Air Service to have received the highest award for gallantry; together with his three Military Crosses awarded earlier in the war, it makes Lassen the SAS's most highly decorated soldier. Considering all that he had been through prior to his death, it makes the fact that he was killed during the last days of the war so tragic, but equally, it would be hard to imagine what he would have done in a peacetime Europe.

Lassen was born in Denmark into a wealthy family. His upbringing of outdoor life on the large family estate shaped the way he developed. From a very early age he was given the freedom to roam and he soon developed his field craft and shooting skills, becoming a master shot with a bow and arrow and excelling in the use of his hunting knife. At school it was his fitness that made him stand out, and not his academic ability, and so he left as soon as he was 18 to work as a cabin boy on a merchant ship sailing to the Far East, and then on a large tanker sailing to South America.

Given his background, it is not surprising that Lassen would go on to join the British Special Forces. He had been incensed by Germany's invasion of Denmark, and even though he was still only 19 he set a course for revenge. He made his way to Britain and in 1941 joined the commandos. Having served with the Small Scale Raiding Force, he went to the Middle East in 1943, where he joined the Special Boat Section, then attached to the Special

Air Service, and played a leading role in disrupting German and Italian forces in the Aegean, adding two bars to the MC he had won during cross-Channel operations with the SSRF.

By early 1945 Lassen had risen to the rank of major and volunteered for service in Italy. At the end of March he was commanding M Detachment of the SBS, attached to the 2nd Commando Brigade, in the north-east of Italy where German forces had been driven steadily northwards through the country and had fallen back to a defensive line on the River Po. After a period of relative stalemate during the winter months, the British Eighth Army was preparing to renew its offensive and advance along Route 16 to break though the Argenta Gap, crossing the rivers Senio and Santerno towards the Po at Ferrara. From there, its armoured units could swing left across country to meet up with the American Fifth Army to push the Germans out of Italy and to cut off the divisions defending the city of Bologna.

Under Operation Roast, the 2nd Commando Brigade, commanded by Brigadier Ronnie Tod, was tasked with crossing Lake Comacchio to make the Germans believe the Allied main thrust was coming from the east, along the coast, rather than through the Argenta Gap. This, it was intended, would draw off German troops from west of the lake where, in fact, the main thrust would take place.

Lake Comacchio and its surrounds is a vast area covering a hundred square miles. The lake is better described as a large flooded area of wetlands and swamp, rather than a large expanse of water, with the seaport of Garibaldi on its eastern side. The lake stretches 20 miles across, with several small and very low islands scattered around, and is separated from the Adriatic Sea by a narrow strip of land no more than a mile or two wide.

The 2nd Commando Brigade comprised of two army commando units (2 and 9 Commandos) and two Royal Marine units (40 and 43 (RM) Commandos), and this was the first time all four commando units were to fight together as a brigade. German defences consisted of around 1,200 men, mostly dug-in along the narrow strip, and so the commandos were tasked with clearing the strip to secure the Eighth Army's eastern flank.

The plan was for the army commandos to cross the lake from the south-west and land on the far side of the Bellocchio Canal, which ran from the lake to the sea about halfway along the strip. Then, 2 Commando was to seize and hold the bridges over the canal, while 9 Commando cleared the strip to the south. The Royal Marine commandos were to work their way up the strip, dealing with enemy positions as they advanced.

Amongst the units attached to the brigade was Lassen's M Detachment of the SBS, and teams from the Combined Operations Pilotage Parties, which were to carry out reconnaissance missions to establish suitable areas for the commandos to carry out their attacks.

The operation commenced during the evening of 1 April, when the SBS and COPP teams set off in their canoes to cross the swamp and mark a route for the commandos to cross the lake in storm boats. The conditions were incredibly hard, making progress difficult. The men had to first paddle and wade through mud, over a distance of nearly a mile, before there was enough water to move more freely. Some became separated from their leaders as they tried to find their way across the lake, the two army commando units ended up bunched together, motors packed up in the mud and slime, and the whole crossing ended up several hours behind schedule. Then, as the commandos tried to go ashore, they became bogged down in mud.

The opening phase of the operation had descended into chaos and confusion. With daylight fast approaching, men scrambled ashore exhausted under the cover of an artillery barrage, but still carried out their attacks. By first light the attacks were ongoing. A mist had appeared over the area making visibility difficult for both attacker and defender, but the men of 2 Commando pressed home their attack, capturing all their objectives with the exception of one bridge blown by the enemy. Meanwhile, the men of 9 Commando had initially made good progress, but then became pinned down by heavy enemy fire as the commandos tried to take a key defensive position. Two troops proceeded down the strip to bypass the enemy position, and then under the cover of a smokescreen turned round to attack the position from the south-east with bayonets fixed. The plan worked and the German defensive position was overrun, although the last hundred yards was completed with little or no cover. Some Germans decided to make a break for it but they fell to the waiting guns of another commando troop.

The assaults by both army commando units proved a success. The Allied front line had now advanced by 7 miles, although it had proved costly for 9 Commando in particular, with nine men killed and a further thirty-nine wounded.

With the men of 2 Commando holding the remaining bridges over the Bellocchio Canal, 9 Commando and 43 (RM) Commando moved forward to the canal. The Royal Marines had initially encountered minefields and strongly defended positions at the southern end of the strip, but resistance was soon overcome, after which the commandos had a long trek up to the bridge.

The following day, 3 April, the Royal Engineers repaired the bridge that had been blown by the Germans to allow the commandos and other British forces, including tanks, to cross the canal that afternoon. The commandos now advanced further along the strip, with 2 Commando holding the western flank on the lagoon side, while 43 (RM) Commando advanced on the eastern side along the Adriatic; 9 Commando was held in reserve.

The commandos reached a further canal, marking the northern end of Lake Comacchio, and it was there that the Germans chose to make a most determined defence. A long stretch of open ground, nearly half a mile long, lay between the commandos and the enemy, with little or no cover.

The commandos were pinned down by exceptionally heavy machine-gun and mortar fire. On the eastern flank, some of 43 (RM) Commando had managed to crawl forward under fire. One of them, 21-year-old Corporal Tom Hunter, noticed there was an enemy stronghold in houses on the near bank only about 200 yards away. Hunter stood up and then charged across the open ground, all alone and firing his Bren gun from his hip. Unsurprisingly, Hunter became the focus of attention for the enemy machine guns. Three enemy gun positions immediately opened up on him, and then half a dozen more joined in from the far side of the bank, but somehow Hunter made it to the houses unscathed.

Hunter then stormed into the houses and silenced the three enemy machine-gun positions. While some Germans had escaped across the canal, others gave in. Hunter then continued to draw fire from the enemy while giving his colleagues valuable time to catch up, but he was now desperately short of ammunition and in an exposed position. It was then that the gallant Tom Hunter was cut down by a hail of enemy fire. It would later be announced that he was to be posthumously awarded the Victoria Cross, making Tom Hunter the only Royal Marine VC of the war.

The dogged German resistance at the canal held up the advance and it was soon realized that a stronger force would be needed, so it would be left to the

24th Guards Brigade to continue the momentum. Nonetheless, Roast had been a success. The commandos had successfully annihilated three enemy infantry battalions and taken just short of a thousand prisoners for the loss of twenty-five dead and a hundred wounded.

While the commandos had been assaulting the strip away to the east of Lake Comacchio, Lassen's men of the SBS were occupying a handful of islands, from where they could be used to carry out attacks on German positions along the northern and eastern banks of the lake. The men had initially managed to remain undetected, but they had been spotted after an enemy patrol boat approached and their position had been given away during the firefight that followed. Despite heavy shelling over the past few days, Lassen's small force had so far managed to remain intact.

With the eastern flank secured, Lassen instructed his men to concentrate on the northern shore. In the early hours of 7 April he sent out two reconnaissance patrols to land on the northern side of the lake, but the combination of a strong breeze and a deep canal, with dykes running parallel to the shore, made it impossible to land. Then, during the following afternoon, Lassen received orders from the Commando Brigade's headquarters to mount an attack on the northern shore. His aim was to cause as much disruption and confusion as possible to give the enemy the impression that a much larger landing was taking place along the shore. This would draw off as many German resources as possible while the Eighth Army launched its major assault on the western shore of the lake.

Later that night Lassen led his small raiding party of eighteen men away from the island. He had split his men into three groups and was leading the first group himself. Without completing a reconnaissance of the north shore it was always going to be a hazardous mission.

Having rowed out to a causeway Lassen led his men on foot along a narrow road towards the town of Comacchio some 2 miles away. With nothing but water either side there was no cover. The men had covered less than half a mile when they were challenged from the side of the road ahead. It was dark, but they knew it would be a German post. An attempt to allay suspicion by answering in broken Italian claiming they were fishermen returning home failed, and was greeted by enemy machine-gun fire from the German position. Suddenly, there was further enemy fire, this time from two more machine-gun positions hidden in the dark.

Without hesitation, Lassen charged forward in the dark while hurling grenades at the first defensive position, which turned out to consist of two machine guns manned by four Germans. By now there was more enemy fire from a further machine-gun post further down the road. Ignoring the hail of bullets sweeping the road from three enemy machine-gun posts, Lassen raced forward to take out the second enemy position under covering fire from his men. Throwing more grenades at the next position he took out two more machine guns in very quick time. The rest of his men had now caught up and they arrived to find two more Germans lying dead and two surrendered.

The raiders had also suffered casualties and were now down to ten fighting men. Still under a cone of fire, Lassen rallied and reorganized his men. While they engaged the third position, Lassen crept forward to throw in more grenades at the enemy. Those Germans still alive decided they had suffered enough and chose to give in, but as Lassen moved forward to just a few feet from their position to accept their surrender he was caught in a burst of machine-gun fire from the left. Lassen fell, mortally wounded, but even as he was falling he flung a further grenade out to his left, wounding some of the occupants, and enabling his patrol to dash forward and capture the final position.

Lassen had single-handedly wiped out three enemy positions, accounting for six enemy machine-gun posts. Eight of the enemy lay dead, others were wounded and two had been captured. Lassen had displayed magnificent leadership and complete disregard for his own safety in the face of overwhelming superiority. Even his men, who had come to know Lassen's ways, were amazed by his heroic actions.

Although badly wounded, Lassen refused to be evacuated, stating that it would impede the withdrawal and further endanger lives. He ordered his men to withdraw and then finally took his last breath. Anders Lassen was dead.

With their leader dead and ammunition all but exhausted, the attack lost its momentum. The raiders needed to withdraw, and by dawn they were back at their starting point. That same day the local Italians removed the bodies of Lassen and the rest of the dead from where they had fallen and took them to Comacchio.

Even by Lassen's own exceptional standards, his action at Lake Comacchio on the night of 8/9 April 1945 was truly remarkable. There was initially concern that the recommendation for the award of a posthumous Victoria Cross for Lassen would not be supported because the request to recognize Tom Hunter's exceptional act of gallantry was already in the system; a second recommendation in such a short period of time may have been considered too soon.

In the end the gallant acts of both men would rightly be recognized with the VC, and the award to Lassen in particular was probably long overdue: he had consistently displayed extreme individual gallantry and his contribution to the war had been immense.

Inevitably, there has been post-war speculation about whether Special Forces should have been used for what essentially was an infantry task. But most importantly, as far as the overall British plan was concerned, the Germans had been forced to move a number of battalions eastwards towards Comacchio to counter the assault, allowing the British to mount its main assault towards the Argenta Gap. Within days of Lassen's death the Allies began its last major offensive of the campaign in Italy. The end of the war in Europe was now just days away.

Chapter Thirty

Midgets Against the *Takao* and *Myōkō*

31 July 1945

The successful X–Craft attack on the *Tirpitz* in September 1943 had paved the way for future midget sub operations. Although only one of the six craft that had gone to northern Norway returned intact, it did not deter the construction of newer and improved craft, with six more midgets built for the Royal Navy during the following year. The newer XE-Class midget submarines were basically the same as the original X-Class. They, too, carried a crew of four, but in addition to the two side charges, each of which contained two tons of amatol explosives, the XE-Class carried six 20lb limpet mines, which were attached to the target by the crew's diver.

The changing war at sea and the imminent end of hostilities in the West meant the new XEs were never used in the European theatre, but the prolonged war in the Far East provided the Royal Navy with an opportunity for the new midgets to go into action.

In early 1945 the submarine depot ship, HMS *Bonaventure*, sailed for the Far East with the six new midgets in her hold. They had been adapted for operations in the region by being tropicalized for the increased humidity and the side charges had been enlarged, which effectively doubled the amount of explosives.

On arrival in Australia during April, the captain of the *Bonaventure*, Captain William Fell, actively sought opportunities for the midgets to be used. Initially, there were no possible targets identified, but the following month Fell was given the opportunity to use his midgets to cut some telegraph cables off Hong Kong. By cutting the undersea cables connecting Singapore, Saigon, Hong Kong and Tokyo, the Japanese would be forced to use radio communications and, therefore, open themselves to message interception.

Missions to cut the Hong Kong to Saigon telephone cables were carried out in July 1945 by two midget subs under Operations Sabre and Foil. The first, Sabre, was carried out by *XE4* after she had been towed to a position 40 miles from the Mekong Delta: her divers succeeded in severing two cables. Meanwhile, the second part of the mission, Foil, had been carried out by *XE5* at the Hong Kong end of the cable, again successfully.

Both midgets and their towing submarines then returned safely to their base. While this was at least a start, it was not the kind of mission for which the midget submarine crews had been trained. However, during the discussions and meetings that followed, Fell was offered an additional operation – one that was far more daring and exactly what the midgets could do best.

Called Operation Struggle, the mission was to destroy two Japanese heavy cruisers – the *Myōkō* and the *Takao* – anchored in the Johore Straits at Singapore. The *Myōkō* was the older of the two ships and displaced 13,000 tons. She had been damaged during the Battle of Leyte Gulf, damaged again while trying to return to Japan, and then sailed to Singapore to undergo repairs. The *Takao* was a newer ship with a displacement of 10,000 tons and had also been damaged during the same battle. She had been so badly damaged that there was no chance of returning to Japan and so she was now moored in the strait as an anti-aircraft battery for the defence of Singapore.

Although the two cruisers were damaged, it was felt that, if they were to be repaired, both would still pose a significant threat in the region; meanwhile, they continued to cause a threat as floating gun batteries. They still needed to be neutralized and so two midgets, *XE1* and *XE3*, were allocated the task of carrying out a joint attack on the two heavy cruisers: *XE1* was to attack the *Myōkō* and *XE3* the *Takao*.

Late in the evening of 30 July, four days after leaving the Malaysian island of Labuan, the two midgets slipped their towing submarines. The *XE1* was commanded by Lieutenant John Smart, an experienced midget sub operator. He had been the passage crew commander on board *X8* during Operation Source nearly two years before, when he had been tasked to attack the German battleship *Lützow*, but the *X8* had encountered problems during its passage when it developed serious leaks in its side-mounted demolition charges. These then had to be jettisoned, but they exploded near the craft causing significant damage and resulting in her having to be scuttled. Now commanding *XE1*, his crew consisted of Sub-Lieutenant Harry Harper,

Leading Seaman Walter Pomeroy and Engine Room Artificer 4th Class Henry Fishleigh.

Commanding *XE3* was 24-year-old Lieutenant Ian Fraser. Fraser had served on merchant ships before the war and had volunteered for submarine service after joining the Royal Navy in 1939. Awarded the DSC in 1943 for his bravery and skill during submarine patrols while serving in HMS *Sahib*, he had then volunteered for the midget submarines and was now in command of an XE-Class. On board the *XE3*, at the controls, was Sub-Lieutenant Bill Smith, a New Zealander, Leading Seaman James Magennis, the crew's diver, and Engine Room Artificer 3rd Class Charles Reed. Magennis was 25 years old and from Northern Ireland. He was an experienced diver and had also taken part in Operation Source when he had been part of the passage crew on board the *X7* bound for the *Tirpitz*.

The long approach up the Johore Straits and through the harbour defences of minefields, listening posts, a buoyed defence and surface patrols, took a great deal of skilful navigation and nerve. Many of the channel buoys were expected to be lit to make navigation easier, but this turned out not to be the case. It was now the early hours of 31 July and rather than risk being spotted in a designated safe channel, or being picked up by one of the many listening posts, Fraser elected to take the *XE3* into a known minefield. Stealthily they pressed on, with Fraser sitting astride the sub gazing at the skyline through his binoculars.

The passage did not pass without incident. First, just before dawn, the *XE3* had to crash dive to avoid an oncoming tanker with an armed escort. Then, having surfaced again soon after, the crew were alarmed to find they were sitting on a mine, which fortunately had failed to explode.

The temperature and humidity on board was almost unbearable. The crews were also getting very tired. They had been fortunate – and surprised – to find the gate of the anti-submarine boom open and the two midgets quickly slipped through. It had taken the crews eleven hours to cover the 40 miles to the target area. The crews now searched for their camouflaged targets but Smart could not find the *Myōkō*. However, Fraser had more luck and now sighted the *Takao*, exactly where he had expected.

Fraser commenced the attack in *XE3* just before 2.00 pm. As the sub closed on the *Takao*, it was initially forced to take evasive action after sighting an enemy motor launch just yards away. Rather than risk being seen, Fraser continued towards the *Takao* blind and before long the *XE3* crashed into the side of its hull. Fortunately, and quite remarkably, the midget sub had not been detected. Fraser then eased the *XE3* back and tried again to get into a better position, but the *Takao* was nearly aground both fore and aft, and so there was little water space beneath the hull. Furthermore, the tide was beginning to fall and so there was now very little time. After trying for some forty minutes, the crew eventually managed to position the midget beneath the midship section; it was the only area where there was enough space to get the midget submarine into position.

It was now up to Magennis to attach the limpet mines. He first flooded the compartment of the sub known as the Wet and Dry, and then tried to remove the diver's hatch, but so tight was the space that he found he could not open it wide enough as the lid was hitting against the hull of the ship. He knew that to try and adjust the sub's position would add further delay and inevitably mean the sub would become trapped beneath the hull by the falling tide. Magennis, therefore, decided to remove his breathing apparatus and squeeze out of the gap between the partially opened diver's hatch and the hull of the ship.

Once out, Magennis replaced his oxygen supply and quickly set about clearing the thick layer of seaweed and encrusted shellfish from the cruiser's hull so that he could attach his limpet mines. In order to secure the limpets he also had to tie them in pairs by a line passing under the cruiser keel, and it took him half an hour to attach all six mines, about 50 feet apart, to the *Takao*'s hull.

This extremely tiring work was not helped by a steady leakage of oxygen, which was ascending in bubbles to the surface; fortunately, no one on the surface spotted these telltale signs of a diver below. A lesser man would have been content to place just a few limpets and then return to the craft. Magennis, however, persisted until he had placed all his mines before returning to the craft. By the time he managed to squeeze his way back on board the sub he was exhausted. His breathing apparatus had been damaged and his hands were nearly raw, having been repeatedly cut on the encrusted shellfish on the hull.

Fraser now went to release the two side charges, each of two tons of explosives, but only the port side fell away. The starboard side was stuck and, unbeknown to the crew of the *XE3*, the *Takao* had fallen further with the tide. The midget sub was now stuck and its crew trapped.

For nearly an hour the crew tried every trick they knew to try and wrestle the sub free. They were on the point of giving up when, almost miraculously, the *XE3* suddenly swung to starboard and the corresponding force of water pushed them clear to one side. They were free, but their troubles were far from over, as the starboard charge was still attached.

Acknowledging that Magennis was exhausted, Fraser decided to go outside to try and free the charge, but Magennis would not have it. Recognizing his own responsibilities as the crew's diver, he ventured outside once again rather than allow Fraser, who was much less experienced as a diver, undertake the job. Equipped with a heavy spanner, it took Magennis several minutes of further hard graft to eventually free the charge. With his diver back on board, Fraser set course to make their escape.

In the meantime, on board the *XE1*, Smart had given up trying to locate the *Myōkō*, and had left his charges next to the *Takao* instead. Then, at 9.30 pm, the charges exploded, ripping a massive hole in the *Takao*'s hull of some 60 feet by 30 feet, and causing significant damage to the cruiser's turrets, while flooding a number of her compartments and completely immobilizing her. She would never sail again, and after the war she was towed out to the Straits of Malacca where she was used as target practice for the Royal Navy before she was eventually sunk.

The two midget subs withdrew safely, although it was a long and tiring journey back to their towing vessels. Fraser and Magennis returned to England as heroes and it was announced they were both to receive the Victoria Cross. The two other crew members of *XE3* were also decorated: Bill Smith was awarded the DSO and Charles Reed the CGM. The crew of *XE1* were also decorated for their part in the raid. John Smart was also awarded the DSO and Harry Harper the DSC, while the two other ranks on board, Walter Pomeroy and Henry Fishleigh, were both awarded the DSM.

Fraser's citation for his VC included the following:

The courage and determination of Lieutenant Fraser are beyond all praise. Any man not possessed of his relentless determination to achieve his object in full, regardless of all consequences, would have dropped his side charge alongside the target instead of persisting until he had forced his submarine right under the cruiser.

James Magennis was the only VC winner of the Second World War to hail from Northern Ireland and he became a celebrity in his home city of Belfast. His citation concluded:

> *Magennis displayed very great courage and devotion to duty and complete disregard for his own safety.*

The midgets had, once again, made their mark, and the heroic crews had performed one of the last courageous acts of the Second World War.

Bibliography

Published Sources

Ambrose, Stephen E., *Pegasus Bridge* (Pocket Books, London, 2003)

Appleyard, J. E., *Geoffrey* (Blandford Press, London, 1947)

Arthur, Max, *Men of the Red Beret Airborne Forces 1940–1990* (Hutchinson, London, 1990)

Arthur, Max, *Symbol of Courage* (Sidgwick & Jackson, London, 2004)

Ashcroft, Michael, *Special Forces Heroes* (Headline Review, London, 2008)

Barker, Ralph, *The Ship-Busters* (Chatto & Windus Ltd, London, 1957)

Binney, Marcus, *Secret War Heroes* (Hodder & Stoughton, London, 2006)

Bishop, Patrick, *Target Tirpitz* (Harper Press, London, 2012)

Bowyer, Chaz, *Bristol Blenheim* (Ian Allan, London, 1984)

Bowyer, Chaz, *For Valour, The Air VCs* (William Kimber & Co. Ltd, London, 1985)

Brickhill, Paul, *The Dam Busters* (Evans Brothers, London, 1954)

Cherry, Niall, *Striking Back: Britain's Airborne & Commando Raids 1940–42* (Helion & Co. Ltd, England, 2009)

Courtney, G. B., *SBS in World War Two* (Robert Hale, London, 1983)

Cull, Brian, Lander, Bruce and Weiss, Heinrich, *Twelve Days in May* (Grub Street, London, 1995)

Currie, Jack, *The Augsburg Raid* (Goodall Publications Ltd, London, 1987)

De la Billière, General Sir Peter, *Supreme Courage* (Little, Brown Book Group, London, 2004)

Downing, Taylor, *Night Raid* (Little, Brown Book Group, London, 2013)

Dunning, James, *When Shall Their Glory Fade?* (Frontline Books, Barnsley, 2011)

Durnford-Slater, John, *Commando: Memoirs of a Fighting Commando in World War II* (William Kimber, London, 1953)

Ford, Ken, *The Bruneval Raid* (Osprey Publishing, Oxford, 2010)

Ford, Ken, *The Cockleshell Raid* (Osprey Publishing, Oxford, 2010)

Frost, John, Major General, *A Drop Too Many* (Cassell, London, 1980)

Gale, R. N., Lieutenant General, *With the 6th Airborne Division in Normandy* (Sampson Low Marston, London, 1948)

Gibson, G. P., *Enemy Coast Ahead* (Goodhall Publications Ltd, London, 1986)

Goutard, A., Colonel, *The Battle of France* (Frederick Muller Ltd, London, 1958)

Halley, James J., *The Squadrons of the Royal Air Force and Commonwealth 1918–1988* (Air-Britain, Tonbridge, 1988)

Harclerode, Peter, *Arnhem: A Tragedy of Errors* (Arms & Armour Press, London, 1994)

Harrison, W. A., *Swordfish at War* (Ian Allan, London, 1987)

Lett, Brian, *The Small Scale Raiding Force* (Pen & Sword Military, Barnsley, 2013)

Lyman, Robert, *Operation Suicide* (Quercus, London, 2013)

Mears, Ray, *The Real Heroes of Telemark* (Hodder & Stoughton, London, 2003)

Middlebrook, Martin and Everitt, Chris, *The Bomber Command War Diaries* (Penguin Books, London, 1990)

Millar, George, *The Bruneval Raid: Flashpoint of that Radar War* (Bodley Head, London, 2004)

Newton, Don and Hampshire, A. Cecil, *Taranto* (New English Library, England, 1974)

Norton, G. G., *The Red Devils* (Leo Cooper, London, 1971)

Owen, James, *Commando* (Little, Brown Book Group, London, 2012)

Phillips, Lucas C. E., *Cockleshell Heroes* (Heinemann, London, 1956)

Pringle, Patrick, *Fighting Marines* (Evans Brothers, London, 1966)

Ramsey, Winston G., *The War in the Channel Islands, Then and Now* (Battle of Britain Prints International Limited, London, 1981)

Ransom, Derek, *Battle Axe: A History of 105 Squadron RAF* (Air-Britain, England, 1967)

Redding, Tony, *War in the Wilderness: The Chindits in Burma 1943–1944* (Spellmount, Stroud, 2011)

Robertson, Terence, *Channel Dash* (Evans Brothers, London, 1958)

Ryan, Cornelius, *A Bridge Too Far* (Hodder & Stoughton, London, 2007)

Schofield, B. B., Vice Admiral, *The Attack on Taranto* (Ian Allan, London, 1973)

Schofield, B. B., Vice Admiral, *Stringbags in Action* (Pen & Sword, Barnsley, 2010)

Scott, Stuart R. *Battle-Axe Blenheims* (Alan Sutton Publishing Ltd, Stroud, 1996)

Southby-Tailyour, Ewen, *Blondie* (Leo Cooper, Barnsley, 1998)

St George Saunders, Hilary, *Combined Operations, The Official Story of the Commandos* (Kingsport Press, USA, 1943)

St George Saunders, Hilary, *The Green Beret, The Story of the Commandos 1940–45* (New English Library, London, 1971)

St George Saunders, Hilary, *The Red Beret, The Incredible Story of Death-Dealing Parachute Volunteers* (New English Library, London, 1973)

Sturtivant, Ray, *The Swordfish Story* (Arms & Armour Press, London, 1993)

Sweetman, John, *The Dambusters Raid* (Arms & Armour Press, London, 1990)

Thompson, Julian, *Forgotten Voices of Burma* (Ebury Press, England, 2009)

Towill, Bill, *A Chindit's Chronicle* (Author's Choice Press, USA, 2000)

Watkins, Paul, *Midget Submarine Commander: The Life of Godfrey Place VC* (Pen & Sword, Barnsley, 2012)

National Archives – Document References

ADM 179/227 SSRF	Operation Aquatint
ADM 199/1844	HMS *Tuna* War Diary
ADM 202/310	Royal Marines Boom Patrol Detachment – War Diary – January–December 1942
ADM 202/399	Operation Frankton
AIR 14/523	Summary of Events, 2 Group
AIR 27/164	12 Squadron RAF Operations Record Book – 1923–December 1940
AIR 27/264	21 Squadron RAF Operations Record Book – January 1943–December 1944
AIR 27/278	22 Squadron RAF Operations Record Book – 1915–December 1941
AIR 27/449	44 Squadron RAF Operations Record Book – January–December 1942
AIR 27/766	97 Squadron RAF Operations Record Book – September 1939–December 1942
AIR 27/830	105 Squadron RAF Operations Record Book – 1941–1942
AIR 27/2128	617 Squadron RAF Operations Record Book
AIR 37/981	38 Group RAF – Operation Order Market
AIR 37/1214	1st British Airborne Corps – Allied Airborne Operations in Holland – September–October 1944
DEFE 2/109	SSRF – Operations Barricade, Dryad, Branford, Aquatint, Basalt, Batman
DEFE 2/842	Folbot/Goatley/Cockles
DEFE 2/952	Royal Marines Boom Patrol Detachment Reports of Operations
WO 106/4417	Early Planning of the SSRF
WO 171/366	HQ 1st Airborne Corps War Diary – September 1944
WO 171/393	HQ 1st Airborne Division War Diary – September–December 1944
WO 171/589	HQ 1st Airlanding Brigade War Diary – January–December 1944
WO 171/592	HQ 1st Parachute Brigade War Diary – January–December 1944
WO 171/594	HQ 4th Parachute Brigade War Diary – January–December 1944
WO 218/158	War Diaries – Middle East Commando Depot, 1 January–31 December 1941
WO 309/551	Killing of Members of British Raiding Party from HM Submarine *Tuna*

Index

Listed below is an index of British personnel, units and operations included in this book. The index also includes personnel from Allied nations who were attached to British units for the operations included. The ranks shown are those at the time of the operation and where an individual is mentioned in more than one mission, the senior rank attained is used. Decorations or awards are not shown.